FIRST PERSON
ACTION RESEARCH

Judi Marshall

FIRST PERSON
ACTION RESEARCH
Living Life as Inquiry

Los Angeles | London | New Delhi
Singapore | Washington DC | Melbourne

Los Angeles | London | New Delhi
Singapore | Washington DC | Melbourne

SAGE Publications Ltd
1 Oliver's Yard
55 City Road
London EC1Y 1SP

SAGE Publications Inc.
2455 Teller Road
Thousand Oaks, California 91320

SAGE Publications India Pvt Ltd
B 1/I 1 Mohan Cooperative Industrial Area
Mathura Road
New Delhi 110 044

SAGE Publications Asia-Pacific Pte Ltd
3 Church Street
#10-04 Samsung Hub
Singapore 049483

Editor: Kirsty Smy
Editorial assistant: Molly Farrell / Lyndsay Aitken
Production editor: Sarah Cooke
Copyeditor: Andy Baxter
Proofreader: Lynda Watson
Indexer: Silvia Benvenuto
Marketing manager: Sally Ransom
Cover design: Francis Kenney
Typeset by: C&M Digitals (P) Ltd, Chennai, India
Printed and bound by CPI Group (UK) Ltd,
Croydon, CR0 4YY

First published 2016

Library of Congress Control Number: 2015953040

British Library Cataloguing in Publication data

A catalogue record for this book is available from
the British Library

ISBN 978-1-4129-1214-3
ISBN 978-1-4129-1215-0 (pbk)

At SAGE we take sustainability seriously. Most of our products are printed in the UK using FSC papers and boards.
When we print overseas we ensure sustainable papers are used as measured by the PREPS grading system.
We undertake an annual audit to monitor our sustainability.

To Mum and Dad, Eileen and Geoff

CONTENTS

ABOUT THE AUTHOR

Judi Marshall is Professor Emerita of Learning and Leadership at Lancaster University Management School, UK. Prior to joining Lancaster in 2008, she was at the School of Management, University of Bath, and a core member of the Centre for Action Research in Professional Practice (CARPP).

In her academic career Judi has followed her developing interests as new questions arose. The topics she has studied include management job stress, women in management, organizational cultures, systemic change, education for sustainability, the gendering of corporate responsibility and sustainability, and careers. Judi's publications map across these and other interests. She has, for example, an international reputation for her work on women in management, publications including *Women Managers: Travellers in a Male World* (1984) and *Women Managers Moving On: Exploring Career and Life Choices* (1995).

Initially a qualitative researcher, Judi also became an action researcher, especially exploring and articulating the principles and practices of first person inquiry, whatever other topics she is engaged with. This has led to a sequence of publications on first person action research approaches. These incorporate the notion of *living life as inquiry* (Marshall 1999), aspiring to treat life as an ongoing experiment, which can be adopted as an approach to learning and to leadership.

How to write academic work which is alive and takes forms congruent with the challenging issues studied has been another enduring interest, leading Judi often to experiment with writing approaches, and to write about doing so.

Teaching and pedagogy have been significant interests in Judi's career. Whilst at the University of Bath, for example, with colleagues, she developed the *MSc in Responsibility and Business Practice* for mature, part-time course participants wanting to put environmental sustainability and social justice at the heart of their practice. The course was innovative educationally as well as in its content, adopting a question-posing, critical and values-aware approach based in principles and practices of action research. This enabled participants to engage with the challenging and contentious issues addressed, and to develop their practice alongside their intellects. Judi was a tutor on the programme and Director of Studies from 1997 to 2007. In 2011, she co-authored *Leadership for Sustainability: An action research approach* which includes stories of seeking to contribute to systemic change from people who had undertaken the MSc. At Lancaster, Judi and colleagues developed the *MA in Leadership for Sustainability* along similar lines. Coaching course participants who are seeking to contribute to change in their organizations, professions and own lives, and helping them to develop themselves as action researchers has thus been a major strand in Judi's academic career.

Judi has also worked extensively with research students undertaking Diplomas, Masters and doctorates. Often this has involved group-based, tutor and peer supervision providing especially rich environments for the development of action research skills as well as understandings. She has enjoyed helping people do work that matters to them, which addresses challenging issues of our times, is radical and creatively meets academic standards.

ACKNOWLEDGEMENTS

In the development of this book, I especially thank:

My many colleagues and Masters and research students at Bath and Lancaster Universities over the years for their companionship in inquiry

Geoff Mead for our conversations in 2004 envisaging a book to bring our different notions of first person inquiry into dialogue, which did not then come to fruition but did generate a special journal issue (Marshall and Mead, 2005)

Bill Torbert for comments on a draft of Part I: **Action inquiry and action logics**

Peter Wagstaff for a conversation about my interpretations of Nathalie Sarraute's work which appear in Part III

Barbara Turner-Vesselago for conversations about writing as inquiry and Freefall Writing which contributed to Part IV: **Writing as inquiry**

The late Gerry Cox for introducing me to Going, Going by Philip Larkin

Elizabeth Adeline for the quotation from Janet Frame's autobiography on the importance of waking thoughts to the aspiring writer

My long-term learning group colleagues who appear in Part V: **Inquiry learning groups and working with feedback**

Ginny Newsham and Sara Shevenell, who have been writing their own books in parallel, for discussions, encouragement and extensive feedback

Rich for myriad forms of practical and moral support

INTRODUCING FIRST PERSON INQUIRY

In this book I offer a notion of research that is thoroughly integrated into everyday life, through which I seek to live with integrity in potentially challenging times. *Living life as inquiry* is at the same time philosophy, orientation and practice, seeking to treat all I think, feel, say and do as experiment (Marshall, 1999). It is a potential contribution to the world of reflective inquiry. In various realms of research, reflectiveness or reflexivity of some kind are increasingly advocated and integrated. As we contribute to making knowledge, individually and collectively, we can seek to make our purposes and the processes we engage in open to review, for our own learning, as inherent quality processes, and to inform those who engage with our work – as long as we accept caveats that full transparency is not possible, is an incompatible aim. Also we can explore the connections and potential incongruences between our theorising and how we act.

This book is especially offered as a contribution to action research. It explores principles and practices of first person inquiry and issues we encounter as we go about doing it. The ideas and practices presented are also more widely applicable to qualitative research which is engaged with what Denzin and Lincoln (2005a) depict as a 'triple crisis of representation, legitimation, and praxis [which] confronts qualitative researchers in the human disciplines' (Denzin and Lincoln, 2005a: 19). Taking these in turn: it is no longer assumed that researchers can capture lived experience, and so attention is directed to how this is 'created in the social text written by the researcher' (Denzin and Lincoln, 2005a: 19). The legitimation crisis 'involves a serious rethinking of such terms as *validity*, *generalizability*, and *reliability*' (Denzin and Lincoln, 2005a: 19). These are being reviewed in a wide range of research movements including action research. The third crisis – of praxis – then follows: 'Is it possible to effect change in the world if society is only and always a text?' (Denzin and Lincoln, 2005a: 20). At these interesting times, there is a vast array of terms, conceptualisations and practices for researcher conduct and the reflexivity which is now required.

Here I explore notions of *first person action research* against this shifting and generative landscape of methodological and paradigmatic challenges and choices, and in the light of the conditionality we now need to live with and embrace. First person inquiry is a worthwhile endeavour in its own right and a foundation for inquiring with others or engaging in more traditional forms of qualitative – and other – research. It can be set alongside second and third person action research, in which we inquire with co-researchers and seek to promote inquiry in organisations and wider social formations, respectively. These forms are elaborated in PART I: **Integrating action research, systemic thinking and attention to issues of power.**

Developing our capacities for reflectiveness and dialogue seems especially necessary now in the world, given the global and local challenges of environmental un-sustainability and social inequality we face, and the dynamics of difference and power we engage if we seek to address them. Action research of some kind provides ways of being and behaving in uncertain and potentially dangerous times, offers disciplines for living conditionally and open to review, and potentially for acting for change.

A range of approaches depict first person inquiry, including action inquiry (Torbert, 2001; Fisher et al., 2003), action science (Argyris and Schön, 1974, 1996), reflective practice (Schön, 1983), action learning (Raelin, 2009; Revans, 1982), critical action learning (Rigg and Trehan, 2004; Trehan and Pedler, 2009), feminist reflective research (Stanley and Wise, 1993), autoethnography (Ellis and Bochner, 2000; Holman Jones et al., 2013; Sparkes, 2002, 2012) and practical reflexivity (Cunliffe and Easterby-Smith, 2004). These notions have their varied accents and tones, reflecting their different heritages, the contexts and lives in which they have arisen, their communities of influence, and their authors' styles of being in the world. Living life as inquiry is offered as a contribution to this array. As the book proceeds I will also make connections with authors of fiction who have similar interests – Nathalie Sarraute and Kazuo Ishiguro – who have sought to portray the conditionality of living experience. Their work has informed my thinking about inquiry sensibilities and practices, and about issues of articulation and representation, and some motifs and examples from these sources are offered in this text.

My approach has been developed through an academic life as a qualitative and then action researcher. I have not distinguished readily between 'research' and the rest of my life, experimenting with the translation processes between the two, with how they are interwoven and inform each other. For example, I acknowledged and worked with the inevitable connections between my life and research as I studied women in management, writing about 'Researching women in management as a way of life' (Marshall, 1992) as one elaboration of this.

As my research life has unfolded I have paid attention to my sense-making, appreciating how I am continually making choices that shape what I can offer. I have tried to explore and articulate these choices in my work, opening them to critical review. As an entangled academic, I feel compelled to apply my thinking in action and to develop my ideas through experiencing. Concerned about environmental challenges, for example, I have been involved in education for sustainability since the 1980s and have sought to influence my institutions to give these issues more attention. These interests appear in this book.

I have come to term this approach 'living life as inquiry' (Marshall, 1999), cautiously expressing my tacit knowing of the processes involved as:

> a range of beliefs, strategies and ways of behaving which encourage me to treat little as fixed, finished, clear-cut. Rather I have an image of living continually in process, adjusting, seeing what emerges, bringing things into question ... attempting to open to continual question what I know, feel, do and want, and finding ways to engage actively in this questioning and process its stages. (Marshall, 1999: 156–7)

This approach also means seeking to pay attention to the 'stories' I tell about myself and the world, appreciating that these are all constructions, glimpses perhaps of transitory purposes and perspectives, and of social discourses within which meanings unfold. I can 'listen' to them with interest, noticing what shapes they take and whether I seem attached or not to their rhetorics.

When I adopt living life as inquiry as an active approach to experimentation, I can take a preoccupation which is not worry or tension necessarily, but is interesting enough to puzzle about, and experiment, turning it into a 'project' of some kind, engaging in cycles of learning, as I seek to understand more and flex my behaviour out in the service of doing so. I make conceptual sense differently because I have allowed research to become multi-dimensional. I seek to track perceptions, sensations – potentially fleeting, potentially recurrent – and to avoid them becoming static, habituated. Often these explorations are in the service of acting more effectively in some way, reflecting too on what that might mean.

In many ways this approach to life is nothing special; it is how people live step by step, trying to be aware of those steps, as far as we are able – an important qualification. But it represents also a challenge, an invitation, of seeking to live a mindful life and learn as we go along.

One of my images of inquiry is that of continually weaving between inner and outer arcs of attention (Marshall, 2001), as I seek to reflect and act fluidly in context, and to 'maintain curiosity ... about what is happening and what part I am playing in creating and sustaining patterns of action, interaction and non-action' (Marshall, 1999: 157). The image is of a figure of eight, on its side, repeatedly written over, the lines diverging maybe, then maybe returning through the central intersection – an image of infinity – in which keeping moving is an aim, a quest for agility of mind, feeling and action. This approach is

Weaving between inner and outer arcs of attention

© Xpixel/Shutterstock

described more fully in PART II: **Disciplines of inquiry:** Scanning inner and outer arcs of attention.

In the next sections of this chapter I consider key issues in adopting first person inquiry, before outlining the book's format.

Inquiry as relational, systemic

Notions of first person inquiry can seem to confer a self-importance on the person as 'individual' or imply too much of a sense of (humanistic) self, neither of which are intended (but may be features of language use). Whilst my approach could be called reflective practice and has been informed over the years by classic sources in this field (such as Schön, 1983; and Argyris and Schön, 1974, 1996), living life as inquiry is also a thoroughly relational notion, with alignment to social constructionist (as well as critical theory) approaches. Processes in and through which we live and make sense are also social.

   In the approach elaborated in this book, a person is always in context, inquiring in ongoing action, curious about connections, interfaces, boundaries and how these are being created. So inquiry is also, for me, about living out systemic thinking, informed by the ideas of Gregory Bateson and others, as I seek to act with integrity in an ever-unfolding, complex world (Bateson, 1973; Marshall, 2004). Alongside systemic thinking, paying attention to potential issues of power is also vital. These aspects of living life as inquiry are explored in PART I: **Integrating action research, systemic thinking and attention to issues of power.**

   The notion of living life as inquiry is of course thoroughly aspirational, and comes with a significant health warning. Taking it seriously can lead people into trouble. And it is also potentially pretentious. It is not an idealisation that I expect to achieve. Rather it is a motif, a dynamic, shifting image of possibility, an invitation to pay attention to and respect what is, rather than to live by projecting, perhaps protecting, what should be. But/and living life as inquiry itself could become a 'should be', and needs to be adopted with caution. As Berman suggests:

> How things are held in the mind is infinitely more important than what is in the mind, including this statement itself. (Berman, 1990: 312)

Inquiry as political process

As will become apparent in this book, living life as inquiry is personal and life process, and it is also political process in various ways. How issues are framed, researched and depicted is influenced by multiple dynamics of power. What voices count and are discounted, what issues can be raised or are muted, what forms of knowing are considered legitimate and illegitimate are reflections of the politics of epistemology. I favour inquiry which is located, embodied, in context in multiple potential senses. This practice incorporates a deep respect for multiple ways of knowing, and commitment to living these out. It eschews the privileging of rational intellect.

As people often want to change the situations they study, in positivist as well as action research, inquiry also means engaging with values; researchers are often attached and entangled. These are not threats to the integrity of research, but we can consider how to hold assumptions, values and frameworks lightly, so that these are open to review and to potential development through inquiry.

Over the years I have sought to give a range of potentially muted issues such as stress (in the 1970s and 80s), gender, equality and sustainability attention in the academy, adopting appropriate forms of engaged, reflective researching. In the politics of epistemology such choices can offend, go against mainstream preferences and templates for acceptable science. I have thus seen this as political work, with attendant issues of how to position myself and maintain senses of purpose and vitality as a scholar–person. My resources for living this academic life have been wide and various. They include action research, as this book will show. I have also been informed by feminist thinking, in its rich variety. Whilst gender is not an explicit theme in this book, a concern for the processes through which power differences might be created and enacted cannot be taken out of my development and so is in some ways inevitably 'written in'.

Self-indulgence or responsibility?

Self-reflection is often suspected of self-indulgence, if not narcissism (Sparkes, 2002). The potential accusation is that the voice of representation is then a 'confessional tale' focused more on the researcher than their field of study

(Van Maanen, 1988), and that the 'research' might have been similarly selective. First person action research can be undertaken with many different purposes. It can be used to develop as a person, address how one is in the world, operate more effectively and gain a sense of agency in a situation that seems potentially over-powering. This does not need to be ego-obsessed activity. How to conduct first person inquiry with due humility could be a focus of attention.

Living life as inquiry is generally not self-reflection for its own sake, but is adopted to inform action in the world around issues people think matter. As some of us go about trying to make the world a better place (amidst ongoing questioning of what that might mean), adopting some form of self-reflective inquiry practice is a responsibility, despite the impossibility of doing this 'perfectly'. How to conduct myself, which issues to pursue and how, are important, continually live questions. The potential for arrogance, misguided interference and damage are great as we become self-appointed change agents to our organisations, societies, the planet, the universe. (Exemplary concerns, but how do we go about them? And might desisting from action be more beneficial than compulsive activity?) We owe it to our fellow creatures to engage in some form of self-questioning, seeking to pay attention to our purposes and patterns, and inviting challenge from others in these terms. My advocacy that inquiry could improve the world is also conditional and questionable in this way.

Inquiry develops in company

Whilst it might imply intense personal process, living life as inquiry is not something we often do well alone (the European–American Collaborative Challenging Whiteness, 2005). It benefits from 'friends willing to act as enemies' (Torbert, 1976: 169), those who will question our patterns, assumptions, actions and cherished beliefs, as well of course as from 'friends willing to act as friends', who support us to unfold who we might become (Marshall and Reason, 1993: 122). The story exploring **Inquiry learning groups and working with feedback** in Part V elaborates what these potentially blunt and simplified terms might mean through nuanced experiences of learning colleague-ship.

My ideas and approaches have developed in relation with various colleagues and communities, especially at the Centre for Action Research in Professional Practice (CARPP), that thrived between the early 1990s and 2010 at the University of Bath School of Management and whose members and work have since migrated and diversified (Marshall, 2014). The postgraduate research programme there, the MSc in Responsibility and Business Practice, and the action research projects formed a rich community of practice and of inquiry, which evolved over the years as new people brought their interests and talents. More recently I have enjoyed the inquiring company of colleagues and course participants in the Department of Management Learning and Leadership at Lancaster University Management School, including working on the MA in Leadership for Sustainability and the MA in Management Learning and Leadership. I have also appreciated belonging to the loose network of those engaged with issues of sustainability across Lancaster University and beyond.

My ideas and developments of inquiry practice have partly been nurtured through my membership and various roles in these communities, and especially through supervising and learning alongside diploma, Masters and doctoral students. Implications for those adopting action research approaches for educational qualifications are integrated through this text and addressed in some separate sections.

Writing as inquiry

This book is as much about *writing as inquiry*, as it is about living life as inquiry. This is for two reasons. Writing has been a key inquiry practice for me and people I have worked with over the years (Richardson, 2000), and so I will offer and illustrate some of its disciplines. In doing so, I will draw on techniques taken from Freefall Writing (Turner-Vesselago, 2013).[1] Also, I tell stories as a major strand in the book to show the qualities of inquiry in action. All of these include sections originally written using writing as a process of inquiry. The stories come from different realms of life, including how I seek to contribute to change for sustainability in my own institution, and to approach puzzles about how to help an elderly relative. Through them I seek to show how inquiry invites openness to the ongoing provisionality of multi-dimensional living. This book is therefore an experiment in representation. I seek to show some of the different qualities of text, offering writing of different kinds and at different stages of development. The stories appear with 'writing notes', explicating writing as an inquiry process.

The politics, quality processes and ethics of producing storied accounts of this kind and of boundaries and revelation will be explored. Action research does not fit easily into positivist notions of objectivity, disguise and distance, and so can sometimes seem a nightmare in terms of gaining ethical consent in formal systems aligned with these principles. But the various genres of action research have their own ethical codes, typically with rigorous attention to issues of power, participation and equality. And I have some right to tell *my* story, with due care for others involved. Sometimes it might become necessary to fictionalise, invent or disguise to tell a version of 'truth', because informed consent and

---

[1]Freefall Writing™ is a writing process devised by Barbara Turner-Vesselago. See *Writing without a Parachute: The Art of Freefall* (Vala Publishing, 2013) for further details.

full confidentiality are not possible. These issues are explored generally and elaborated in relation to specific stories told here.

Choices of form and voice

This book brings together themes, issues, informing ideas, stories and possible practices. A major dilemma in writing from first person inquiry is whether I can avoid, control, balance out or justify the over-insistent 'I'. Living life as inquiry is a practice for fitting into the world, for seeking to act with integrity; it is not about focusing attention on myself. And yet the personal, political and systemic are interwoven in inquiry, arising differently in specific biographies. Living life as inquiry is therefore also autobiographical and so some elements of this seem relevant to tell. How I discern what boundaries to adopt will be discussed. Also, as I seek to exemplify living life as inquiry through accounts richly told, I have fullest access to my own experiencing, giving me opportunities to elaborate con-tradictions and tensions in this approach, perhaps thus reaching towards more generic issues through the particular.

This raises interesting issues about what it therefore means to write myself in, and reflect on my perspective(s). Of course my attempts to account for my sense-making are also partly futile. For the glimpses I can achieve, there is a vast mystery that is unknowable beyond (Bateson and Bateson; 1987; Flood, 1999; Weick, 1979). And yet I think, act and so on. So what are the quality processes by which I treat my understandings as viable enough to speak and act from? These are addressed in various sections, especially in PART II: **Dimensions of inquiry**. Always I rely on the protection that I do not have to 'get it right', that I can treat any move, including a much cherished viewpoint, as an inquiry that can be open to feedback and reviewed as I proceed.

Book format

This book has developed as a collage of different forms, as I have worked in parallel on various depictions of the principles and practices of first person inquiry, on ancillary material highlighting specific features, and on stories of inquiry. Alongside these, I offer some expressive material from novelists and poets. The sequencing offered is one way to tell and review the potential practice of living life as inquiry. But the chapters are in parallel rather than a coherent tale; they can be read in any order. As model, I have in mind a well-illustrated guidebook, to Paris say, in which I can open any page, find material in different forms – maps, cutaway drawings, overviews and in-views, references across to other sections. I find my way through it, as I do the city, as an active process. I hope that you will do so with this book. With this in mind, it is organised into six Parts following this Introduction. In each there are unnumbered chapters, some of which flow from their predecessors, some of which stand alone. There is therefore substantial cross-referencing. This uses Part numbers: and chapter and subsection titles. If, for example, in the chapter on **Inquiry in Action** I wish to make a connection with adopting writing as a process of inquiry I would reference across to it thus:

See PART IV: **Writing as inquiry:** Drawing on creative writing approaches.

Page numbers have been included only where the section referred to is not in the book's Contents list.

Following this chapter, to complete the introduction I offer a poem by Philip Larkin, standing for my concerns about current un-sustainability and social justice challenges, which inform my purposes for and approaches to inquiry. All we now do is in the knowledge of climate change, loss of biodiversity and global inequalities. As Naomi Klein (2015) says uncompromisingly about climate change in her book (entitled) '*This changes everything*'. Later in the book a second poem, by Wendell Berry, echoes this theme.

Part I **Integrating action research, systemic thinking and attention to issues of power** outlines living life as inquiry through these interwoven dimensions. A separate chapter depicts the allied approach of action inquiry, and its associated framework of action logics.

Part II is a compendium of issues and practices in implementing first person inquiry, in **Dimensions of inquiry**. Chapters consider notions, disciplines and inquiry in action. Some images of aspiring inquiry practice are also offered.

Part III considers working with ideas, theories and images as inquiry. Alongside attention to academic theories, it draws on the work of two novelists – Nathalie Sarraute and Kazuo Ishiguro who explore the nature of experiencing and representation – for their potential relevance to living life as inquiry, especially to themes of interaction, self-reflection, memory and life narrative.

Part IV explores writing as a practice of inquiry, a key approach as explained above. It also considers some of the issues in writing as representation, especially those of finding appropriate form to articulate what we have to offer. This Part incorporates two examples of experimenting with selected Freefall Writing practices (Turner-Vesselago, 2013): **Learning to Microlight** and **Walking the River Dart**.

Part V contains stories of inquiry, informed by and illustrating principles and practices of first person action research offered in earlier chapters. The stories refer to: working in inquiry learning groups and with feedback; seeking to contribute to systemic institutional change for sustainability; and wondering what to do about an elderly relative. Issues of ethical consent are outlined in each story.

Part VI contains some brief closing reflections, showing inquiry continuing.

There are three Appendices:

Appendix A considers arenas of action we can scan when we seek to contribute to change. Offered as an action research approach, it is informed by systemic thinking, notions of power and theories of institutional change.

Appendix B is addressed to those presenting first person inquiry for Masters and doctoral work. There are relevant threads throughout the book.

Appendix C is an experiment in fictionalising an inquiry account. This might be a choice for some researchers for several reasons, including concerns about ethics and disclosure. Its topic is processes of change in seeking to influence organisations to extend attention to corporate responsibility.

'GOING, GOING' BY PHILIP LARKIN

Working with the notion of living life as inquiry, I am seeking to act for change in a changing world. This book's contribution is set in the context of current profound challenges of un-sustainability, as indicated by scientific analyses of climate change (Intergovernmental Panel on Climate Change, 2014), warnings that we are close to or exceeding planetary boundaries in terms of a 'safe operating space for humanity' (Steffen et al., 2015; Whiteman et al., 2013) and reports of mass extinction of species and biodiversity (Hooper et al., 2012), with associated global inequalities, economically and materially (for example, Banerjee, 2012). Whilst there is now more rhetoric and some impressive action in relation to climate change and corporate responsibility, we also seem well able to turn away from these challenges, to continue with 'business-as-usual', leading some to explore the dynamics of 'denial' (Norgaard, 2011; Foster, 2015).

The following poem stands here for some of the sense of concern I then feel, which contributes to my questions about what integrity as a scholar means as we research and live with the challenges of un-sustainability and inequality.

Going, Going

I thought it would last my time –
The sense that, beyond the town,
There would always be fields and farms,
Where the village louts could climb
Such trees as were not cut down;
I knew there'd be false alarms

In the papers about old streets
And split-level shopping, but some
Have always been left so far;

And when the old part retreats
As the bleak high-risers come
We can always escape in the car.

Things are tougher then we are, just
As earth will always respond
However we mess it about;
Chuck filth in the sea, if you must:
The tides will be clean beyond.
– But what do I feel now? Doubt?

Or age, simply? The crowd
Is young in the M1 café;
Their kids are screaming for more –
More houses, more parking allowed,
More caravan sites, more pay.
On the Business Page, a score

Of spectacled grins approve
Some takeover bid that entails
Five per cent profit (and ten
Per cent more in the estuaries): move
Your works to the unspoilt dales
(Grey area grants)! And when

You try to get near the sea
In summer …
It seems, just now,
To be happening so very fast;
Despite all the land left free
For the first time I feel somehow
That it isn't going to last,

That before I snuff it, the whole
Boiling will be bricked in
Except for the tourist parts –
First slum of Europe: a role
It won't be so hard to win,
With a cast of crooks and tarts.

And that will be England gone,
The shadows, the meadows, the lanes,
The guildhalls, the carved choirs.
There'll be books; it will linger on
In galleries; but all that remains
For us will be concrete and tyres.

Most things are never meant.
This won't be, most likely: but greeds
And garbage are too thick-strewn
To be swept up now, or invent
Excuses that make them all needs.
I just think it will happen, soon.

Philip Larkin (2012: 82-3)

Written 25 January 1972

PART I

LIVING LIFE AS INQUIRY

Living life as inquiry is my attempt to act with integrity, context-sensitivity and agency in an ever-unfolding, complex, always largely unknowable world. This approach draws on principles and practices of action research. It is always lived out in context, in ongoing inquiry into connections, interfaces, and emergent action. It is therefore thoroughly informed by notions of systemic thinking. Alongside sits attention to potential issues of power. The resulting experimental approach is at the heart of this book's offering. As already admitted it is highly aspirational. Engaging life in this way can, at different times, be a steady approach to learning, exciting, or feel vulnerable and potentially unbounded.

In the next chapter I offer key notions in relation to action research, systemic thinking and power that inform the principles, practices and crafts of living life as inquiry. This chapter sits alongside the more elaborated dimensions of inquiry in Part II. Both are companions to the stories of inquiry in Part V. These various offerings and resources can be read in any order or in parallel.

As additional material in this Part of the book, I outline action inquiry (Fisher et al., 2003) which is an appropriately demanding framing on first person inquiry. It is accompanied by related notions of adult development and action logics.

Each person creates their own version of first person inquiry as an ongoing experiment. Each of us draw on our own distinctive array of influences and interests. Throughout this book I offer mine as potential resources, explaining how I find them helpful, and demonstrating the processes of crafting an inquiring approach to life, through which I am always seeking fresh learning, including to enhance my skills of inquiry. You will have your own influences and ways of going about the continuing process of development in inquiry, which I trust you will bring to your reading.

INTEGRATING ACTION RESEARCH, SYSTEMIC THINKING AND ATTENTION TO ISSUES OF POWER

In this chapter I set out some key reference points I draw on as I integrate action research, systemic thinking and attention to issues of power into living life as inquiry. My preferred way of working with this material is to take the frames along to an interactive workshop, to talk from them adding amplifications, contradictions and nuances as I go, illustrated copiously with stories from my own and others' experiences, and then to elaborate in relation to participants' interests. The sources of this material and how I hold it are reflected in how this chapter is written. The frameworks are offered relatively succinctly and schematically. Some sections are expressed through lists of bullet points, taken from PowerPoint slides I have developed over the years. Speaking this material interactively I feel I can keep it light, help it flow, make any statement that is too absolute in relation to the spirit of living life as ongoing inquiry shimmer briefly and fade so that it does not become too substantial. I cannot do this well here, without extensive chattering that would seem unseemly and inappropriate in print. The form adopted in Part II is thus a close companion to this chapter. Through short pieces on specific aspects of putting inquiry into practice it seeks to amplify, qualify, layer and interconnect the themes expressed here. The stories in Part V then provide extended illustrations.

In the following sections I explore action research, systemic thinking and issues of power in turn, building up a sense of how I integrate these into living life as inquiry.

Action research in brief

As backcloth to the approach of living life as inquiry there are a wealth of frames and resources for undertaking research generally and action research more specifically. These can all be tailored to given experiences and circumstances.

Action research is an umbrella term applied to a range of richly diverse approaches with their different heritages and informing ideas. In different depictions it can include organisational development (with Kurt Lewin, 1951, cited as one key source in the 1940s in the USA), the emancipatory participatory action research movements of the south (e.g. Fals Borda, 2001), action science (Argyris and Schon, 1974, 1996), teacher 'self-study' (e.g. Whitehead, 1989; McNiff and Whitehead, 2009) and the Scandinavian workplace democracy heritage (e.g. Gustavsen, 2001). Action research approaches are informed by and aligned with a wide range of other movements, intellectual and practice, such as feminisms. Connection is expressed through a host of regional and international networks and conferences. Work is collected together in Handbooks (Bradbury, 2015; Cooke and Wolfram Cox, 2005; Reason and Bradbury, 2001, 2008a) and review articles such as Cassell and Johnson (2006), which draw a variety of potential boundaries. Different actors and authors would place themselves differently in terms of research paradigms. Most are unlikely to align with positivist approaches and assumptions, although some might, many express interpretivist, social constructionist and critical theory dimensions to their work, and some connect fully to a participatory paradigm (Heron and Reason, 1997).

Action research is not then a world apart. Many of us would see 'it', and have lived its development in the last 20–30 years, as aligned with movements away from positivism towards more post-modern, post-structuralist, socially constructed, critical, participatory and action-oriented notions of social science. These changes are depicted in many publications across all disciplinary areas, whilst the continuing strength of positivist notions of science and their predominance in 'mainstream' circles is also noted. A relatively early contribution to moves away from positivism was the then radical *Naturalistic Inquiry* (Lincoln and Guba, 1985) posing alternative notions of researching and quality. The *Sage Handbooks of Qualitative Research* (Denzin and Lincoln, 1994, 2000, 2005b, 2011) have been major definitional contributions. Also in terms of the research topics they study, action researchers are engaged in many diverse worlds, thus involved with debates about appropriate notions of science and open to myriad influences.

Core characteristics of action research for me are that it:

- is concerned with knowledge in and for practice;
- involves engagement and being part of the action, with an interest in contributing to change;
- both adopts chosen disciplines and respects and works with emergent process;
- often operates through cycling between action and reflection;
- often seeks to promote participation and collaboration – although not all action research is participative co-action;

- is values-aware, rather than espousing objectivity or neutrality, wishing to contribute to human and ecological flourishing in some way;
- respects and works through multiple forms of knowing, being cautious about inappropriately privileging intellectual, analytic knowing;
- pays attention to issues of power, in multiple ways;
- is sensitive to context and to timing, judging whether it is beneficial in a given situation to blend with or challenge prevailing ways of being and social practices.

(Marshall, 2011; Reason and Bradbury, 2001, 2008)

Working with these broad intentions, how to create an action research approach for specific inquiry questions in a given context is a creative, iterative process.

The research process: an action research perspective

Figure 1 seeks to show the dynamic interplay between the main dimensions of any research when taking an action research approach. The dimensions are interactive, always open to revision as learning develops. Inquirers generate and refine questions or issues and find appropriate ways to explore them. Learning is fed from one phase of inquiry into new questions and inquiry processes for the next phase, in emergent, strategic design. Fieldwork, whatever this means in a given project, happens as learning cycles, with periodic reviews informing and shaping each next cycle, rather than being wholly intellectually pre-determined at the outset. Any feature of the researching can be radically reviewed and changed, as an inherent, iterative quality process.

How the research is conducted is significantly influenced by the research paradigm(s) with which you are working. Whilst some consider that action research is inherently linked with a participatory paradigm (Heron and Reason, 1997), paradigmatic positioning is open to a variety of possibilities, with more diffuse boundaries between options than many scholarly attempts at mapping imply. Action research might well, for example, incorporate and blend influences from social constructionism and critical theory. In action, it might nest aspects of positivist analysis, such as attention to the material conditions of participants' lives or planetary climate effects, within participative designs. How the research is framed is also influenced by the specific context within which it is conducted, and the issues of power that operate across it.

The repeated questioning in relation to each dimension as the research unfolds is: *In what ways is this inquiry?* This is an important reminder to those who are undertaking research with an intent of contributing to change, as advocacy can take over, can reduce the potential for learning, mutuality and perhaps for systemic impact. We can, of course, always inquire with critical reflection into our attempts at advocacy.

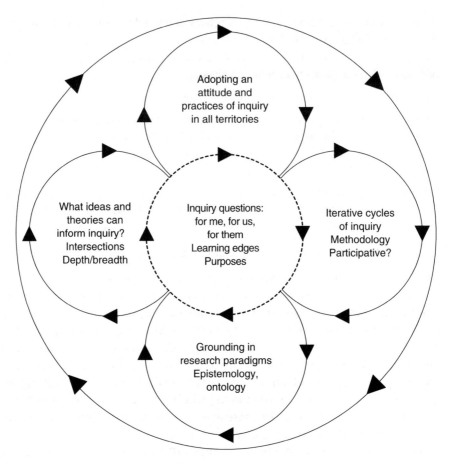

Figure 1   A dynamic model of action researching

In relation to all the research dimensions in the model, options need to be charted, and choices are then made, articulated, followed through and reviewed again, in explicit reflective sense-making processes.

How to scope appropriate topic literature is an interesting issue. Any researcher presenting their work for Masters or doctoral accreditation or wishing to publish in an academic journal will be asked what contribution they are making, with an emphasis on theory. Often people are advised from mainstream rubrics of research to focus, specialise, bound the issues they explore and identify relevant literatures. Containment of some appropriate kind is vital to engage with chosen kinds of depth and quality. Saturation – a notion that one has thoroughly explored in a given area, that researching further yields only repeated patterning and themes – is potentially relevant from grounded theory (Charmaz, 2005); and what this means can be reviewed, developed, articulated. Each researcher can explore in what ways such a notion might apply for them.

But often action researchers work at intersections and their literatures and theorising reflect this. They may bring diverse sets of ideas with different heritages into conversation. It is helpful when they know and articulate this, saying how they are scoping different elements. (It can be confusing when ideas with different heritages are forced together, appear alongside each other, without apparent awareness. 'Would these authors want to be in the same paragraph?' you might wonder, and comment.) Rather than detracting from quality and contribution, this explicit work of creative juxtaposition generally enhances conceptual quality.

Writing from this dynamic modelling of researching can tell the learning journey, a potentially hackneyed phrase, but much Masters and doctoral research has this quality. Research in this frame is not about having an initial idea that then needs *proving*, or about 'getting it right'. Rather it is about experimenting, encountering tensions and dilemmas, and learning more about these as facets of the issues being explored. Engaging requires allowing immersion to inform and expand the learning.

Given the potential richness and nuance of the research as experienced, there are usually dilemmas about how detailed any account of learning should be. The reader probably does not want to know every twist and turn, a 'blow-by-blow' account. Yet the unfolding development shows the learning, analysis and enacted quality processes. It is helpful to show some inquiring in rich enough action for the reader to judge the claims of quality for the work undertaken. Some stories in this book seek to show detailed inquiring selectively in this way. For example, please see PART V: **Acting for sustainability: Planning** *Global Futures*: **Meeting vignette** and PART V: **Wondering what to do about an elderly relative:** Experimenting with possibilities.

Territories of action researching

One way to tell the story of action research is to outline the qualities and implications of different territories of action, considering inquiry as first, second and third person. Often research is an integration of these (Marshall, 2011; Reason and Bradbury, 2008b; Reason and Torbert, 2001). This framework offers scope and flexibility. Chandler and Torbert (2003) chart the riot of proliferating forms of inquiry available from cross-matching first, second and third person inquiry into a three-dimensional array of options – identifying '27 flavors'. The potentially interwoven strands in inquiry can be seen as simultaneous attentions. This is a challenge to reflect in writing.

Living life as inquiry can be seen as especially offering a contribution to first person action research, with continual consideration of implications in second and third person terms. There are many potential connections with reflexive qualitative research, in terms of action and processes of interpretation (Denzin and Lincoln, 2011).

First person action research involves a person cultivating an approach of inquiry to all they think, feel and do, including being curious about their perspectives, assumptions and behaviour (Marshall and Reason, 2007). Their intent would be to develop their awareness, practice, choices and effectiveness in context, through developing their abilities to bring inquiry into the heart of ongoing action. This is a highly aspirational notion, and yet first person inquiry of some kind is vital, in my view, for all approaches to research that do not align with positivist presumptions of objectivity (Alvesson and Deetz, 2000; Denzin and Lincoln, 2011), especially those that engage with other people directly and open up issues of potential change in any way.

Seeking some form of self-awareness is a bold intention. 'Of course, the whole of mind could not be reported in a part of the mind' (Bateson, 1973: 408). So this is necessarily provisional, ever incomplete work, as other sections of this book show and discuss. But if we accept that we cannot give a 'full' account, that does not absolve us from integrating critical reflection into our work, in order to give some sort of account.

In the range of first person inquiry approaches, autoethnography can be seen as a cousin, with many similar intentions of reflexivity to first person action research, but from a different heritage. Tempting as it is, I am cautious about using the two terms interchangeably. Ellis and Bochner (2000) depict autoethnography as 'an autobiographical genre of writing and research that displays multiple layers of consciousness, connecting the personal to the cultural' (Ellis and Bochner, 2000: 739). The commitment to see the political in the personal and to articulate and explore this is especially valuable, and links with first person action research. Sparkes (1996), for example, critically considers masculinities through exploration of his experience of being an injured elite sportsman and associated insights into spoiled identities. Resonances between autoethnography and living life as inquiry thus include embodiment. Autoethnography seems, however, less likely to integrate experimental action into its approach.

Second person action research entails people inquiring together, formally or informally, into questions of mutual concern. One or more people might initiate the research, but the aspiration is to develop a community of inquiry with all participants becoming co-researchers, shaping research processes as well as topic(s). This is no simple matter, and the dynamics of group development with their associated issues of inclusion and power have to be addressed as well as reflected upon.

Co-operative inquiry is a clearly expressed form of second person action research, articulating how to move between disciplined cycles of action and reflection (Heron, 1996; Heron and Reason, 2008). Its principles and practices can be adapted to different situations, to help joint inquiry take forms appropriate to issues, context, purposes and participants. Collaborative forms of inquiring are often integrated into wider organisational or community initiatives. McArdle's (2002) research with young women managers provides an especially accessible and frank account of what co-operative inquiry might involve and the thoughtful, participative processes through which it can evolve. She worked with a group of young women in a corporate environment engaging in several cycles of reflection on their everyday experiences of gendered organisational processes. Through the research they generated and tested out alternative ways of operating that helped them become more resourceful in work relationships, enhancing their self-confidence.

Adopting the language of second person action research raises issues of power in participative research (Gaventa and Cornwall, 2008). Intentions of co-research cannot be naively and easily achieved and are an accomplishment for all concerned if they do become possible. One complication is the use of language involved. 'Participation' is both a descriptive term – we are in relationship, even if that is antagonistic, for example – and it is also a powerful normative ideal, invoking the potential for mutuality, engagement on equal terms. The latter may be difficult to achieve, as people engage from their different agendas, not least of which is the 'investment' the initiating researcher brings, including perhaps the wish to write the project up for their dissertation or for articles. Research can incorporate direct attention to these potential differences and their implications for living out 'equality'. Heron's (1999) proposal that when facilitating meetings and events we seek to achieve an appropriate blending of authority, participation and autonomy in a situation, at a given time, is a reminder not to over-idealise participation, and, as always, to review and account for choices made. This notion of balancing dimensions of action also has challenging implications for developing the skills of conducting research and facilitation in action research, in which engaging with others in egalitarian power relationships is an important espoused intent.

People sometimes too readily claim the title of second person inquiry when they engage collaboratively with others, especially when presenting their work for postgraduate qualifications. For this to be fully the case the other parties need to be overtly aware of the mutuality and shared influence intended and able to shape the processes and sense-making of inquiry. Often a claim of first person inquiry in collaborative relationships with others would be more appropriate, especially if large group dynamics or organisational politics are involved, and would point to more appropriate quality criteria for the work.

Third person action research seeks to prompt and support widely participative inquiry over time, for example in an organisation (Coghlan and Brannick, 2014) or in a geographic region, as demonstrated in the Scandinavian action research tradition with its strong emphasis on promoting democratic processes (e.g. Gustavsen, 2001). As with second person, the forms third person inquiry take are tailored to context and purposes. Publications can be intended as contributions to third person action research, by posing questions, stimulating debate. Often a core intent of third person action research is to promote and nurture a sensibility of inquiry amongst participants. In initial phases of a research initiative such capacity-building might take priority over other objectives. In a third person inquiry as others join in, become mutually questioning, take their own inquiring action, the project can become amplified, take light, spread. Often the initiating researcher(s) lose(s) track of all that is happening. This can be exciting, generative and a sign of the project's success. And any initiating researchers may lose a sense of control, which could be challenging for them, and require ongoing reflection on their needs and approach, and some adjustments.

Inquiry and systemic thinking go hand in hand

First person action research is always lived out in context, in ongoing inquiry into connections, interfaces, and emergent action. In my interpretation it is therefore thoroughly informed by notions of systemic thinking. This section sets out key ideas and practices in integrating inquiry and systemic thinking. (How these came to be my theories of choice is explained below. Other people make parallel selections such as complexity science with similar intents.) Elsewhere I have offered a specific story of systemic inquiry, integrating quality notes about conducting first person action research (Marshall, 2008).

Systemic thinking is a general term for a wealth of ideas amongst which there is much variety. It is foolhardy in a way to seek to define or explain it, as the ideas which most attract me have an ineffable, elusive quality in relation to which clear definition is a suspect activity. As Flood warns:

> Systemic thinking … is not something that can be explained easily and understood comprehensively. It is not recommended to rush into rationalisation of this sort. Very quickly we will lose touch with the notion of wholeness in a trivialised account of its so-called properties. (1999: 82)

I therefore offer some reference points here and exemplify them in the companion stories in this book which seek to bring this approach to life. These themes are also considered in PART II: **Dimensions of inquiry**.

My attachment to systemic thinking has grown through experimentation. I hold a loosely connected constellation of ideas and practices informed by concepts I have savoured and explored in practice during many years. I have engaged especially with the work of Gregory Bateson (Bateson, 1973, 1979; Bateson and Bateson, 1987), and similar others such as Berman (1981, 1990), Capra (1982, 1996), Charlton (2008), Flood (1999), Harris (2007), Meadows (1991, 2009), Senge

(2006), Senge et al. (1994), Watzlawick et al. (1974) and Weick (1979). These offer dynamic and complex impressions of the world. They place actors and sense-makers as participating in the patterning they are seeking to understand, rather than apart (Bateson, 1973; Watzlawick et al., 1974), a dimension which is vital for those engaged in inquiry. A wider realm of relevant work includes: explorations of how social practices are maintained or shift (Shove, 2010; Shove and Walker, 2010) arguing against notions of attitudes–behaviour–choice as a viable theory of social change; and critically systemic thinking as a competence aligned with notions of active civil society (Ulrich, 2000).

I draw on these ideas as both clues to the co-created nature of the worlds in which I engage as inquirer and to inform my senses of possible action and ways of being. Systemic thinking is then an integrated strand in my everyday behaviour and a key dynamic in living life as inquiry. How I have worked with this material has been translated through my specific life and experiences. Aspiring to continual learning has involved plenty of 'life training' in systemic living, and this continues. The materials offered in this chapter are akin to ingredients which I then draw on selectively and dynamically, step by unfolding step, as I engage in inquiry.

Thinking systemically for me involves:

- often holding in mind ideas of connectedness, systemic properties and dynamics, persistence of patterns, and resilience;

- respecting emergence and unfolding process;

- believing that often 'parts' cannot change unless there is some kind of shift in systemic pattern, but/and that sometimes 'parts' can change and influence change in the wider 'system'.

(Marshall, 2004: 308–9)

This is a view of dynamic patterns unfolding over time; of delays, non-linearities, lack of firm boundaries and so on. I need suitable resources to help me think, feel and be amidst it.

I distinguish *systemic* thinking from approaches influenced by mechanical, engineering, modernist assumptions which are more often called 'systems' thinking (Flood, 1999). (Although some authors, notably Senge (2006) and Senge et al. (1994) use the term 'systems thinking' for ideas I consider systemic.) In systemic thinking there are no clearly delineated 'things' or 'systems'. How we 'punctuate' the world we seek to understand and attribute boundaries is open to critical review (Bateson, 1973). We can work with notions of systemic patterns, recurrent flows of behaviour, assumptions and structuring which may be characteristic but shift and change. These may be considered 'emergent properties' if this does not unduly fix and cohere them. A sense of apparent order might appear in the moment, only to dissolve the next. In this framing there are no clear boundaries between 'inside' and 'outside'. For example, a person is not a separated entity, but connected through cycles of exchange to the world around them.

Systemic thinking eschews limited linear, cause and effect notions and talks in terms of feedback loops. Negative feedback damps down and controls, like a thermostat regulating temperature. Positive feedback amplifies. It can lead to escalating change, as is often depicted in relation to environmental phenomena. *The Limits to Growth* (Meadows et al., 1972) and its sequels (Meadows et al., 1992, 2004) especially highlight exponential growth in the interactions between global population, food production, industrial production, resource consumption and pollution, and their planetary implications (Meadows et al., 1992: 14). Similarly, carbon use and carbon emissions continue to accelerate upwards, despite our attempts to moderate them, partly because of rebound effects (Berners-Lee and Clark, 2013).

The term 'feedback' might give a misleadingly neat impression. Often flows of effects seem more like multiple ripples, of different amplitudes, working on different time phases. For example, I might think that an action I have taken has had no wider repercussions, perhaps only to discover later that effects are in process, triggering other effects in unfolding patterns of potential consequences that were initially beyond my view.

Seeking to understand action in complexity our attention is often drawn to 'unintended consequences'. In systemic thinking the intended/unintended distinction becomes highly questionable. Expecting all consequences to be intended is rather discordant, as if we can be in control, as if messages have clear, unambiguous meanings that are received faultlessly by listeners and so on. Such assumptions are open to critique. Bateson, as often, offers an appealing image. He points out the difference between kicking a stone, to which the actor then gives energy, and kicking a dog. The animal has its own collateral energy (a criterion of distributed mental process), interpretations of the situation and range of potential next actions. 'In the "control" of action by information, the energy is already available in the respondent, in advance of the impact of events' (Bateson, 1979: 101). We cannot predict what will happen. This is a fitting, if unnecessarily violent, analogy for everyday action.

One illustration of applying systemic thinking can give a flavour of basic elements in this approach. It is a typical, poignant, environment–human example. Fishing with nets caught dolphins as well as the intended tuna. A move to long-line fishing, with individual baited hooks, was introduced trying to avoid this unintended consequence. But then large birds, such as albatross in the southern oceans, saw the hooks when they were near the surface (before they sank lower), flew down to eat the bait, and were pulled down into the water and drowned (Marten, 2001). A global study (RSPB and Birdlife international, 2011) estimated that 300,000 seabirds are killed each year (of which 100,000 are albatross) by long-line fisheries.

Often an intended problem solution creates ripple effects of this kind. Potential mitigation measures have been developed, including: use of 'bird scaring lines' with flapping streamers, setting long-lines at night when birds are less active, and weighting lines so that the baits rapidly sink below the reach of seabirds. These also help increase fish catches as fewer baits are taken by birds. There is talk of an international treaty, and of the need to convince fishing people of the economic and conservation benefits of taking mitigation measures. This seems work in progress, at best.

We should however generally be wary. Any 'solutions' can themselves have further unintended consequences. Also we might wonder if premises on which action is based, and 'solutions' are framed, need questioning in order to think 'upstream' and operate with more systemic wisdom. Here assumptions about humans' rights to fish to maximum capacities, with industrial approaches, may be left unchallenged.

Analysing systemic patterns is intriguing and can be informative. And we need always to review whether it is legitimate to think of ourselves as 'outside' the patterns. As I eat fish, for example, even if I try to be selective, am I implicated in the deaths of birds in the southern oceans? Or can I legitimately see this as a tragedy happening at a distance?

In living life as inquiry I am always engaged in some way in any dynamics I seek to understand, if only through my interest. Typically I am entangled in organisational and other patterns, even those I decry. In seeking to understand I must appreciate the functionality of current forms (Watzlawick et al., 1974), that we are all 'doing our best' and that I may well be helping to keep things the same (see below). Also I have to live with incompleteness; I cannot know any situation wholly, from all perspectives (Bateson, 1973).

Inquiry is, then, a vital approach if I wish to learn and act within 'the unknowable that is wholeness' (Flood, 1999: 142). When I adopt systemic thinking my aim is not usually that of seeking control, however this might be defined, as control is an incongruent aim from a systemic view. Rather I am seeking to live with integrity and some appropriate influence in an unfolding, co-created world, given that I can only perceive, and act by, arcs of circuits of effect (Bateson, 1973). A key dimension of inquiry for me is, for example, whether change of some kind is possible in a given setting, whether this is a propitious moment or situation to be worked with, or not.

If I *am* seeking control in some way – for example, wanting to help certain options in decision-making become more likely to be considered and chosen – how do I then operate? Working with systemic principles in mind, I might make information available to all involved, taking care in how I frame what is offered, opening it to response and re-framing. I might talk through choices with other actors I consider influential, putting my views. Even when expressing a strong advocacy, I seek to twin this with inquiry (Taylor et al., 2008). But somewhere along the line I have to work in and trust ongoing process and the outcomes it throws up. I then generally continue to pay attention as things unfold.

Also, I might attempt to contain my vulnerability to potential harm, recognising that I have a right to self-care, and reflecting on what this means in the circumstances.

Living life as inquiry integrating systemic thinking is an aspiration to continual engagement, holding any emergent sense-making as provisional and reviewing this as action, reflection, feedback and fresh encounters with alternative perspectives unfold. I need the disciplines of first person action research for approaching openly, interpreting and then acting/inquiring again. Theories and ideas of systemic thinking are soft guides, contributing to potential sensibilities which can be tuned and developed through life experience, and through engaging in collaborative sense-making when this is available. They also offer conundrums to be worked with, as explored below.

Reaching for systemic thinking, complexity science and other such approaches in the face of the limitations of linear cause and effect thinking in a complex world not amenable to our control is, however, inherently paradoxical. We might espouse uncertainty whilst also seeking ways to know things 'for sure', or sure enough. For example, we might seek to know how to bring about systemic change. We need to learn the humility that such knowing is not available to us. Thus we must always act from inquiry, with a deliberate learning intent and appropriate individual and collective processes.

We need also to beware of interpreting or claiming solo impact in complex interactive systems. Some measure of influence might be as bold as is justified. How then can I possibly say that anything I and people I work alongside have done has had an impact? This risks potential arrogance. Some attribution of contribution might just be possible – retrospectively, in a long long-term, accompanied by a challenging conversation about multi-causality, systemic lags, timescales and criteria for what makes a 'better' world. Judging that prospectively is difficult, if not foolhardy. And yet we act. So we might seek more proximal indicators of potentially 'good' or good-enough process – open, inquiring, inclusive, politically questioning and so on. If we can submit these too to ongoing critical review.

We can also reach for notions that help us pay attention; give us some possibilities of looking just a little 'around the corner'. I have found frameworks from Senge (2006) and Senge et al. (1994) helpful for introducing notions of systemic thinking to students and practitioners. Whilst the frames can seem over prescriptive and narrowing if held tightly, they have the potential to encourage people to develop their systemic sensibilities, just as practices for meditation are disciplines to be learnt with and transcended into richer practice. Some key frameworks from these sources are therefore offered next, on this basis.

Senge (2006) collects together frequently recurring 'patterns of structure' (2006: 93), calling these 'systems archetypes' or 'generic structures', that we can learn to see in our personal and organisational lives.

> If reinforcing and balancing feedback and delays are like the nouns and verbs of systems thinking, then the systems archetypes are analogous to basic sentences or simple stories that get retold again and again. (Senge, 2006: 93)

Being able to identify these recurring plotlines offers opportunities, Senge suggests, to identify 'leverage in facing difficult challenges' (2006: 93) and ways to discuss these with other people.

The systems archetypes include the Tragedy of the Commons (Senge, 2006: 397), in which individuals seek to maximise their gain and so, perhaps inadvertently, crash the communal resources on which they all depend (Hardin, 1968). Another recurring pattern is that of 'fixes that fail' (Senge, 2006: 399), in which an attempted solution to a problem, such as putting water on a squeaky wheel, appears initially to be working, only to exacerbate the problem in the longer-term (with rusting in this case). Other archetypes with significant implications for potential change include: 'Shifting the burden' and 'Success to the successful' (Senge, 2006: 391 and 396).

Senge (2006) articulates several aphorisms of systemic thinking 'distilled from the works of many writers in the systems field', some of whom he then names (Senge, 2006: Note 1: 408–9). These principles are reminiscent too of the work of Bateson (1973) and Watzlawick et al. (1974). We can bear these in mind as we think about situations in which we are embedded, and we devise experimental next steps in action. Senge terms these 'laws' of the Fifth Discipline. They include:

- 'Today's problems come from yesterday's "solutions"'
- 'The harder you push, the harder the system pushes back'
- 'Behavior grows better before it grows worse'
- 'The easy way out usually leads back in'
- 'The cure can be worse than the disease'
- 'Faster is slower'
- 'Cause and effect are not closely related in time and space'

    (Senge, 2006: 57–63)

From this perspective, the first attempt at a solution may well be a symptom of the problem; so as we reach towards action it is especially helpful to notice our first inclinations and potentially to pause or divert them. Thus despite our best intentions and efforts, attempts at change can often lead to 'more of the same' (Watzlawick et al., 1974: 31); systemic rules may be replicated or even reinforced. This can be expressed as:

Plus ça change, plus c'est la même chose

[Translated as: 'the more it changes, the more it is the same thing'. An epigram used by Jean-Baptiste Alphonse Karr in January 1849 in his journal *Les Guêpes* (*The Wasps*) (Karr, 1849).]

Watzlawick et al. (1974: 37) offer a picture of two sailors steadying an already steady boat as a reminder that our behaviour may well be part of any 'problem' we identify (see image below). Each sailor is reacting to the other's behaviour, or their anticipation of the other's behaviour, contributing to an escalating pattern of mutual adjustment which seems likely to be uncomfortable, unproductive (the boat might well be stalled) and be heading for trouble.

Two sailors frantically steadying a (steady) boat

Source: *CHANGE: Principles of Problem Formation and Problem Resolution* by Paul Watzlawick, John Weakland, and Richard Fisch. Copyright © 1974 by W.W. Norton & Company, Inc. Used by permission of W.W. Norton & Company, Inc.

As illustration for what might be happening in this image, Watzlawick et al. (1974) give the example of one partner having the impression that their spouse is not being fully open with them, becoming suspicious of their behaviour and so asking for information and assurance. The other partner might find such questioning intrusive and withhold information defensively. This helps feed the first partner's worries. This example shows how patterns of interaction of this kind are often influenced by assumptions people make about another person's behaviour and their attempts to then make corrections for this. Sometimes these corrections happen with no regard to what the second person is actually doing or saying.

In such circumstances circuits of behaviour are more important than how the situation originated. So changes can possibly be prompted by any party adjusting their behaviour. If I find I am pulling away in a situation, for example, I can experiment with moving towards, in an attempt to stop patterns escalating and to allow fresh possibilities to emerge.

I enjoy this image, finding it a helpful attentional device. I have put a copy of the picture on my office wall as a reminder. When, in what ways, am I acting like this? Can I notice as it is happening? Can I review my interpretations or assumptions and how these are informing my behaviour? Can I consider or ask about other people's potential assumptions? Can I simply experiment by countering the pattern, by acting differently? And so on. Such questioning links closely to inquiring into whether to persist or desist, as considered in PART II: **Disciplines of inquiry:** Finding resonant phrasing. See also Living and acting in context in this chapter.

We may wonder how many of the remedies for sustainability and social justice applied in the name of corporate social responsibility will prove in time to have been 'more of the same'. One repercussion of this patterning is that languages and energies for change can become devalued and co-opted, as experience repeatedly fails to match rhetorics of intended development.

But what one person sees as the inappropriate persistence of old patterns, or even resistance, might appear to another as 'resilience'. Caution is therefore needed in these attributions. What criteria are being used? Who defines, and is excluded from defining? In what ways is power at play? Can we project potential criteria into the longer-term? Helping arrangements carry on when they are precarious could be 'good work'. But it could, alternatively, be both futile (as soon as you stop doing it, they will collapse) and inappropriate, because once things fall apart new, more fitting, possibilities might emerge. Being willing to let things fall apart, and live through the consequences is challenging systemic work, especially if it seems that other people might be hurt in the process.

Focusing back on the potential to act for change, Kim (1995: 8–9) offers a multi-level model for understanding situations and considering appropriate interventions. He distinguishes events, patterns of events, systemic structures and mental models, each more generic level shaping those nested within it. We can ask whether we are thinking and intervening at the appropriate systemic level(s). Being able to influence mental models and systemic structures is valuable as these set conditions that can then shape sense-making and action. One of Meadows' touchstones for systemic change works from similar principles.

Almost always, the most effective restructuring means putting information into a place where it doesn't now reach, or changing goals, rewards, incentives, and disincentives, so that the same people, in the same positions make decisions a different way. Restructuring a system means changing what's in people's heads. (Meadows, 1991: 59)

Condition-setting then becomes important, as initiatives seeking to encourage sustainable practices show. Although, again, we should be very cautious about thinking we can predict or control outcomes. For example, taxes influence behavioural preferences and can be more or less ecologically helpful; they can also have perverse effects of their own. In the UK, Landfill Taxes were first imposed by central government on local authorities in 1996, as the UK's first environmental tax, to encourage recycling. The tax rates have risen progressively over the years to influence behaviour, with some success in increased recycling rates achieved. But their effects are not simply causal. For example, they increase the incentive for small businesses to dump rubbish in the countryside illegally to avoid charges; and people may think recycling is sufficient, and not reduce their original consumption. Recycling could even seem to legitimate increased consumption.

Deploying a model of this kind, we can seek to ask questions of effectiveness with different systemic levels in mind. Kim argues that 'The highest leverage lies in clarifying the quality of life we envision for ourselves, and then using that as a guide for creating the systemic structures that will help us achieve that vision' (Kim, 1995: 9).

Helpful as such frameworks can be, they may also become mechanical and over-determined. They have to be lived with inquiry to become pliable resources. For example, whilst the multi-level model implies that often we should 'go upstream' to find appropriate solutions, we need an attuned sense of what this means in different circumstances, of when it might not be appropriate and of how to inquire as we go. Perhaps, say, overtly seeking to influence systemic structures could draw unhelpful attention that then polarises issues which had previously operated fluidly. This could prompt some people to defend their positions by exerting power over others in ways which will then consolidate their dominance, even reinforce it through procedural or structural devices. Seeking to anticipate if action could unfold in such ways, whilst not expecting any certainties, is part of the play of inquiry.

Systemic thinking in action

In this section I draw together potential glimpses and rubrics of what it means to live life as inquiry integrating systemic thinking, and paying attention to potential issues of power (as outlined below in Taking power into account). Over many years of trying to communicate this approach I have arrived at PowerPoint slides with lists of potential implications and choices for practice. These are expressed as first person action research, but can apply also as second and third person approaches. Acting from systemic notions is relational practice, recursive, always in dialogue with others and embedded in systemic patterns.

The list below is a prompt to be presented alongside elaboration and story. I offer it here as a succinct guide to some of the key facets of living life as inquiry. The next two sections (Living and acting in context, and Anticipating, priming attention) help illustrate what it means to adopt these approaches to life. Other sections of the book then elaborate, or cast them in a questioning light.

The list is organised under three sub-headings. Some features are matters of orientation – the underpinning approach. These seek to show the conditionality of living life as inquiry, and its priority of pursuing learning. The second section of the list articulates what seeking to act in the service of systemic wisdom and 'good' effects implies for the individual who can only see and work with arcs of circuits of effect (Bateson, 1973) and has to open all they do to continual inquiry and updating. Any actions are necessarily experiments. A third cluster depicts characteristics of ongoing inquiry approaches, showing how these are seeking pliability in an unfolding world that can be viewed from multiple perspectives. Paying attention to potential issues of power influences interpretations and action throughout.

Combining inquiry with systemic thinking and attention to power can involve the following approaches to action and being:

Orientation

- Treating action as always experimental, open to review and learning
- Working with both intention and emergence
- Pursuing purposes and interpretations within a wider framing of inquiry, so that these can be reviewed and revised
- Holding ideas and interpretations lightly
- Realising one cannot do straight line, control-oriented, interventions, however well intentioned, and that trying to typically leads to so-called 'unintended consequences'
- Questioning when to persist and when to desist

Enacting systemic principles and practices as experimentation

- Putting information into systems where it has not been before (Meadows, 1991) and seeing what arises
- Connecting up new feedback loops so that chains of consequences become more apparent, and ongoing monitoring and learning are enabled
- Tracking and questioning systemic patterns
- Paying attention to how I and we might be helping to keep things the same
- Developing notions and goals of effectiveness appropriate to systemic levels

Ongoing inquiry approaches

- Engaging in repeated cycles of: anticipation, planning (perhaps), acting, reviewing
- Appreciating inter-relationships, complexity, systemic patterns, and that we cannot know everything

- Tracking, questioning, adjusting purposes, strategies, behaviours and effects (including requesting feedback); reflecting on their (in)congruence, See PART I: **Action inquiry and action logics**: Action Inquiry

- Treating what emerges as 'data', as potentially valid information, rather than as getting things right or wrong

- Being non-judgemental (people are doing the best they can, I am doing the best I can), noticing how challenging this can be

- Not being ego-attached; this too can be challenging, especially if I think I am likely to be misunderstood, or might lose positioning that had enabled me to operate

- Seeking to act with integrity: including judging the appropriateness, in any given situation and time, of trying to fit in, acquiescing to current patterns, critiquing what is happening or contributing to creating new patterns.

- Being opportunistic

This scanning of dimensions of attention and action seeks to express the inherent conditionality involved in living life as inquiry. If things seem under control, I am not doing inquiry live. Change can be considered the way life is. Processes will unfold, often in what seem perverse ways, and I seek to maintain my abilities to treat this with curiosity, and my own attempts at life with amusement. Helpful reminders are phrases such as:

It is what it is

We are where we are

This, too, shall pass

Living and acting in context

As I draw on the approaches to action and being outlined above, I seek to pay attention to broader patternings within which I am operating (through processes of co-construction), and how these inter-relate with my senses of purpose, which inevitably unfold with time and engagement. In this section I outline some factors I am generally attending to as I continue to tease out the implications of informing inquiry with systemic thinking.

What sense can I develop of 'context' in relation to my co-construction of it? Do I seek to fit in, or explore the crafts of being different? Is this sufficiently my space? Are these people I want to be amongst? How can I conduct myself if I choose to stay?

Living out systemic thinking involves having patience and judging timing; deciding sometimes not to 'interfere' and allowing patterns to unfold as they do, so that consequences are experienced by those involved. It may appear that things will 'fall apart', but trying to hold them together may not be wise, for me, for others, for the longer-term health of systemic patterns, of their purposes and potential.

Wondering whether to persist or desist is a key conundrum of living life as inquiry. How do I know if/when to persist (especially with what seems impossible or futile) or to desist, as letting go means fresh shape might then emerge – or at least I will not spend my energies in futile trying? Several times I have chosen to stay in a situation I found impossible because the possible consequences of letting go seemed too much to bear. I would now say that was an appropriate choice sometimes, but not in every situation. See PART II: **Disciplines of inquiry:** Finding resonant phrasing.

Taking a systemic perspective, I am much more wary than I once was about valiantly setting out alone to try to improve something, although I might do, after reflection. But now I more often check sideways and ahead to see if circumstances and timing seem at least in some ways propitious. And I might seek to help them become more propitious. See APPENDIX A: **Scanning arenas of action in change.** This circling of inquiry is helpful, can build others' commitment to consider change as well as confirm mine. But I will now more often than I used to let things go.

Letting things be, although usually still paying attention in some way, may then help allow space in which different kinds of response can take shape, although these are likely to be in tension with attempts to re-establish what previously seemed 'normal'. Whether new order is possible is a perilous question. Often unexpected beneficial outcomes arise, as people step in and out and things unfold. Often they do not. Living in such ambiguous spaces, I am always making choices, noticing, adjusting, and considering how to be kind (enough) to myself and compassionate to others.

Systemic inquiry can be a rocky path: A cautionary tale

Whilst I was redrafting this chapter, I was very challenged by difficult times on the management committee of a voluntary organisation. In my role, I had been adopting the notions of acting for long-term, systemic well-being outlined above. I was seeking to contribute to fulfilling the organisation's aims and to helping develop the committee's potential effectiveness. Things had never been easy, but they became more difficult. I hung on but my patience for what was happening and for the stress I was experiencing wore thin. After several tense months, with people pulling in their different directions, there was a particularly tempestuous meeting. We staggered through tiredly to some decisions and went our separate ways.

(Continued)

It is inappropriate to explain any details. But this experience seemed a fitting reminder of the complexities of living life as inquiry, the potential messiness and vulnerabilities, and that if inquiry is 'for real' systemic thinking is no remedy against hassle and pain. Working through the aftermath of the bruising meeting it took days for images of the event and my sense of upset to subside. I sifted through my impressions from different perspectives: how I had behaved, concern for other people, whether the meeting outcomes were alright in the circumstances and so on.

I wrote a reflective note and discussed matters with learning group colleagues, trying to find an alternative future approach. By a week later I could put the event further away from me, decide not to rekindle it too much. 'It was what it was', as my colleague Vivien often wisely says about a complex experience after which we are wondering if we could have acted differently. Influenced by the learning outlined in PART V: **Inquiry learning groups and working with feedback:** Ongoing Inquiry, I decided to step back, become a peripheral member, not an easy choice for me when I care about the quality of outcomes. I am still working with what this means in practice.

Anticipating, priming attention

Whilst living life as inquiry is not about control, we may be able to increase the scope of anticipation, and so reduce the likelihood of encountering totally 'unintended' consequences, by 'walking through' potential unfolding events in imagination or more formally through processes such as scenario planning.

At times, I try to play through what might happen next, and next, to consider potential ripples. If, for example, I raise issues of sustainability at a meeting, what positions might others take? Will some want to curtail the conversation? How might they go about doing that? What choices of behaviour will I then have? Where might they lead next? And so on. One intention in doing this is to increase my abilities to work with an array of attentions as situations unfold, to relax into what is happening, to pick up cues more readily, and to respond with pliability, rather than be focused on pushing a point of view. I might take special care with where I sit in such meetings, who else I can see and so on, wanting a physical mirroring of the wider scope of vision and choice I am seeking mentally.

One factor I pay attention to is whether, in a given situation at a given time, making things more explicit is likely to be generative or possibly degenerative [see the box on the next page]. Might delineating what is happening and inviting people to take different points of view make something more apparent beneficially, or apparent and threatening to those who might question it? Resistance is often dormant until change starts to unfold. Being explicit, despite the good practice of action inquiry in opening framing to view and review, is not always helpful, in my experience. See PART I: **Action inquiry and action logics: Action inquiry**.

Generative and degenerative

I use notions of potentially generative and potentially degenerative process frequently, and so these require some explanation. In the forms of inquiry I am outlining, little can be clearly categorised as 'good' or 'bad'. Many processes have the possibility of leading to outcomes which contribute to ecological and human flourishing in some way. But all initiatives always also come with a question mark, especially as processes unfold over time. What might have seemed 'generative' can prove damaging in the longer-term. Perhaps, for example, members of an organisation advocate for corporate social responsibility reporting and this is introduced, but in time the language and measures used stultify, avoid difficult issues, fooling the organisation into thinking it is radical when it is not. This would shift from potentially generative to potentially degenerative. Often it is how processes are conducted that gives them the potential to become generative. Initiatives that incorporate a learning approach; attend to process as much as outcome; have integrated quality processes; are participative, engaging a wide array of voices; are power-aware, seeking to balance out differences in power; and are progressive, achieving initial goals and then setting new targets that surpass these, have enhanced potential to be generative, in terms of conduct and outcomes.

In this use of language, any designation is, however, always open to question. Reviewing the criteria against which the terms are judged is a dimension of inquiry.

Combining inquiry with systemic thinking offers me an orientation in the world and a palette of potential action and being. Acting from these aspirations raises issues of identity. If I see myself as acting in the service of sustainability and social justice, who am I? Where do I belong? How will others see my efforts and probable inconsistencies as I navigate between multiple worlds? I need to be willing to work at margins (hooks, 1990) rather than yearn to be 'mainstream'. See PART III: **Working with academic literatures**. Reviewing and staying connected to potential multiple identities and affiliation groups is an aspect of inner work and self-care.

In some situations I know I am likely to be misunderstood. Does that matter? Or in what ways might that matter? For example, I might consider my behaviour in a specific situation inept, but recognise that I was acting and framing my purposes against the codes of another situation, group or issue altogether, and that, perhaps, I did the best I could and would have felt compromised if I had not tried to raise issues others were not attending to. If I can judge my integrity against alternative perspectives, and in the service of a longer-term 'game', I might be able to be kinder to myself. Although I can still review the crafts with which I act. Difficult times have to be lived through; new possibilities may emerge.

As I try out different perspectives on shifting landscapes and on myself within them, I find that holding notions of action logics lightly can be helpful, to expand my range of points of view. See PART I: **Action inquiry and action logics:** Action logics. For example, I find sometimes an achiever-oriented mind takes over, and I notice that I am trying very hard to help something happen, perhaps against what I am interpreting as resistance (but which might alternatively be considered resilience). Whilst I might enjoy the agility of overcoming apparent obstacles, when this proves extremely difficult I need to back-up and take a more encompassing, emergent point of view. I might, for example, wonder what it would mean to adopt an alternative action logic which invites a longer time-frame, ironic distance in devising action, curiosity about how things unfold.

'Dancing with systems' (Meadows, 2002)

One core aim in adopting an approach informed by systemic thinking is that of finding resources to live with pliability. The greatly respected systemic thinker Donnella Meadows (2002) called her approach to living from systemic understanding 'Dancing with systems', communicating the sense of artistry involved. To encourage us to learn to dance, she offers 'the practices [she sees her] colleagues adopting, consciously or unconsciously, as they encounter new systems' (Meadows, 2009: 170). This guide to 'Living in a World of Systems' is summarised in the chapter subheads listed below. Meadows suggests you should:

Get the Beat of the System

Expose Your Mental Models to the Light of Day

Honor, Respect and Distribute Information

Use Language with Care and Enrich It with Systems Concepts

Pay Attention to What Is Important, Not Just What Is Quantifiable

Make Feedback Policies for Feedback Systems

Go for the Good of the Whole

Listen to the Wisdom of the System

Locate Responsibility in the System

Stay Humble – Stay a Learner

Celebrate Complexity

Expand Time Horizons

Defy the Disciplines

Expand the Boundary of Caring

Don't Erode the Goal of Goodness

(Meadows, 2009: 170–84)

Doppelt (2003) draws appreciatively on Meadows' work in offering guidance to aspiring leaders for sustainability. He critiques and re-orders Meadows proposals, and thus identifies his own seven 'greatest leverage points for change towards sustainability in a social system' (Doppelt, 2003: 85). The first is to 'change the dominant mind-set out of which the current system arose' (2003: 85). Thoughtful and thought-through as these proposals are, following such suggestions faithfully could have a perverse effect, could attempt to pin down or routinise, rather than encounter, rich variety and unpredictability. Systemic thinking implies that these are possibilities to be lived as active experiments, experienced fully, with associated risks, rather than formulae that can be imposed. Living live as inquiry is, rather, a craft adopted as continuous learning.

Whilst systemic thinking is a potential resource, we need also to question how we use it. Aspiration can lead to potential arrogance. Can we be discerning? Can we be attuned to a sense of purpose beyond individual, potentially egoic, interests, and beyond current measures of success and meaning, as the latter could inhibit our attempts to act for systemic change? Adopting systemic thinking can be appropriately heroic in the sense of speaking and acting outside dominant discourses, taking a stand, and helping others to explore and inquire beyond currently favoured frames of meaning. But it can never be only heroic, taking on responsibility for wider systemic patterns, setting oneself above others and other concerns.

Adopting systemic ideas in theory–practice constellations, raises a host of questions which I can take into living life as inquiry, to guide experimentation rather than to be resolved.

How do we know what sorts of change (for equality, for sustainability, say) are needed? How radical must change be to be in any ways sufficient to the challenges?

How can we tell when to persist and when to desist in micro encounters and macro initiatives? What cues can we use? How can we test out our impressions, learn as we go along?

When is apparent change really 'more of the same' and how can we anticipate, at the time, any glimpses from a longer-term view?

Might we be misleading ourselves about our impacts in relation to what matters?

How can we judge effectiveness?

When? how? is prompting disturbance productive?

Does provoking resilience/resistance reveal systemic patterns and open them to change? Or might it reinforce them?

Who pays what prices? Often architects of change lose battles but move on. Their supporters at lower organisational levels might be left to cope with the consequences.

Taking power into account

Notions of systemic unfolding are appealing, and often appropriate, but they might also be naive if we do not take account of power in its different potential conceptualisations and manifestations, which is always implicated. We need to see our thinking and action within broader perspectives, to be interested in power and politics and the potential questions these pose. Systemic patterns are held in place, challenged and changed through complex and multiple dynamics of power. Attention to potential issues of power and its enactment can be thoroughly interwoven with systemic thinking and thus becomes a further resource informing inquiry.

In this section I outline some frames on power and illustrate some of their relevance for the practice of first person action research. (They do, of course, also have implications for second and third person action research.) You will make your own theoretical choices, informed by your history and experiences. As with other ideas in this book, those below are ones I have savoured, and tested out conceptually and through practice. I use them to think through experiences and initiatives, and to question what might be happening and what parts I might be playing in ongoing action. A key inquiry question throughout is whether and in what ways dynamics of power can be contested.

A range of authors conceive power as multi-dimensional, and thus as more or less overt and amenable to challenge (for example, Gaventa and Cornwall, 2008, 2015; Hardy, 1994; Hardy and Clegg, 2006; Lukes, 1974, 2005). Any attempt to summarise issues of power is bold, but I will take this frame as an initial heuristic device in the exploration that follows. Through my own academic history, I also draw on feminist theorising that explores power in various ways, such as the work of Acker (2004), Calás and Smircich (2004, 2006), Martin (1990, 2000), Plumwood (2002) and Waring (1988). This attunes me, for example, to the potential dynamics of co-option, to how new initiatives can be subsumed into dominant frames or forms, and their radical potential muted.

I will now explore multiple dimensions of power, offering indicative but speculative illustrations related to sustainability, social justice and corporate responsibility.

Lukes' (1974, 2005) classic framework maps three dimensions of power. One-dimensional power is conceived as focused in decision-making, in which any conflict is overt. One party manages resources and dependencies, and others are aware of arising issues and able to enter the decision arena should they wish. The capacity to effect outcomes relates to abilities to mobilise resources in this arena.

Exploring one-dimensional power I can deploy all the disciplines of first person inquiry outlined in **Disciplines of inquiry**, such as scanning inner and outer arcs of attention. I might, for example, review relational dynamics in a situation which is proving challenging, notice what assumptions I am acting from and question their appropriateness. As I seek to act effectively, I might well scan the four territories of experience outlined in PART I: **Action inquiry and action logics: Action inquiry** and consider how I use the four parts of speech to seek to be clear in my framing and open to mutual inquiry. I might consider whether I am feeling sufficiently resourced and skilled to act inquiringly in the situation, or whether I am encountering issues in the dynamics that would benefit from exploration off-line to support me, for example discussion in an inquiry learning group.

Awareness of agenda control adds a second dimension to understanding potential power dynamics in this model (Lukes, 2005). Issues can be framed and the decision arena managed to avoid overt or covert conflict. Acquiring access to the decision arena and contributing to agenda-setting become major interventions. The language of the model implies formal meetings, with explicit agendas, and rules about how these are managed (for example, that all items for discussion must be identified and approved ahead of the meeting). This helps delineate the patterns involved. But the dynamics of second-dimensional power can apply as well in any informal conversation in which some options are given weight and others are excluded from consideration or devalued, and devices are used to suppress conflict and egalitarian participation. For example, in some conversational dynamics one party controls topics allowed to be discussed, maintaining those they favour and dismissing those raised by others as irrelevant in some way. This is a simple everyday example of two-dimensional power in action. Often recourse is made to norms of appropriateness of some kind to demarcate acceptable and unacceptable views; these may well be implied to be beyond contest. Aware of such norms, participants might be easily disciplined. For example: 'We need a rational debate, thank you, not to get into emotions on this one.' Such conversational patterning can threaten others' confidence and warn them to conform. It may be difficult to challenge overtly. Developing consciousness about the dynamics involved might be helpful, and open up the potential for inquiry about whether and how to address this situation. Not all potential battles need to be fought, some disputes of meaning dissolve.

It may be possible to contest the demarcations and norms people have tried to establish, drawing on approaches to inquiry outlined in PART II: **Dimensions of inquiry**, and taking due regard for potentially recursive systemic patterns as explored in this chapter. 'Well, I think we need to engage with the issue of values in this decision-making, corporate responsibility is not just rational choice. What do other people feel about this?' This approach might become more likely if we know others around will support the questioning we open up.

Formal images for seeking to contest two-dimensional power, also give clues to potential informal possibilities. Gaining 'a place at the table' is a key motif in enabling people to challenge agenda-setting power. Action may then need to mimic formal processes sufficiently to be allowable, whilst seeking not to become co-opted and have one's efforts defused. In one form of resistance to corporate power some activist organisations have bought small numbers of shares in companies to gain access to their Annual General Meetings, to raise sustainability issues, vote and protest. Friends of the Earth, activist comedian Mark Thomas and Kerim Yildiz (spokesman for the Kurdish Human Rights Project) did this to protest in 2000/2001 at UK-based Balfour Beatty's potential involvement in the Ilisu dam project in Turkey because of the environmental and human rights issues involved. Balfour Beatty withdrew; but the dam project went ahead (www.ilisu.org.uk/news23.html; http://en.wikipedia.org/wiki/Il%C4%B1su_Dam).

Power can also be conceived as acting covertly, symbolically, through the management of meaning, Lukes' (2005) third dimension. Apparent co-operation masks potential latent conflict. Those affected are unaware of ways in which they might be disadvantaged by prevailing social and institutional arrangements and do not resist, for example in situations of internalised oppression in relation to racism (Gordon, 2007). People can become more empowered through consciousness-raising and strategies for de-legitimising dominant frames of meaning. Adopting this approach invites deeper questioning.

Illustrating in relation to corporate responsibility, some attempts at resistance to three-dimensional power seek to argue for attention to environmental issues within dominant meaning systems and the language of economics. For example, the Stern Report (2007) on *The Economics of Climate Change* pointed to the urgency of addressing climate change and sought to show that deferring attention will impose a bigger financial burden than taking action now. Similarly Triple Bottom Line accounting adopts prevailing, accounting, language. Whether initiatives of this sort help change mindsets and thus operate at a three-dimensional level of power, or are too readily co-opted into established frames of meaning is an interesting matter for inquiry (Henriques and Richardson, 2004; Richardson, 2004). As people seeking to act for change we can ask these questions, and seek to conduct activities with reflexivity about the potential power dynamics involved. Three-dimensional, meaning-making power is pliable and adaptive, very likely to play out through 'more of the same'.

Seeking to contest power enacted through meaning-making is a major challenge and conundrum. Points of inquiry might be what approaches to adopt, but also how to conduct oneself with agility and not end up burnt-out or a martyr. Some of those interested in promoting awareness of societal challenges have sought to use irony to reveal hidden assumptions and power dynamics in everyday practices, depict the tensions they incorporate and make them more open to review. The Yes Men (undated), for example, adopt the approach of culture jamming, devising media interventions to draw attention to social issues and uses of institutional or other powers they see as problematic.

It may be, however, that many of us are well-able to live with tensions and contradictions (Allen et al., 2015; Foster, 2015; Norgaard, 2011) and so may not find such interventions discomforting or feel we need to change our behaviour.

As we treat our conduct as inquiry, frameworks on power and systemic thinking caution against thinking we are achieving significant change, given the insights into the dynamics of resilience they offer.

Finally, in the frame adopted here, we can also conceive of power as structural, embedded in systems which then frame the landscape for decision-making, agenda-setting and interpretation (Hardy and Clegg, 2006), and shape what seems 'normal'. Those affected may be aware or unaware, but unable to resist. Resisting and not resisting both reaffirm the status quo. The prospects of acquiring power to counter dominant discourses and institutional patterns are limited. Can we act outside current systemic patterns or paradigms? Those with privilege are unconscious beneficiaries of current arrangements, mindsets and so on. Whilst they may also be adversely affected by them in some ways, they are unlikely to welcome change. These are some of the paradoxes of embedded agency (Garud et al., 2007). We can see the power of established, unaware privilege in current climate politics. People in affluent western societies benefit from carbon-intensive economies and a long history of expansive resource appropriation and use. Most experience this as a right, which they are being pressured to relinquish. They thus see any change in their behaviour as discretionary, as a potential loss, and argue that it will have little effect as developing countries increase their environmental impacts.

Structural power is not readily open to influence, or to inquiry. Resistance would require shifting structural and systemic patterns. Those seeking to act for change must question how this can happen. Can we create different systemic conditions? Self-appointed change agents are engaged in this experimental work, taking a variety of approaches. Some people offer alternative conceptualisations, which would have different implications for frames of meaning and action. For example, the so reasonably argued framework of 'contraction and convergence' (Meyer, 1990) proposes that the global total of greenhouse gas emissions from human sources should be shrunk within an agreed time period to zero net-emissions, and that emissions entitlements should then be shared equally planet-wide.

These are demanding issues to engage as individual inquirers. It helps to be involved with people and networks to address such issues. And this brings its own complications if inquiry is your intent.

This chapter has set out principles, practices and questions in combining action research, systemic thinking and attention to issues of power as an approach to life and to seeking to act for change. These inform and can be related across to the thinking and action depicted in the stories offered in Part V of this book.

ACTION INQUIRY AND
ACTION LOGICS

Action inquiry and the action logics framework elaborated below are, like all other notions in this book, offered to be held lightly, as potential contributions to disciplined experimentation, not only within these frames, but with curiosity directed at the frames themselves.

Writing note: An early draft of this chapter was shared with Bill Torbert who approved its depiction of the work he and colleagues have undertaken, and offered additional comments, which have mostly been integrated. The frameworks introduced below have recently been revised (Erfan and Torbert, 2015; Torbert, 2013), adopting new terms. Here I have chosen to use the earlier versions I have known and worked with over many years.

Action inquiry

One of the models I hold in mind as a valuable contribution to first person action research is that of action inquiry, developed by Bill Torbert and colleagues (for example, Fisher et al., 2003; Torbert and Associates, 2004). [This is now formally known as Collaborative Developmental Action Inquiry.] It is a paradoxically clear framework inviting us to expand our awareness and potential behaviour. Its intentions are to be in the service of mutual engagement in the world and of sharing transformative power organisationally and societally (Torbert, 1973, 1976, 1987, 1991). It is depicted as a format for personal and organisational transformation, no less.

Action inquiry has connections with the action science of Chris Argyris (Argyris, et al., 1985), a term which Torbert first coined (Torbert, 1976). Argyris' version of action science specifically referred to creating a kind of conversation that can reflect back on its own assumptions and norms, and potentially change them. Torbert's notion of action inquiry included this idea and practice (second person research/practice), but also delineated first person awareness practices and third person organisational theory and practice, which all together aim at making current interactions timely within ever more complex and enlarging frames.

Action inquiry is highly aspirational, and provides grounded practices to engage in development. These are the scanning of territories of experience, and associated attention to balancing parts of speech. Action inquiry can be explained clearly, it seems, and adopted as if formulaic, as an initial way in. As soon as anyone experiments with this approach, however, it can become more nuanced, unpredictable and potentially more demanding, forcing the person to create practice in their own distinctive idiom.

Scanning territories of experience

Action inquiry suggests we develop our abilities to track four territories of experience simultaneously (Fisher et al., 2003: 18). These are:

Purposes or intentions

What are you trying to do or achieve?

What purposes do other people have?

Could there be more discussion of purposes to develop people's capacities, learning, mutuality, and a more deeply shared vision?

Strategies

What different approaches could you adopt?

How can you choose an approach which seems appropriate?

Behaviours

How can you put the strategy into practice?

Do you have the necessary skills to do so?

Effects of your behaviour

Noticing what happens

Obtaining feedback

You can then consider:

- Whether your purposes, strategies, behaviours and effects are aligned or not aligned and what consequences this has (not that alignment is an unreflective ideal)

- The timeliness of your behaviours

- How much you are willing or able to make yourself vulnerable in a given setting and how wise it is to do so

- What information you gain from interventions which seem 'unsuccessful' (and how to be more curious than regretful about these)

- Whether your contributions can invite other people to be more collaborative or open – either by modelling such behaviours or by explicit invitation (see below)

- How to gain more feedback about your behaviour or the effects of your contributions

I find the notion of purposes especially intriguing and elusive when applied in practice, adding challenge to inquiry conduct. There is often not one identifiable and clear purpose. Often a plausible surface purpose, which at least set me exploring, disaggregates into a cluster of ancillary, more fundamental and/or conflicting purposes. For example, in wanting to learn to speak more effectively at the University Senate (Marshall, 1999), I found myself wondering if I might risk my career prospects by being too out-spoken. These unfolding re-frames are interesting to explore rather than dimensions I seek to clarify and pin down.

Also, from experience, I know how disruptive it can be when people repeatedly question purposes and open things up to re-framing. Sitting on formal committees, for example, it may be appropriate to go 'upstream'. And I can see that those who invite this repeatedly can be a pain, really. People just want to get on and for the meeting not to last forever. They do not want to have to challenge the way the organisation runs itself every minute, or debate its role in society. They do not have the energy, the time. They expect some things to be accepted the way they seem to be. If these questions matter to me, I could wear myself out and get nowhere. Also, if I intervene often, I wear out people's patience, might help set new rigidities in place, be unable to access the interaction and pliability of discussion when needed. So I need to judge if this is an achievable reflection on purposes, here and now. And when might it become power politics, or a form of self-oriented showing off?

In my own conduct of inquiry, I have found pushing to receive feedback of some kind to be an important practice, but this is not always straightforward. Sometimes situations are so charged that we cannot ask directly. The issues of vulnerability explored in PART II: **Inquiry in action:** Vulnerability in inquiry apply. Also, the frame another person comes from will shape what they offer me. I need to consider this, and whether I will find that helpful. For example, if I interpret that there are interpersonal power dynamics in an exchange, I may well not ask the other person what they thought of my effectiveness in our joint action. My openness could give them an opportunity to re-enact the power-over behaviours I have been seeking to side-step and thus not to accredit. I might though ask, out of curiosity, and take a somewhat self-protective approach to how I hear the answers.

The four 'parts of speech'

Alongside the rubric of territories of experience is a complementary framework through which the attentions can be enacted and deliberately cultivated. Action inquiry invites us to notice and experiment with how we use four 'parts of speech' (Fisher et al., 2003: 23–5). These are not intended as a linear, prescribed sequence but are typically thoroughly intermingled.

Framing

    Explicitly stating purposes

    Testing assumptions

    Re-framing

Advocating

    Explicitly giving opinions, expressing perceptions or feelings, or proposing actions

Illustrating

    Giving details which ground and give direction to advocacy

Inquiring

    Questioning others

    Opening any of the above to question

Action inquiry suggests that these align respectively with purposes, strategies, behaviour and effects, although it may not necessarily be as neat as this.

You can consider what parts of speech you use. Torbert and his colleagues suggest that advocating and illustrating are most common, and therefore conversations can often be unclear because their framing is not explicit (Fisher et al., 2003) and there is insufficient mutual inquiry to explore framings and re-framings. For example, as someone tells me a lengthy tale of difficulties, I may well not know if they want me to do something with their problems or are taking an opportunity to air them and will then feel un-burdened. Also, if inquiry is muted, assumptions go unexplored. Cultivation of these skills could mean considering how to use framing and inquiring more often and productively, and whether your use and modelling of inquiry can invite other people to be more collaborative or open.

The four 'parts of speech' frame is also valuable for guiding writing. Framing and context are seldom well enough articulated in early drafts, and the conditionality of knowing, expressed through various forms of inquiry, is often key to quality. In academic writing it may be worth adding a fifth strand of *themes and issues*, the naming and teasing out of analysis, so that the writing is not weighed down by detail, explores and synthesises rather than primarily advocating, and achieves critical analysis. Themes identified can then connect with relevant academic literatures.

Adopting an action inquiry approach, we can also be cautious about any assumption that all issues can be made more explicit, through framing, and that this is necessarily for the good. As discussed elsewhere, life is also full of mystery. We need to accept that much is unknowable, so mutually engaged intelligence and action are more robust than acting alone, each from our partial view. Also, being explicit is not a universal, cross-culturally transferable value. Tacit framing often sits behind whatever we do and think – including behind any advocacy of the benefits of being explicit, and behind the textured practices of leaving things unspoken. Hall (1977) explored this in his notion of hi-context cultures, in which guides to meaning are embedded in contexts, so that small actions or signals can invoke understanding. He was working with the inter-cultural communications puzzles of his time, and contrasted hi-context with lo-context cultures in which he saw framing as explicit and available for negotiation. Hall typified Asian cultures as hi-context and western cultures such as the USA and UK as lo-context. But any culture can be seen as having hi-context features and we should be cautious about treating these as necessarily 'good'. In inquiry, I might find these issues in play as I seek to explore, and need to treat them with due curiosity, and consider what skilful practice might mean when attempts to be explicit are inappropriate in a given situation.

Action logics

Action inquiry is grounded in notions of adult development expressed through the Leadership Development Framework (Torbert and Taylor, 2008). The latter is informed by the psychometric research of Loevinger (Hy and Loevinger, 1996) and Cook-Greuter (1999), and has been validated in the field by Torbert's quantitative, qualitative, and action research (Torbert, 2013). The Leadership Development Framework outlines a tentative sequence of action logics with their organising principles through which people perceive and enact the world (Rooke and Torbert, 2005). [This was recently revised to the Global Leadership Profile, GLP, Torbert, 2013; but I will use the previous nomenclature here.]

The proposed dynamic is that people develop increasingly complex action logics as their earlier ways of operating prove ineffective for challenges they face. Previous action logics are still available within a more encompassing picture. The sequence of labels is: Opportunist, Diplomat, Expert, Achiever,

Individualist, Strategist and Alchemist (Rooke and Torbert, 2005). The Diplomat action logic, for example, aligns with group norms, and avoids conflict; that of Expert prioritises rationality and efficiency in chosen knowledge systems, believes it is possible to be objectively right. Later action logics (Individualist onwards) are depicted as post-conventional, actively questioning bases for judgement. Even if there are reservations about the elitist implications of such a model, it is possible to see the action logics as available frames, and to consider what adopting each might involve.

The transition between Achiever and Strategist action logics implies a significant shift in cognitive frames, behavioural complexity and enthusiasm for inquiry, and so is elaborated briefly here. It resembles the movement from Learning II to Learning III as described by Bateson (1973), and opens the way for double-loop learning (Argyris and Schön, 1974).

> The Achiever is passionate about accomplishing goals ... [the] Achiever frame ... focuses not just on how things work on the inside, but on how to be effective in one's wider surroundings. (Fisher et al., 2003: 52)

Despite this significant accomplishment, there are potential limitations:

> [The Achiever] views the framework of assumptions he or she 'inhabits', not as a framework at all, but rather as 'the way the world really is'. (Torbert, 1987: 111)

An Achiever action logic thus assumes aims as given, and so focuses on considering what strategies and behaviours might help achieve them; purposes are not readily open to review.

Moving towards post-conventional thinking, the Individualist action logic questions what had previous been taken-for-granted, opening more of the world to review. People adopting this frame are curious about and willing to express their own distinctive principles, and to be 'seen as different' (Fisher et al., 2003: 65).

The Strategist action logic [entitled 'Transforming' in the GLP] takes these moves further and consolidates them. It appreciates that people operate from diverse perspectives and that action has to be achieved within contested space. The world is seen as highly conditional and multi-perspectival, and adaptation is an inherent quality of effectiveness. This involves:

> becoming aware that different persons, organizations, and cultures are not just different from one another in visible ways but also in terms of the frames through which they interpret events. The evolving **Strategist** begins to realise that all frames, including his or her own, are relative. No frame is easily demonstrable as superior to another because there are no objective criteria outside all frames. Frames are constructed through human interaction, not given by nature. These sorts of realisation, experienced not just as intellectual statements but as emotional truths, attune the evolving **Strategist** more deeply than managers at any prior

stage to the uniqueness of persons and situations. But they also leave the evolving **Strategist** radically unanchored in any particular, taken-for-granted frame. (Torbert, 1987: 143–4)

Questioning and reviewing purposes is thus a key aspect of skilled performance. It is possible that this might not be a deliberate intent, but following the offered practices of the action inquiry framework enables this kind of questioning to become available, in the flow of ongoing action/reflection, contributing to development. Like all aspirational inquiry notions this is not a state to be achieved, a mechanical practice. If I think I know how to do it, I risk not engaging with full attention and openness. Inquiry that is fully under control is not fully inquiry. I must then often accept and live inquiringly with being 'radically unanchored' (Torbert, 1987: 144).

I introduce the action logics frame here to explore for its possible contributions to thinking and action rather than to consider as true or to use as a grid through which to analyse the world. The framework itself invites us to be curious and reflective about how we hold frames.

Living life as inquiry would appear quite differently enacted through different action logics, and notions of skilled inquiring performance would also shift. An Achiever logic might emphasise goal achievement, for example. A Strategist logic might continually question purposes and seek contextually sensitive framings and re-framings. An Alchemist approach is in the service of transformation, whatever that requires. As will become apparent as this book unfolds, living life as inquiry is offered with the latter two images of possibility more in mind, appreciating that, in any experience, we might well move through multiple action logics.

PART II

DIMENSIONS OF INQUIRY

A compendium of facets, glimpses, choices

This part of the book explores a variety of dimensions of first person action research. It includes potential rubrics distilled from many years of living with inquiry as a guiding motif. I draw on these as reminders to myself, in peer conversations and when coaching others in first person action research. These are not clear guidelines. My intention and advice is always to hold these possibilities lightly. You could imagine them offered in conversation, with a tone of 'well, maybe ...', and in dialogue with you saying how inquiry is for you, or wanting to consider how to extend and deepen your practice. Inquiry involves identifying, making and charting choices. This material offers some signposts as resources in these processes. It fills out the overview of living life as inquiry given in Part I.

Devising processes of inquiry is akin to research design in other methodologies. Finding suitable forms to align appropriate ways of exploring with searching inquiry questions is a process of discovery and creation. Inquiry requires disciplines of some congruent kind, it is not a matter of 'anything goes'. Scope is important. How can we shape inquiry so that it addresses interesting and researchable issues, is not trivial, but is also not overwhelming, potentially too diffuse? Also I aspire to inquiry in which it becomes possible to explore what I could not possibly imagine, to reach beyond encountering only my own shadow. Can I listen enough, be alert to what else is going on besides what I bring? Can I partially set the latter aside in some form of phenomenological bracketing? What practices of inquiry will help me engage fulsomely?

Throughout the book aspects of living life as inquiry are selected for moments of separate focus. There are many caveats to this approach. Living process is integrated, whole. One could say 'multi-dimensional', but that would imply separable dimensions, and we create these as a matter of dexterity, through 'how the sequence of experience is punctuated' (Bateson, 2000: 293), to which we bring purposes, conscious and unconscious. So pulling at any apparent thread to examine it is a contrived process. All else may follow close behind that which we take as temporarily figural. And, but, the contrivance of focusing can be part of our practice, seeking to discern what is going on here, now, with its textures, which we provisionally name.

The dimensions of inquiry below can be read alongside the stories in Part V of this book. We can talk, a lot, *about* action research, but matters of heart, spirit and tilting into wind and taking the consequences are not so easy to communicate. I hope the stories provide senses of inquiry unfolding dynamically over time to complement these chapters which could seem somewhat static and generalised.

The format in this Part has been chosen for its congruence with the content. I am seeking to articulate facets and glimpses. There is no intent to pin down a mythical 'whole'. It is contrived to sequence dimensions of inquiry that may well be relevant simultaneously. So you have choices of what paths to follow through the compendium of entries, and the accompanying stories.

NOTIONS OF INQUIRY

Crafting your style, disciplines and practices

Notions of inquiry, theories and frameworks, come from different contexts and lives. You can be open to your form(s) and its (their) development, rather than prematurely judgemental or conformist. You can explore, borrow, adapt, innovate. Sometimes developing inquiring practice requires consenting to an offered approach enough to learn about it from within, and then adapting it as you wish. Sometimes it means cleaving to your independence, belligerence even, asserting repeatedly what is *not* your way, until some form arises that is, and has that mark of 'you' that will make people who know you smile.

Advice – like suggesting that people keep a research journal – is both sound and has limitations. Each person has to generate their own forms, ways, times of and for inquiry. However, finding some time and space for reflection and styles for this that suit you are key. People do this differently. And for different purposes. Those who want to offer their first person inquiries for an academic qualification – a Masters degree or doctorate, for example – need to consider what their versions of 'data' and of 'evidence' are, how they will show them and affirm the quality of their processes of research, what sorts of account they will give.

Concern for quality of inquiry is inherent. I want the knowing I live by to be appropriate, robust according to its genre. And quality is always in process, requiring ongoing attention, discipline, review and creativity. When academic criteria need addressing alongside life criteria taking charge of this process is imperative. This involves framing what one is doing, and using and potentially creating appropriate criteria, informed by the wealth of relevant resources now available. (These include Bradbury, 2015; Denzin and Lincoln, 1994, 2000, 2005b, 2011; Reason and Bradbury, 2001, 2008a.)

Whether inquiry engages multiple ways of knowing and is fully embodied are two indices of quality for me. I, and many of the colleagues and students I have worked with over the years, have in some way been challenging the privileging of propositional knowing over other forms, such as experiential, practical and presentational knowing (Heron and Reason, 2008). I see emotional, intuitive, embodied, experiential, practical, spiritual and intellectual ways of knowing as integrated, interwoven. We are, for example, always feeling in some way, in my view. Whilst we might, still, bring attention to different facets of experiencing, I am wary about clearly demarcating them. These are significant issues of the politics of epistemology, and relate to how research paradigms and forms of knowing are considered acceptable or unacceptable in different contexts.

A loosely organised range of conceptual and practice-based influences, accumulated over the years, informs my approaches to inquiry. These include feminist perspectives (such as Acker, 2004; Calás and Smircich, 2004, 2006; Martin, 1990, 2000; Sinclair, 2007, 2009; Spender, 1980) and other realms of theorising that are alert to power and politics, for example in relation to global issues of inequality (Banerjee, 2008, 2012; Dar and Cooke, 2008). Such approaches especially give questions of epistemology a critical edge, raising issues of voice and knowing. As you design inquiry, you can consider your heritage of interests, and what these bring as informing epistemology(ies) to your development of inquiry approaches.

Initiating inquiry

How do we identify issues for inquiry?

How do we recognise when inquiry seems to have arisen, as if of its own accord?

How do we discover what has real interest and energy for us?

How do we scope inquiry somewhere between vast, entangled and focused, contained?

Identifying issues for inquiry is inquiry in itself, an iterative process of noticing, working with, shaping, testing out, revising. Inquiries can start in many different ways, deliberately or unintentionally. Often inquiry arises from following curiosities, interests. I notice a repeated fascination or puzzle; I want to pay it more attention. Typically I want also to develop my crafts or capacities in some ways too. For example, Marshall (1999) reports on taking learning to speak effectively as a new member of University Senate as an inquiry project. Sometimes inquiry involves addressing what might otherwise be problems or diffuse worries and giving them clearer edges so that they can be explored in some way. This opens the possibilities for typical behaviour patterns to move on.

Framing inquiry may appear instant. Sometimes the rich question arises clearly for us to articulate and enact. But often it is a slower, more emergent, process with tantalising glimpses of what might be interesting and have energy that then take time to form a shape we can work with. Testing out our potential framings of inquiry on supportive, critical, friends can be helpful. Sometimes the immediate phrasing of an issue does not hold continuing energy, and revision is needed to identify the exciting challenge.

Scoping the territory of inquiry

In identifying something as a topic for inquiry we need to be cautious in several respects. We may identify when a theme in inquiry started, for example, only to find reflective notes from much earlier showing that this was already on our minds. There are seldom neat starts, or ends. Our ways of punctuating the time stories of inquiry are choices, which we can reflect upon and open to review. We can lose sight of the, often multiple, overlapping contexts within which inquiry occurs, simplifying the picture. Looking back at any point, we may interpret, but this is to fix the fleeting moment, innocent of other influences, mirrors and connections that we were not consciously aware of at the time. Or our sense-making might create meaningful figure against implied ground, when the ground is more influential, it should not be relegated to background (Weick, 1979).

From what might be termed a positivist research perspective (Guba and Lincoln, 2005), any diffuseness about how inquiry arises might be considered a fault. From the perspective of living life as inquiry this is, partly, just the way things are. I can be curious, amused, thoughtful about it. I can seek to expand the realms of my attentions. I can invite different perspectives from others in the field of inquiry. But completeness is not an option. Nor, except in exceptional circumstances, is one coherent account agreed amongst all those involved. (Whatever 'involved' means.) Inquiry cannot be known, or spoken, fully. And we have to live with, and seek to speak from this, without pinning dynamic processes down into things.

Propitious circumstances

Sometimes specific situations or sequences of activities seem to offer especially propitious conditions for engaging in inquiry (Marshall, 2001). I might, for example, attend a conference on an intellectual or action topic I am puzzling away at, or might meet with a friend I have not seen in a while and we each try to express succinctly what is currently important to us, the arising phrasing offering me fresh perspectives that I then want to inquire into. In propitious circumstances, key issues and themes seem to come together or be made apparent in what I am doing, reflections bubble up. See examples of arising inquiry themes in PART II: **Disciplines of inquiry:** Finding resonant phrasing. I can then more intentionally adopt the disciplines of inquiry outlined in the next chapter.

I do not know when prompts to engage in inquiry will emerge. Thus it is difficult to know what digression is in a life lived as inquiry, when anything can be treated with curiosity or can take on potential significance. For example, chance remarks can echo, setting off trains of reflection. When a learning group colleague said, as if a fact about me, 'of course, you are always in a hurry', I later found this phrase ringing in my ears as I walked the platform at Birmingham's New Street station waiting for the 10.15 train wondering if I should be doing something 'useful' (and noting some associated childhood messages). See PART V: **Inquiry learning groups and working with feedback** Moments such as this draw my attention, help me notice a pattern that shows through like an habitual gesture, and invite me to adjust it – like loosening if I notice my shoulders tensed. See PART III: **Drawing on the work of Nathalie Sarraute:** Tropisms.

When such reflections arise, what do I do with them? If I let some glimpses be said, then others emerge. I am interested in pausing to notice, and curious about whether experimentation or change might then arise. But I do not want to overplay the significance of such experiences. If all I find out through inquiry is that I try to fit in too much, and try too hard, that is not necessarily insight.

Living this way implies then accepting a looseness of boundaries, congruent with systemic thinking, and not seeking control. So life can seem out of control much of the time, and I notice how my efforts are therefore sometimes directed at creating temporary enough order to keep on going on.

Being is 'action' too

Inquiry includes, for me, experiments in being, although the term *action* research may mask the importance of this. It could entail, for example: experimenting with a shift in perspective; deliberately not-talking at a meeting; reviewing and changing my assumptions or expectations when something does not turn out as hoped; accepting a pattern of relationship as it seems to be, rather than pushing to develop it; and being kinder to myself. All of these can be experiments in living as inquiry. In the stories of Acting for sustainability and Wondering what to do about an elderly relative in Part V, for example, biding one's time and playing 'wait and see', respectively, are ongoing experiments in being, which involved continual active attention whilst not seeking to unduly shape or jeopardise unfolding action. Often the 'outcome' of living life as inquiry is a shift in someone's sense of self, rather than some 'achievement' in terms of action.

Treating an issue as inquiry is not about giving priority to trying to make something happen. It is holding an attitude of curiosity as I go about trying to make things happen. I include myself in the circle of curiosity, and so I am seeking always to be open to reviewing purposes, strategies and behaviours as well as apparent effects. See PART I: **Action inquiry and action logics:** Action inquiry. The broader purpose is to have a richer existence rather than to sort life out and reduce its variety.

Designating something as inquiry, wondering how to stay alive to it, and to further questions that then arise, can be a potential release of any tension, or can shift inquiry into a different modality. And, amongst other questions, this raises issues about the potential nature of integrity and effectiveness, and how to explore these notions in appropriately contexted ways. Cause and effect are not implied. If the situation changes it is typically inappropriate from a systemic perspective for me to claim credit for my potential contributions in an egoic way, although I might affirm how I stayed present, or something of that kind.

Vicious or virtuous cycling?

If inquiry comes alive when there are 'problems' to work with, does living life as inquiry risk being a continually worried way of being in the world prompting dissatisfaction, disappointment or self-punishment? (Especially in contrast to the recent growth of appreciative inquiry and its warning that the nature of the questions we ask ourselves is fateful; Ludema et al., 2001; Ludema and Fry, 2008.) Could persistent inquiry mean losing a sense of pleasure and ease with being alive? Well, maybe yes, of course, but not necessarily. I see living life as inquiry as a floating choicefulness, always seeking to be self-reflexive. It is a practice for being curious. Mostly it is fun. As I probe away at something, allowing that all 'outcomes' are interesting and can be worked with in some way, I feel more resourceful. I can treat disappointment, say, with curiosity, be kind to myself and see what then arises. I do not have to try hard to influence for specific outcomes, as what emerges is way beyond what my efforts alone can achieve, and will be interesting systemic data. And I can choose whether or not to designate something as inquiry; I can leave aspects of life unprocessed and rest awhile.

These issues raise an important health warning. Perhaps inquiry can become obsessive, too self-engrossed. We need to take care if this seems likely and to invoke support from co-inquirers to challenge such patterns, and help us take other paths. We could ask *in what ways* do we each do inquiry, and do the forms we adopt express something interesting about us, that we may also want to experiment with, to open to development?

Often Masters, doctoral students and others who find living life as inquiry an appealing notion, 'admit' to having been quite controlling, previously more positivist in their notions of research. So, perhaps encouraged by complexity and similar theorising, they seek to work with more emergent processes. But a pendulum swing is not obligatory, or necessary, and they may find this a struggle. It may also be highly inappropriate as the person finds themself fighting concerns about being out of control. They could instead seek a 'meta' position in which they have more choices of strategy and approach, disciplined *and* emergent. These are potentially exciting aspects of deciding *how* to work with inquiry, with the research design process.

Amongst this welter of possibilities, how do we know when inquiry is alive? This is an ongoing question. In brief, I suggest that it is when the issues addressed are current puzzles rather than largely historical, when something is at stake, when I experience a combination of excitement and fear. If I repeatedly forget what I have committed to inquire into, that is a potentially important sign; perhaps that intention and energy have moved on; perhaps that I am avoiding something. As we move into and through inquiry we can be curious about whether we are addressing core issues, or might be into displacement away from difficult territories. But if we are critically reviewing, and open to re-framing as we go along, perhaps we can start almost anywhere and lead ourselves into inquiry that has meaning. Inquiry that lacks meaning is not so likely to thrive, will become arduous and empty to maintain. But foolhardy 'bravery' is not necessarily inquiry, especially if pursued in a punishing way. In which case the light of inquiry could be cast on the way of conducting the exploration and the attitude to self it seems to express.

Multiple ways of knowing

Inquiry as offered here is a whole person, embodied experience, respecting, working with and expressing multiple forms of knowing. How I feel is a key channel of understanding to be set within a wider array of modalities, and I will seek appropriate ways to do this, including in academic work and representations, then considering quality judgements of appropriate kinds.

As I live inquiry, there are cues I can review as I scan, judge and adjust different forms of attention. The qualities of my breath, for example, how I sit and stand. Inquiring is not about getting something 'right', but about noticing what *is*. For example, perhaps some avoidance of an issue or what someone is saying may show up physically, as I find myself pulling back in my seat. What do I do if I notice this?

People often take the permission incorporated in inquiry to affirm their own voice and knowing. They may extend this to assert that whatever they feel or think is 'true'. It may well be so for them, although they might like to test this out. But cleaving only to what Belenky et al. (1986: 54–5) call 'subjective knowing' has limitations, especially in the space of degree-related research projects. We gain from moving between and combining different forms of knowing. In these authors' terms, that means integrating the different voices of subjective, received and procedural knowing (the latter as separated or connected, Clinchy, 1996), to articulate 'constructed knowing' (Belenky et al., 1986: 137–9). This is highly conditional, open to revision, incorporating its own quality processes.

Working with multiple forms of knowing inevitably engages the politics of epistemology and issues about what forms of knowing are considered acceptable and unacceptable in different contexts. Academia and research have tended to favour rational, distanced, propositional knowing, but this can now be open to contest.

Voice

Issues of voice pervade inquiry. The politics of voice have implications for inquiry, form and representation. Partly brought up through the feminist debates of the 1970s and 1980s, I am especially alert to issues of terminology and valuing, potential polarisation, potential silencing and more. Dale Spender's *Man Made Language* (1980), is an icon for me of those times, with its analysis of how gender associations enhance or demean value.

Inquiring practices can be seen as inferior to assertive action. Behaviour intended as inquiring can be interpreted differently by others. I may appear uncertain or even anxious, when that was not my intention or experience. Carrying off being inquiring can thus be an interesting accomplishment. This could have different dimensions in relation to issues of diversity. For example, a tall, white man with a senior role of some kind might find people's expectations thwart his attempts to be openly inquiring. Or a woman whose style is based on questioning and participation could find it hard to side-step people's concerns that she might be hesitant and unable to maintain appropriate 'control' and order.

DISCIPLINES OF INQUIRY

Once inquiry has been initiated, how do we then shape it? I use the notion of disciplines for broadly based approaches to inquiry which have inherent quality processes and can be applied systematically. These include engaging in cycles of action and reflection, and interweaving inner and outer arcs of attention. They are outlined below, following consideration of some factors influencing how we adopt and enact disciplines. I sometimes use the term 'practices' for more specific activities within the broader notion of discipline.

Disciplines do not come ready formed, but need crafting to person and circumstances. Developing them is akin to learning basic practices of meditation such as paying attention to breath and posture, and letting thoughts pass rather than clinging at them. I initially consent to the basic form, to hold myself to its rules, and I also adapt and extend it to become my own. Working through disciplines of inquiry is always also a creative dance, respecting and working with what emerges.

In relation to both disciplines and practices we can develop our skills, doing this through applying the individual and collaborative learning processes of action research. Such developments are life-long processes. And our capacities to inquire are not simply matters of quantity, to which we can add incrementally. Living life as inquiry is an integrated approach which can be qualitatively developed through practice, and can involve shifts in our framing on the world. Inquiry might thus become more challenging and disruptive with experience, as a sense of expanding competence encourages us to choose to make ourselves more vulnerable, to seek deeper engagement and learning.

In the early stages, inquiry may appear neat, as someone finds their way, following guidelines they have chosen. Gaining more confidence, they can let their processes of inquiry flourish, develop into more varied forms. At the other extreme, inquiry may initially appear messy and fragmented, with a lot going on but little discernible pattern. The inquirer can then review what is happening and shape it a little more, to extend their disciplines. Any terms that might be applied to the forms inquiry takes, like 'clearly focused' or 'sprawling', are not inherently good or bad, but can be reviewed for their appropriateness to the issues being explored, for relevant quality processes, for how they consolidate or extend current skill patterns.

Published accounts of inquiry usually do not help us know what experiencing it might entail. They may imply it is deliberate, rational, and clearly shaped. It may also appear as if inquiry is a high-energy persistent activity, somewhat mechanical even, never flagging, as the author recounts engaging in cycles of action and reflection and so on. Well sometimes this is so, although not heartlessly. And often it is not. We can notice the emerging forms inquiry is taking, including phasing over time, and whether these have meaning of some kind.

Finding resonant phrasing

Cloaking an inquiry impetus with appropriate words to frame and pursue it is a delicate, interesting, potentially playful and definitional process. My sensory experience of what is puzzling might not be initially amenable to clear expression. I may want to pause tentatively for some time, trying to establish what shape the dilemma is taking, what words can hold its ambiguities and nuances. And when I can give a shape to the initial grains of inquiry that makes it hurt almost or be thrilling, or sometimes both, then I feel I have experience that is more engaging to inquire into. I enjoy word play in these processes. Key phrases capture an issue I am working with, often have an edge of ambiguity, conundrum or challenge that I want to keep on engaging. Realising that I am often inquiring into whether to 'persist or desist' had this ring for me when it arose (Marshall, 1999) [see the box on the next page].

As illustration, the following are fictionalised examples of inquiry intents (immediate or longer-term), drawn from my experiences of helping people give their inquiries shape:

How do I need to conduct myself in order to stay generatively in this organisation that I am seeking to flee?

What notions of sustainability can be fostered in this organisation at this time?

How do I know when enough is enough?

When and how do – and can – I enact the kind of leadership I respect?

How can I build a more effective relationship with my control-oriented boss?

How can I raise ethical issues without being considered too rebellious or crazy? What does it mean to do this skilfully?

First person action research is not necessarily about making major interventions for change in a situation, although it might be. Often inquiry is about the micro practices of behaviour, as some of the themes above illustrate. This does not mean that micro inquiry is unambitious. Systemic change can be influenced by small shifts in behaviour. See the two sailors image on page 16.

Finding resonant phrasing:
How can I know when to persist and when to desist?

Evocative images or phrases sometimes arise to organise my sense of inquiring, helping me pay attention and engage in ongoing review. I welcome this, and the associated embodied impression of living questioning.

The sense that I am often inquiring into whether to persist or whether to desist took shape for me in the 1990s, and continues as a valuable motif. I had been reflecting on this theme, from a macro scale of whether to continue certain activities to the micro level of how to act in specific situations. Forming the phrase and recognising its repeated relevance gave this stream of inquiry heightened energy, focus and capacity to challenge me.

Several influences had come together (Marshall, 1999). Whether individuals can affect complex systems or contribute to other peoples' development, and if so how, are key questions which recur across my personal and professional practice. In the late 1990s these were relevant in various domains of my life. For example, I had been treating how to speak effectively as a new member of University Senate as deliberate inquiry; and a colleague and I had been trying to help revise our Department's annual appraisal processes, to somewhat mixed reactions.

Also, I had been analysing research data that suggested some senior women managers had stayed over-long for their own well-being in hostile circumstances as they tried to enable change (Marshall, 1995). I concluded that in some cases the women had discounted their perceptions that organisational processes and senior colleagues were tracking against potential change, and had ignored their own needs, disregarding their own safety.

These various experiences and reflections can inform my sense of what inquiring into whether to persist or desist means. The research on senior women managers, for example, invites me to consider what sources of data I am and am not paying attention to, and how selectivity might limit my abilities to inquire. Any such exploration takes shape within an appreciation of systemic thinking, mindful of the dynamics of resilience. This also informs choices and crafts of what persisting and desisting might then mean in action.

Using a rubric such as 'inquiring into whether to persist or desist', helps me pay detailed attention and experiment. Whatever then happens is potentially interesting 'data'. Sometimes I decide to persist when there are strong countervailing factors, seeking to give possibilities a chance to become realised. I try to do this with some awareness and subject to ongoing inquiry, but hoping for effects can take over. How can I tell if my approach is appropriate and timely? If a person stays over-long in a draining situation, this can erode their capacities for insight and behavioural flexibility, and may damage both them and the issues they sought to act for. Intending change agents can become co-opted, innovative moves difficult to frame, jeopardising future potential effectiveness. Making such calculations, a person might choose to pay the price and wilfully persist. It may be possible to reduce the costs, for example by setting a time limit to activities or adopting an inquiring detachment. It is interesting to discover what does then happen through persistence, and this can be contrasted with other times of choosing to desist, contributing to systemic learning.

Inquiry can, then, be carried in questions that become articulated, framed, and can be pursued long-term, may wane and increase in significance. Eventually a question can become emptied of energy, satisfied enough. Warming up inquiry questions that have lost their vitality is not advised; we can instead note their passing.

As we frame and review emerging inquiries, we can wonder if a potential topic and research approach mirror each other. For example, if someone is exploring their role in organisational change processes, might their experience of a chosen emergent research approach challenge their needs for control? Could this provide insights into dynamics of resistance and resilience that relate to their chosen topic? We do not have to see such potential resonances as tightly coupled to be curious about them. Exploring how different dimensions of researching might mirror each other might offer richer learning than would taking an objectified approach. Although we need to be cautious about interpreting inappropriately, beyond the realm of our 'data'.

Potential resonances might influence how we make sense, and therefore benefit from review. Perhaps, for example, the sense of loss that permeates my work on environmental sustainability, and thus my life, whilst based on plenty of data in my view (such as Hooper et al., 2012; Intergovernmental Panel on Climate Change, 2014; Rockström et al., 2009; Steffen et al., 2015), may also reflect or be amplified by my own ageing. How then do I carry this awareness of possibilities into my sense-making?

All such factors might become open to review as we inquire, and are more likely to do so richly if we engage in some practices of co-inquiry, opening our sense-making to discussion with others. But this also shows how inquiry is often a whole-life process and boundaries are difficult to draw. It is potentially rich, fascinating but also demanding and challenging.

Combining intention, discipline and emergent form

I approach inquiry partly by having an attitude of acceptance. I am not, despite any sense of intentionality, attempting control, which I see as limited and often degenerative in a complex, systemic world. Gentle direction is fine; intending, persisting, following disciplines. And I need also to notice if I am holding an approach too tightly, giving a lot of energy to maintaining a pattern of engagement which is not really working that well, whilst life might be trying to take a different shape. Then I hope to notice when it is appropriate to let go and allow different possibilities to arise. Although I may also, at times, after review, choose to hold some things tightly, be these interests or disciplines of inquiry.

In any situation we can ask 'what form is inquiry taking here' and/or 'what form could it take?' Noticing what emergent form inquiry is already taking helps us consider what is being expressed through inquiry and how to craft a congruent discipline rather than impose something different, potentially alien and idealised. For example, is inquiry taking the shape of an almost breathless rushing forward, with someone asking questions everywhere they go, of every dimension of their life? Is it clearly demarcated and adopted step by step, following an articulated model? Is it a priority one week, nearly forgotten the next? Does it change shape, the core questions regularly revised? Does it feel light, a little ethereal? Does it feel heavy, a weight nearly impossible to carry? In any of these cases, we can seek to discern our learning intentions and consider how generative or potentially degenerative the arising form of inquiry might be, reflecting on the criteria of appropriateness used. Emergent form can then be respected, worked with, allowed, or encouraged to shift shape if appropriate. Sometimes inquiry has become diffuse and I need to become more disciplined, returning to or creating anew an iterative process that takes me through different dimensions of attention, helps me cycle between action and reflection, and reminds me to pay attention to others' voices as well as my own. At other times it may have become too routine, with no apparent heart. I can explore what impetus is being expressed, whether it could be relinquished or is still relevant learning for me. If the latter, I can then work with what is happening and help to craft it into an appropriate genre of inquiry with vitality.

So there is the both/and-ness of seeking to surrender oneself to what the inquiry needs to be and also the sense of needing to contain or focus it enough to achieve a depth and quality of engagement about issues that really matter. This involves integrating broadly based scanning with selective tracking (Marshall, 2001), lest I become swamped by trying to take on everything. Sensory cues help me gauge what appears important, and avoid inquiry that is well practised but inappropriate or dull.

People undertaking action research dissertations especially face such dilemmas. They also need to consider how to do only one dissertation rather than engage so richly that they have material enough for two or even three. Even if the exploration is difficult to limit, they can at least be selective in the story they then tell.

Bearing the above considerations in mind, the next sections consider some potential disciplines of first person action research in more detail.

Attentional disciplines

Drawing on co-counselling

We each have our range of practices for paying attention and learning. Mine are apparent throughout this book. Here I want to briefly outline an influence on them to which I repeatedly return.

I am very grateful for having learnt and practised co-counselling in the 1980s, along with exploring a range of other process-based approaches (Marshall, 2016). Co-counselling (Co-Counselling International, UK, 2014; Heron, 1979) is a reciprocal, peer counselling process in which all parties are equal, once they have undertaken initial training in practices and principles. The basic form involves two people working together in a space they create through an agreed contract about timings and the form working will involve. They then take turns to be client and counsellor, the latter paying attention, holding the space and occasionally asking questions, whilst the former talks or works in whatever way they choose. The client is self-directed and in charge of their session. From this approach I learnt about paying attention; creating a safe-enough space for me or another person to work in; heeding, moving between and expressing multiple ways of knowing; and acting into fleeting emotions, images and thoughts in order to learn more about them. I found that even what might seem potentially 'bottom-less' emotions or persisting thoughts can change form and move on if they are expressed, experienced and reviewed non-judgementally. Co-counselling certainly does not imply that my experiencing is 'true', rather the processes might help me engage it with critical reflection.

I have adapted co-counselling practices so that I can do them alone as a potentially silent internal process, and can apply them in learning conversations with others, if I consider the space sufficiently safe. For example, as I take the bus home, I might notice a tag of lowered affect flit through my attention. I can let it go. Or I can take a gentle look. What is it about? If I ignore it, repress the image, will the associated mood become detached from its potential trigger and persist? Can I turn the experience in the light and see it a-new? Is there some inquiry I need to pursue about this? See PART II: **Notions of inquiry:** Multiple ways of knowing and PART II: **Inquiry in action:** Vulnerability in inquiry.

Practices for staying curious

Working from a range of attentional disciplines, I have tried to tune myself to stay alert and curious in situations which seem tense, chaotic, incoherent and difficult, for me and others. That I need to adopt a different approach is some-times cued for me by my impression that I am somehow trying too hard. See the two sailors image on page 16. In such situations tensions, contradictions and difficulties may need expressing rather than blocking. How might I, we, know? Can we live out the potentially turbulent consequences without grasp-ing after all for control? In such situations, wondering what is happening, I adjust. I deliberately relax a little, scan around me. I listen to context and oth-ers as well as myself for potential cues, prioritising attention to feelings and process over topic. I wonder about potential patterning (knowing that this can though be an inappropriate imposition of ordering). I try to sit with what is occurring, embodying inquiry, metaphorically, and stepping back a little to gain a wider view. I move towards more questioning, seeking mutual review, even if advocating (Taylor et al., 2008).

These are all, of course, aspirations for practice, potentially helpful reminders, and sometimes there are moments when I think I achieve this.

Scanning inner and outer arcs of attention

One of my images of inquiry is that of continually weaving between inner and outer arcs of attention (Marshall, 2001), working with an image of a figure of eight, repeatedly over-written. See Introducing first person inquiry on page xvii. Through scanning inner arcs of attention I seek to notice myself perceiving, framing issues, interpreting, making choices about action and so on. I want to glimpse my assumptions and purposes; am curious about potential patterns, repetitions and themes; and notice my feelings and energy and how these shift. I also wonder what and who I am *not* attending to, what I might be missing. And I notice my tendency for (in)action and consider how it may and may not be appropriate. Am I impatient, for example, wanting to push into action or to leave a particular situation? What is that about? Do I need to allow this, or to countermand it?

Simultaneously, I am seeking to engage in outer arcs of attention, by which I mean acting and sensing outside myself. This includes questioning others, raising arising puzzles for mutual exploration, and taking experimental action. I might thus seek to test out any interpretations I am developing, always seeking to hold these lightly. I often try to transpose what might be concerns or dilemmas into cycles of active inquiry, devising these to address issues and hoping to move my understanding of them on. I might overtly frame my attempts to others as inquiry, learning more about others' positioning through mutual conversation.

Engaging simultaneously in inner and outer arcs of attention is an attempt at a discipline, but not about perfection, or about claiming pure access to a stream of consciousness as this is impossible (Bateson, 1973; Marshall, 2001). Given this significant caveat, these practices offer me opportunities, and challenge me to make what I do, think, feel and experience experimental in some way.

Engaging in cycles of action and reflection

The notion of engaging in cycles of action and reflection is axiomatic to action research. At its most basic, this cycling means I alternate between taking action and reflecting on this in some way – alone, through writing as inquiry or through conversation with others. My reflection informs a next phase of action. There are a wide variety of models, varying in their terms, which suggest that, individually and/or collectively, we plan, act, review, with additional side-steps in some models and nuances from different heritages. Coghlan and Brannick (2014: 9) in their approach to doing action research in your own organisation, for example, incorporate a 'pre-step' in which the researcher seeks an understanding of context, purposes, and political and other forces driving change, and establishes potential collaborative relationships. They then outline a spiral model of recurring research cycles of constructing, planning action, taking action and evaluating action.

There is simplicity to the notion of engaging in cycles of action and reflection which appeals. People can initially adopt this approach with some sense of structure, experimenting with an appropriate framework or blending different models, and then elaborating their approach as they develop. If someone explores in this way it can take them further than they ever imagined because they will have to create a practice, a craft, of their own of some kind, hopefully one that is both congruent with them and also challenging. For example, if someone is a quick-fire person, they can develop disciplines that both allow their preferred approach to life and also provide additional recursive loops that invite review, reflection, taking a pause of some kind. Often people start out following action–reflection cycles somewhat mechanically, and then these become a significant process of learning, more nuanced and pliable, and people cannot imagine discontinuing this approach to life. Courage is relevant here. Such disciplines can open up spaces in which we can acknowledge and encounter what we have previously set aside and our unknowing, let go and allow new sense to arise.

Engaging in research cycling of some kind, I can pay attention to how I use and blend convergence and divergence as a quality process (Heron, 1996). Convergent inquiry travels territory I have already explored, deepens, enhances understanding, may seek saturation as a cue to completeness of some kind (borrowing this notion from grounded theory, with due caution; Charmaz, 2005). Alternatively, I can follow divergent pathways, checking out boundaries, following new leads, going off at apparent tangents, enriching through juxtaposing multiple images.

Interweaving agency and communion

As I seek to blend being active and receptive in living life as inquiry, this can be expressed as an appropriate combination of agency and communion in Bakan's framework of complementary ways of being in the world (Bakan, 1966;

Marshall, 1984). Agency, in Bakan's frame, is a movement of independence through self-assertion, self-protection and attempting to control the surrounding environment. Communion is based in receptivity, interdependence and integration as ways of coming to terms with uncertainty. It involves aligning with situations and other people. Both have generative and degenerative possibilities. I seek to combine these ways of being, and to sense and reflect on their integration. Thus I may persist in a chosen pathway of inquiry, developing disciplines to pursue this. I then engage arising action and what I encounter with acceptance, interested to sense what forms it is taking. Perhaps what I then notice in how I act, in what I say, can inform my sense of being and my perspective. Tendencies of agency and communion are always in dialogue, a dynamic combination in any given moment; sometimes blended with fluidity, sometimes in tension. I may consider if I am over-accenting one approach inappropriately and seek to adjust this. See PART III: **Drawing on the work of Nathalie Sarraute:** Tropisms.

Speaking inquiry as potentially vital process

I find it very helpful sometimes to speak what I am feeling and thinking to others as a form of inquiring. 'How can I know what I think till I see what I say?' (Wallas, 1926: 106). See PART IV: **Writing as inquiry.** As I do so, sense-making, emergent perspective and so on can unfold. I can experience and hear in my voice what holds energy and what may now not. And the listener(s) can feed back their impressions. I can give myself the opportunity to 'behold', in Bakan's (1966) terms, what I might otherwise split apart. As I speak, I am paying gentle attention to what the boundaries are here, to containment. How deep do I want to go, what is legitimate in this space, what is taking some sort of risk, and why would I do that? This is inquiring. Sometimes I decide to tell some form of truth that seems to be pushing the boundaries, in that place at that time. I can monitor this fit as I speak, adjusting as I go, perhaps meta-commenting explicitly to others.

As I articulate what seems to be on my mind, and notice the wording, tone, stance, I might then adjust or experiment with these, perhaps choose to amplify or contradict. I am cautious about telling an overly coherent or heroic tale. I want to speak just enough but no more, to maintain a sense of appropriate connection to my experiencing. Paying such attention to discerning and working at edges as I speak or write is a quality process in first person inquiry (Marshall, 2004).

Finding the right words in this speaking, and in any description of it, is vitally important to me. I sense their nature, weigh them. Surfacing the apt term or phrase is a dimension of the inquiry. This might then carry energy I need to pursue. I am seeking somehow to keep the conversation on an edge, speaking what intensely matters, at that time, and to ensure that it is fresh, not rehearsed. I adopt some co-counselling principles (Co-Counselling International, UK, 2014): of speaking to explore, noticing as I go, testing boundaries, learning by what I hear myself saying, playing into and amplifying hints of feelings or positions in order to explore them, expecting energy and insight to move on rather than what I say to become fixed, being willing therefore to explore apparent distress and see where it leads. I sometimes then feel a slight sense of disorientation when speaking inquiry. I find I have to listen carefully to learning colleagues' questions and comments, want to write down their precise wording (rather than translate into familiar phrases), to catch the flavour.

Such practices of conduct raise the issue of containment. In co-counselling there is a two-party agreement, a contract about the nature of the space created together, rules. When I speak as inquiry in this way, I may have to contain my own space for doing so, to take care of myself.

Sometimes inquiring in circumstances I thought potentially hostile, but in which I was willing to take the risk, has been surprisingly generative. I find someone else who shares my interests, we drop into a deeper discussion than expected. For example, I remember the uneasy moments of entering the coffee room before a research seminar in London (early morning start, unpleasant journey). It was just as a new academic year was starting and I had had too little holiday and was tired already. Instead of pleasantries, I said something of this sort to the stranger who had said 'hello'. She was feeling similarly, we discussed the issues involved and our feelings. I felt much freer to enjoy the day's events because I had acknowledged my initial experiential truths, and felt reaffirmed that the issues I was experiencing were partly systemic rather than personal. Having acknowledged them, and been heard well, I could move on.

Tracking inquiry processes

Engaging in inquiry typically involves tracking this in some ways. This can take a wide variety of forms, including note-taking, research journaling, email trails, recorded conversations and blogs. The kind of notes written can also be very varied, including descriptive accounts, developments of ideas, reflections, critical analyses and arising connections.

People have their different practices of note-taking and writing from ongoing research. Some are already journal keepers or take readily to this in some form. For others it is a trial, a should-do that does not initially fit easily into their lives. Reading improving texts on what form reflective journaling might take may be helpful. Or might not be. A few brief notes of this kind are nonetheless offered below.

Sometimes committing to inquiry involves obtaining a physical notebook that feels right, can be carried easily and so is ever-available. Some Masters and doctoral students accumulate a shelf of such notebooks as physical testimony to their research engagement. For others, electronic devices play this role.

Some potential practices include:

Writing morning pages, respecting arising images and thoughts (Goldberg, 1986)

Writing and leaving some blank pages on which later reflections can be developed

Having a practice for going through journals and notes (monthly perhaps), reviewing them and adding reflective and analytic comments

Developing note-taking as a discipline, finding ways to write speedily, take down key phrases verbatim rather than translate them, include ancillary detail to give nuance and help recall

Incorporating a commentary stream of arising sense-making and questions

Circulating selected notes or accounts to others: for feedback; as a contribution to collaborative, second person inquiry and its research cycling; or to promote inquiry in a wider institution or community as a form of third person action research

If you are engaged in first person action research and also taking on a facilitation role as a coordinator of second or third person research, it is important to consider the power issues involved in activities that may appear as simply practical. Is offering to distribute notes to other research participants to encourage joint engagement in cycles of action and reflection appropriate, for example? Whilst it might be in the initial stages of a project, later this may reinforce your role as the initiating researcher, and could limit others' engagement. Note-taking and consultation might need to become a shared responsibility for the collaboration to flourish. You can consider and negotiate these issues with co-researchers.

Again the key image here is of finding appropriate form – for you, wider purposes and the situation – and engaging with arising questions about this as you go along, rather than treating yourself as bad or deficient in some ways. You can explore, continually, whether forcing reflective writing is a helpful discipline or inappropriate, and you need to claim your authority to devise more congruent processes if necessary. You can create and push experimental disciplines.

But, a cautionary note, if you are researching for a dissertation or similar, you will need to find some form, to have a trail of your equivalent to 'data', to 'evidence' for claims you are making, if only because life inquiry can prompt change and you may find it hard later to recreate sufficiently richly the questions and issues you were previously working with.

INQUIRY IN ACTION

In this chapter I consider a range of loosely associated issues in relation to enacting inquiry. Approaching life with the disciplines and practices outlined in previous chapters involves continual attention and improvisation. We are repeatedly making choices, including those of how to integrate openness and self-protection appropriate to the situation and our capacities at that time.

'Go fearward' (Turner-Vesselago, 2013: 34)

Continually exploring takes energy, attention and often courage in some form as we seek to keep alert to new experiences and perspectives, to be ever open to learning of some kind. In her advice about Freefall Writing, Barbara Turner-Vesselago (2013: 34 and 70–2) includes the injunction to 'go fearward', to reach towards what needs expressing and is on the edge of acceptability. She cautions, however, that this is one dimension of the more generic precept of 'Finding where the energy is' (Turner-Vesselago, 2013: 70), and that that sensing need not be limited to fear alone. See PART IV: **Writing as inquiry:** Drawing on creative writing approaches.

This motif applies well to living life as inquiry, but in this application it needs to come with a health warning. Inquiry is about *having practices* for being brave, for exploring at the edge of knowing and competence, and having the capabilities and support processes, such as learning colleagues, to go fearward, *should you choose*. This is not a prescription. Courage is another bold aspiration, to be adapted and applied appropriately. In what ways to be overt about inquiry, and to whom, are related choices.

I may well not live up to all my aspirations for inquiry, then. But this too is an aspect of inquiry practice. I might, for example, declare that I will inquire into xxx. I seem plausible and tell people how I will start doing this. We meet again weeks later and actually not that much seems to have happened. I may well have explanations of what got in my way. Rather than beat myself up for not sticking to plan, I and my patient listeners might switch the focus of curiosity to that list, to what did arise, to where the energy is and is not in my account of what happened, to the inquiry process itself and whether to maintain it. And so the questioning might shift. My original formulation of inquiry was not 'wrong'. In its way it helped me move. But it has the potential to evolve into something with more heart and relevance that I then have a choice to explore.

How then do we know when an inquiry is completed? Sometimes an inquiry I think I am pursuing becomes emptied of energy or mechanical. I might need to heed this. Or a question could become dormant but be re-stimulated later in an appropriate context. Some threads of inquiry seem to be expressions of ongoing issues we are living out, such as how to have agency in our organisational and professional lives. They may also be reflections of life patterns and what we carry. And so I may keep on meeting myself, doing my stuff.

Whatever the initial process, it helps to notice what is happening and choose then whether, and if 'yes', how, to give the inquiry shape, envisage different routes and media for working with it, arrive at disciplines which have the potential to engage the issues concerned.

Vulnerability in inquiry

Living life as inquiry inherently incorporates vulnerability. If what I am doing has no edge of (twinned) excitement and fear perhaps I am just going through the motions without placing myself fully available in the process. Unless I am willing to accept this I do not have much faith in inquiry. If it is not going to open me to learning then why would I do it? But excitement at learning might lead me into potential danger. If that is my choice, how can I hold myself there, possibly exposed and vulnerable, but still able to take sufficient care of myself? If, for example, I am about to receive feedback I especially need but am also shying away from, can I open myself to someone being potentially direct, even attacking (intentionally or unintentionally), and maintain my capacities to listen and discuss? Unless we make ourselves vulnerable in an inquiry process in some way, we are not then open to learning. That does not mean being self-destructive, although sometimes it might feel as if it does, and may prove difficult.

Can inquiry become dysfunctional then? Potentially. Especially if I allow a self-critical voice to take over and so undermine my sense of self. If this happens, it can be a fleeting phase, to be noted and adjusted, through inquiry, with potential learning to offer. If it persists, it may be time to call on learning disciplines and companions to help us find more generative approaches.

Sometimes it does seem as if by declaring inquiry I invite more unsettlement into my life than I expected, or can immediately cope with. For example, I might set out to review my approaches to leadership and conflict, only to find that new experiences make these especially challenging issues. This experience of heightened salience can make me feel vulnerable, but also usually excited. This can generate tension, but could also be evidence of inquiry in a way, that I have experienced more than my own shadow (or perhaps my shadow potentially available for exploration). Sometimes inquiry brings what was asked for, but it is in a different language from the question posed, may not be initially recognisable. I might feel a kind of thrill: 'oh yes, all right then, you said you wanted to inquire, did you? And look what the universe has offered you?!'

And we can choose to leave some of life unprocessed. See PART II: **Images of aspiring inquiry practice:** Facing into wind.

Relational work

As **Integrating action research, systemic thinking and attention to issues of power** in Part I has shown, my inquiries are always into being in the world in some way, whatever issues I am pursuing, and so into how I unfold my understanding and conduct myself. They thus have a relational intent. In terms of supporting inquiry, it is perhaps a predictable paradox that it is a challenge to do first person action research wholly alone. However developed our self-reflective practices, we benefit from having learning companions who are 'friends willing to act as enemies' (Torbert, 1976: 169). They can challenge what we say; question potential patterns of which we are not apparently aware; question our assumptions; help us critically review purposes, strategies and behaviours; and invite us to see alternative viewpoints and perhaps to relinquish our grip on apparent imperatives that are not serving us well.

But any intent to be a critical friend must be held with caution. We do not necessarily have the right to adopt such a relationship, and must check these dynamics in action. Relationships of this kind take time to develop, are earned, and are typically integrated into long-term mutual support. (They may also be integrated into formal relationships such as those between doctoral students and their academic supervisors, but these too require careful process attention.) Giving and receiving feedback are matters of skill, dimensions of developing practice.

And we need 'friends willing to act as friends' (Marshall and Reason, 1993: 122) to support us in the development we are seeking, to help us surface and honour purposes, and to listen to muted voices and themes in our accounts of what matters.

Such challenging support can come in a wide variety of forms, from the transient to the long-established. It includes peer support groups, coaching, mentoring, engaging with learning buddies, and research or professional supervision. The story in PART V: **Inquiry learning groups and working with feedback** shows and explores some potential qualities and practices of learning groups as one of these potential forms.

Learning groups

These are small groups of people committed to meeting regularly, but not necessarily frequently, and developing their inquiry practices and capacities. Typically this involves general discussion and review and each person reporting what they have been doing, thinking, feeling; reviewing current issues and challenges; and considering next steps. Some academic courses integrate learning groups or sets (in action learning terminology) as key processes. These spaces are achievements. It takes time and appropriate work to develop sufficient trust for groups to function well, and this needs continual renewing to maintain vibrant learning spaces.

Such relationships are generally mutual, heterarchic, in the sense that participants can both hold the space for inquiry, and also themselves be held and supported. This involves a form of peer supervision, learning from and with others. Appropriate practices of inquiry, such as co-operative inquiry (Heron and Reason, 2001, 2008), can enable this. The European-American Collaborative Challenging Whiteness (2005) writes evocatively about practices of radical co-inquiry they established, meeting long-term to explore white privilege by telling and reviewing their experiences. They affirm how vital the peer group space was for learning on issues of race and white privilege when self-concept was at issue and challenged.

Community membership of various kinds is important to many action researchers. Communities can be local, networked, international. Some arise from a course experience. These remind us of the wider world community of people, akin to a Sangha, who affirm and engage in similar practices. Whatever our local circumstances, email lists and other online forms can provide a burbling stream of such connection.

Quality processes: working with feedback

See also PART IV: **Writing as inquiry:** Deepening inquiry through working with writing and PART V: **Inquiry learning groups and working with feedback.** Attempting to pay attention to ongoing process is integral to action research. This includes seeking out and working with feedback of some kind as an inherent quality process. We can deliberately invite feedback from others as input into critically questioning, reflective cycles. But eliciting feedback is no simple matter. Other people may well not affirm my perspective on a situation, given that there is no one reality and people will have their different and equally valid views. When asked whether they think my contribution to a venture has changed, for example, others might think me less helpful, whilst my version may be that I have improved my capacity to manage my boundaries with integrity. Or, I may have worked hard at developing some quality of interaction, which others then seem not to notice.

How I ask for feedback is significant. 'What did you see me doing?' is likely to gain richer impressions than 'did I do ok?' (Although the latter might be the question I decide also, later, to ask.)

When I go about inquiringly, this might be confusing for people, and I need to bear this in mind. For example, if I want to learn about how I conduct myself in a given setting, and ask people how they see me acting, they might take what I intend as developmental inquiry as a lack of confidence or form of inadequacy. Perhaps craftful framing of my intentions can overcome this possibility. Or I may decide it does not matter, they can think what they will. But I might well not want to open myself in some circumstances. How people respond to requests for feedback might be framed by the relationship I hope to explore. For example, if I ask my doctoral students for feedback, what patternings in our relationship(s) might shape any conversation? Might key issues, such as those relating to dimensions of power, therefore seem beyond exploration or require thoughtful negotiation? How would I know?

It may well not be possible to make mutual sense in a complex, multi-perspectival situation. It is appropriate that divergent views stand. In receipt of discordant feedback I can still, if I choose, affirm my own interpretation, especially if it is from a critical perspective, for example about potentially gender-associated dynamics that others might not have interpreted as such. But I can do so alongside and more informed by others' views, and having enlarged the scope of our conversation by telling my own. If agreement cannot be reached, I need to consider what forms of validation it is appropriate to use in relation to my systemic sense-making.

In inquiry, we need then to consider if, when and how it is appropriate to seek feedback, for reviewing the quality of our inquiry and for continual learning. In writing about inquiry, we can note the issues involved and how we have addressed them.

Creating and protecting spaces for inquiry

Living life as inquiry involves attending to two (at least) layers of interaction simultaneously. You often have to help create the space as a 'container' for inquiry and also to be openly inquiring within that space. You might also be facilitating someone else's capacity to be inquiring alongside you. Sometimes there is a potential tension between signalling that being radically inquiring is quite a normal thing to do, that there are potential rules of engagement for it, and you invite people to join you, whilst also modelling what it entails (otherwise the space mirrors procedure not vitality) and so becoming potentially vulnerable. Whilst I might seek to slip deftly between these layers of framing activity, fellow participants might not see things in the same way, and wonder what I am doing; might even see me as anxious, or potentially intrusive. The attempted modelling might open me to vulnerability that seems 'too much' to others I am engaging with.

Spaces intended for critical inquiry can be experienced as transformative. But they might also be seen as controlling, in which rules are set by others (potentially me) and certain kinds of behaviour, such as expressing emotions and attending to process, are rewarded and others sanctioned, and in which some people know the rules and have rehearsed, habituated ways of acting, but others do not.

We may be able to test all these issues out, through framing and re-framing, and negotiate appropriate ways to operate together. We can invite others to hold spaces mutually for inquiry. We can offer potentially helpful rubrics, guidelines, formats and practices and can develop these with co-learners. Learning groups or sets, with their varied informing pedagogies such as action learning, are common practice on many courses, especially Masters for more mature course participants, and come with appropriate guidelines and typical patterns of behaviour.

Life patterns

Often themes we identify for inquiry relate to questions that resonate through our lives, issues we consider potential life patterns, ways we typically behave in certain circumstances, preoccupations which also shape how we inquire and what we notice. We might be able to tell a story of hearing the associated messages early in our lives; or point to how the contexts we operate in affirm, even demand these ways of being and acting. We do not have to treat these as fixed, who we 'really are'. And even if we do interpret some as recurrent themes these are likely to take different forms in different contexts and at different times. Perhaps, instead, the curiosity can be how I am holding certain potential patterns in my life at the moment. In what ways are they shaping my inquiry? How are they appropriate or not, here and now? Are they amenable to review? I imagine specific issues into which I am inquiring, generic themes such as issues of power which thread through them, and possible life themes and puzzles as interwoven strands, echoing each other. I can be reflective and discerning about the relative attentions I give them, about how I work with them in inquiry. See PART III: **Drawing on the work of Nathalie Sarraute:** Tropisms.

In the work for change I review in this book, for example, there is a recurring issue for me about feeling responsible, wanting the world to be a better place – to be kinder, more egalitarian, more willing to listen to multiple voices and taking sustainability, rather than economic 'value', as the fundamental metric. I think that I should do what I can towards this. I can see how such themes influence my behaviour, my choice of career, the educational approaches I have adopted in courses I have developed. This impetus can apply in the moment – can I be helpful in some way to this person here and now? – and in a broader sweep of how I see activities as meaningful, or not. Aware of this tendency, I can question its appropriateness in micro and macro forms. Am I trying too hard to be of service to this person? At a more macro level, have I seen several valiant initiatives in a certain cause fail, and do I need the discernment not to contribute to repeating this pattern as the issue is raised yet again as a challenge to be addressed? I might, for example, ask instead what helps to keep things the same.

If reflection takes us to patterns we think are influencing our lives, we do not have to turn this into self-scrutinising inquiry. We can decide not to inquire into some things. *Whether, when* and *how* are all choices. And framing is paramount. Some ways of framing key life issues are unpropitious for inquiry, too polarising, too judgemental perhaps. If self-criticism underlies our first question formulation, we might need to wait and see if a more curious, open, articulation arises, one that is sufficiently compassionate to self to prompt generative inquiry. This could mean exploring with curiosity when different approaches might be appropriate, and reviewing potential criteria of effectiveness.

If we are engaging broader life issues, anything we take as inquiry may be connected to 'everything else' and if we are sensitive to potential systemic patterns, where do we draw any boundaries? Demarcating territory might make an inquiry more containable, but could also leave other issues vibrating in the background as potentiality, and potential 'interference'. Scoping inquiry and research design are thus important.

The following story is an example of knowing that life patterns are rippling through a specific phase of inquiry. I noticed some years ago how ambivalent I was about going to the next event in an international conference series on corporate responsibility. Rational as attending was (to promote our sustainability programme and activities), I felt very reluctant and experienced it as a potential burden. Talking with a colleague, I said how I was feeling, and surfaced what I then termed the issues of class and gender which affected my sense of whether I could operate effectively in the conference space, whether I could be 'me' sufficiently to breathe. The rather formalised image of 'men-and-some-women-in-suits' was my dominant impression of the culture and social practices.

I vowed that I could only go if I treated the whole experience as inquiry. And so I did. Attending the conference with this agenda made it more interesting. It freed me to notice patterns around me, and of me in interaction, and to experiment. I realised that I especially felt a little out-of-step in relation to a few key players in the association. Not needing them to notice or affirm me, I did not seek their company. I allowed myself to hang out with people I felt more akin to, rather than network as I thought I should, and chose to spend some time alone. I could also then view proceedings at a little distance, notice who was talking to whom, patterns of inclusion and distancing. I heard some other people's stories about how they fitted and did not with the culture, and learned more about differences amongst people who had previously seemed to me to be aligned. My experience of the event shifted from my worst anticipations to such an extent that I enjoyed myself and found the conference fascinating. Afterwards I realised how little I had experienced 'personal' issues in relation to 'class', 'gender' and inclusion, but I had noticed these dynamics in action in nuanced, multi-faceted ways. Treating the experience as inquiry helped me feel resourced, curious, engaged.

From the perspective of living life as inquiry and curiosity about potential life patterns, I can notice the way I construct transitory impressions and patterns that seem unhelpful, that I might want to review. Not holding images of 'who I really am', seeing that as a chimera, I do not have to look for deeply embedded originating causes. Living in and through fleeting moments is my aspiration. A companion challenge is how not then to appear too inconsistent or whimsical to others.

Inquiry might feel different in form at different ages and stages of life. The initiating questions might seem differently phrased, the energy different in quality, although I am not seeking to stereotype. Such differences might also relate to enacted action logics. See PART I: **Action inquiry and action logics: Action logics**.

Striving, and not striving, for outcomes

Living life as inquiry can sound like an heroic quest, and can sometimes, choice-fully, have these qualities. But there is also something paradoxical about highly goal-directed inquiry that is agentically trying to resolve issues. Striving for an outcome is incongruent. Often what arises is not what we expected, but is what 'needs' in some ways to occur next.

A key and treasured lesson for me arose through a silent meditation retreat I went to at the Western Chan centre in Maenllwyd in Wales, UK. The aim was to encourage mindfulness through Zen meditation practices, and I hoped that I might develop a clearer sense of things in some way. That did not happen as I had imagined it might.

For four days we were woken by the Retreat master's clacking boards, met in the chill yard in the early light, did physical exercises, chanted, meditated, took tea, did our allotted tasks, ate meals together, walked, rested, wrote in our note-books, and meditated again. Gently pursuing the offered disciplines involved a lot of consenting, a sense of community. Rather than the clearer conceptual 'mind' I had hoped for, something else happened. What arose instead was a kinaesthetic sense of a fresh and grounded orientation in the world, a sense of myself that was more important than cognitive, intellectual insight. I experienced this, for example, walking out of the meditation hall, standing in the often-muddy yard and beholding the world around and just breathing – and it all just 'was', vividly, intensely, beautifully. By the end of the retreat I felt a change in the way I saw things, so the experience had an impact in the realm I had expected, but only because 'everything' seemed to shift, a little but significantly. Sometimes significant change seems only a shift of the light away.

There is something here about the paradoxical nature of living life as inquiry. It might pull me/you into continually seeking to rectify things. But it needs a light touch, to allow the process to be both disciplined and emergent. And for me or you to be able to be surprised. The purpose of inquiry, then, is to have a greater capacity to operate rather than to reach an end goal. My image is of inquiry through fleeting glimpses and moments, of allowing interests to arise, change shape and fade as appropriate.

I do appreciate that if you are engaged in action research for an educational qualification this may not be an easy story to tell your examiner. You will need to be explicit about what then constitute quality processes. See PART IV: **Writing as inquiry** and APPENDIX B: **Presenting first person inquiry for Masters and doctoral work**. So, is trying to change the world really inquiry? Or, in what ways is it? In Part V of this book I tell stories that show me trying to influence situations and institutions. This could be considered purely political activity, goal-directed. What makes this activity inquiry instead, in my view, is the emphasis on living through process, seeking out and adopting quality practices in inquiry, being on the edge of knowing and being open to learning and change in all that is involved, including purposes. Of course, nearly everything is in some ways political at the same time.

And there is an appropriateness to discern here, again. How do we know when our commitment to 'emergent' processes of inquiry means that 'anything goes'? We may delude ourselves about the significance of what arises, we may rationalise, we may side-step challenging ourselves. And if I respect emergent inquiry, how can I keep it coming back into focus sufficiently, but also recognise if it has changed shape in terms of the nature of inquiry and/or the nature of the issues being thrown up?

Is inquiry always possible?

Can I inquire 'well' if am tired, depressed, unwell? If I call myself to inquiry, am 'I' there and willing and able? Living life as inquiry is not only a high-energy activity. It takes what form it takes. I can inquire in some way whatever my situation, or choose not to. It is not about being 'well' or 'not well'. Inquiry will somehow be informed by one's state of being, and therefore one's sensory profile and capacities at that time, in that context. I can be depressed and know that I am engaged in inquiry, in some congruent form. How then to maintain disciplines of inquiry becomes an issue. These may have to be small, achievable movements. If I am feeling dull in some way, I may not trust my senses or the clues that something is interesting as clearly as I otherwise might: so my choicefulness might become dulled too. These are all sensory impressions I can notice, respect and work with. Life is no ideal, my attentions are always frag-mented to some extent. What this means will be a very individual matter, for each of us to surface and explore. For example, our propensity to engage inquir-ingly with others and to ask questions of purposes in challenging contexts might fluctuate.

Boundaries then become especially important. If inquiry means opening up challenging territory in some way and thus threatens my safety, it is appropriate to consider if I need to contain this. I may focus inquiry on what resources I have and how to enhance these. How to lead a healthier life, encountering all that sits in the way of doing so, could then for example become an exploration in its own right.

If my senses are not functioning 'well' in my terms, things seem to go flat; I find that I am not moving impressions around lightly, am not readily seeing from different perspectives; these processes become somewhat mechanistic. Partly, the capacity for inward reflective attention is lowered, but the capacity to be contextually aware is also dulled. If this is so, acting inquiringly with others or taking initiatives can seem quite risky, because my knowing and testing is not as agile as I think it is in other contexts, at other times. I might take additional action (such as inviting input from a critical friend) to 'cover' for that.

I am phrasing this cautiously, as inquiry can be directed gently at these senses of me seeming 'different' in some ways. Feeling tentative, open to differ-ent sorts of cues and sensations, might well be wholly appropriate. It is also worth considering if we have different propensities, strengths and vulnerabilities as inquirers, as we bring our unique individual histories, our membership of varied knowledge communities, and affinities with others. See PART III: **Drawing on the work of Nathalie Sarraute:** Tropisms.

Exploring unbright mind:
Impressions of an untold reflective account

See PART IV: **Writing as inquiry.**

A busy week. A demanding day ahead. A couple of small practical stumbles already, indicating I was not functioning that well. Symptoms of an impending cold. On the train I wrote a reflective note, allowing myself to explore, to notice and express traces of previous days' problems and lowered emotions that I was carrying along with me. I enjoyed the event I then attended, felt alert, well able to connect, to be present and play my part. My mind refreshed by allowing the down energy into the light. Tired afterwards. Allowing myself to collapse on the homeward journey, to nurture the depleted soul that had left the flat that morning.

IMAGES OF ASPIRING INQUIRY PRACTICE

I have various aspirational images for how energies can align in living life as inquiry. They each show the embodied nature of inquiry. I offer them here as illustrations, trusting that you will surface and work with your own versions.

Heron

Attentive, head at an angle to catch movement. Standing scrupulously still on one leg at the waterside, poised to place the other foot gently, carefully, in a pre-tested, barely disturbed space. Quick to strike when something has caught its attention.

Tapping dynamic root

In my limited experience of Tai Chi the posture and notion of 'tapping dynamic root' appealed. A diagonal line through the body from raised arm and hand pushing back against supposed attack to leg rooted down through the back foot into the earth, well-grounded; reflecting an alignment between posture, purpose and attempted action in the world. All aligned with the breath.

Just as in Tai Chi practice this is a sensation, can be felt and adjusted, in inquiry too I have a sense that alignment and misalignment can be felt, explored and experimentally adjusted.

Facing into wind

One image of whether I am fully into inquiry is whether I have my face into wind. I once tried to learn to fly a microlight. Created from aluminium tubing, brightly coloured plastic wing panels, clips and bolts, microlights are elegant, definitionally light-weight, and thus very wind-sensitive. We could only attempt to fly if the ground wind speed was less than ten miles per hour, and so typically at dawn and just before dusk. We were learning in a single-seater, as these were early days for the type, initially doing tow-training behind a truck to experience take offs and landings, before being allowed to take fully to the skies. We trained and took off directly into wind for safety and to gain optimal lift. So it was important to know the wind direction exactly. Even though there was a wind-sock we would also check. We were taught to stand with our faces into wind, seeking an even flow on each cheek.

If an inquiry loses its edge it may well be because I am not facing into the challenging issues, I do not have my face directly into wind. If I notice, I can adjust this, or, perhaps, sometimes, accept my apparent inclination to reduce the stakes and allow myself not to take the more difficult path. When I feel I am facing fully into inquiry, this is strongly sensory. It is thrilling, embodied. *This* is what I am really curious about and I want to know more. Challenging feedback may be quite hard to take, but it is welcome. I feel alert and there is a strong sensory pull to keep myself there at the point of inquiry, excitement and fear twinned. And this can be a collective experience as people inquire together, on the scent of exciting learning.

PART III

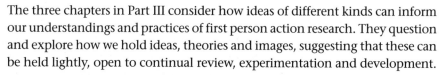

WORKING WITH IDEAS, THEORIES AND IMAGES AS INQUIRY

The three chapters in Part III consider how ideas of different kinds can inform our understandings and practices of first person action research. They question and explore how we hold ideas, theories and images, suggesting that these can be held lightly, open to continual review, experimentation and development.

The relevance of academic literatures to action research is perhaps obvious, especially to those involved in academic work of some kind. The next chapter considers how we work with theories, in the light of many action researchers' intentions to integrate different forms of knowing and not overly-privilege propositional knowing.

Taking living life as inquiry's aspirations to engage with integrity in an uncertain, ever-changing world, I am curious to explore appropriately flexible notions of persons, narratives and lives. Some novelists address these issues richly and with subtlety. Their work informs and nurtures my ideas about and imagery of conducting inquiry, and contributes to ongoing experimentation. Here I briefly consider the works of Nathalie Sarraute and Kazuo Ishiguro which have these qualities for me. Their explorations especially connect with my senses of self-reflection, which seek ongoing conditionality and do not invest in a coherent notion of self. I also appreciate the care both authors deploy with their crafts as writers to offer nuanced impressions of living.

The Sarraute and Ishiguro chapters are offered to complement other material in the book, standing for the inherent conditionality of living life as inquiry and of seeking to account in such terms. They counter any implications that life processes can be known and articulated unproblematically. These are not outlined as ideas you should then adopt, but as examples of my experiments in enriching inquiry in organisational and management scholarship. I hope you have your own parallel examples of sources and resources from realms beyond your focal interests that illuminate and deepen your notions of first person action research.

WORKING WITH
ACADEMIC LITERATURES

As depicted in Figure 1 in PART I: **Integrating action research, systemic thinking and attention to issues of power:** Action research in brief on page 6 topic related ideas and theories have important parts to play in a dynamic, multi-faceted action research process. How these are chosen depends on purposes and interests, and on the issues being explored through action, and can involve innovative juxtapositions of concepts and frameworks from different academic and practice-based areas. These are all choices to be scoped, explored, articulated and critically reviewed.

This chapter offers a brief token exploration of some of the issues of working conceptually in action research, to stand for this significant dimension of exploration. It is illustrated with ideas relevant to one of the first person action research stories in PART V: **Acting for sustainability** – and so uses the theme of systemic change for its examples.

It has been suggested that action research often pays too little attention to theory (Knight, 2002: 39). I think this a simplification, for several reasons. Underpinning and often somewhat tacit in action research are significant issues of paradigm and epistemology, of how we see the world. Whilst these are not always expressed theoretically in everyday research accounts, these issues are relevant in taking an action research approach (Reason and Bradbury, 2008b). As it is not the easy option in terms of mainstream academic work, creating action research as your approach might well take more engagement and working through theoretically than would following local methodological conventions.

In action research too, we are thoughtful about how we work with theories, not wanting to inappropriately privilege ideas and propositional knowing over other forms of knowing (Heron and Reason, 2008). This involves being critically suspicious of extended abstraction, especially when it might overwhelm other senses, such as our embodied and emotional sensibilities, and might obscure concerns for praxis. Collaborative, participative forms of action research are especially likely to be cautious about the kinds of intellectualising that exclude people and devalue local knowledges, and to treat such issues as matters of research design. For example, working with citizen juries is intended to rebalance expert and local knowledges (Pimbert and Wakeford, 2003; Wakeford and Pimbert, 2004). In collaborative research there are also questions about who holds and works with any theories informing the research. Is it only the initiating researcher(s)? If so, how do they do this with integrity? Or is the conceptual work of the research shared – how and to what extent – with other participants through whatever means make this possible?

When we do work intensely with ideas, we can review the forms of scholarship we apply. Whilst the doubting game is a traditional hallmark of good scholarship, we can also cultivate practices of the believing game, working through connected knowing and engaging with an 'empathetic, receptive eye' (Clinchy, 1996: 206) so that we work appreciatively too.

In the rest of this chapter, I briefly review practices for working with ideas, illustrated with some frameworks which offer intellectual and practice questions as I explore how to contribute to systemic change.

Whatever domain I am inquiring in, I am interested in what ideas and *what kinds of ideas* might be relevant as resources for interpreting situations and conceiving action. I need to be thoughtful about their provenance, about how different theoretical frames fit and do not fit with each other epistemologically, and willing to review this critically. Working with ideas involves movement in both directions: literature and ideas inform ongoing inquiry and are tested out in action. Ongoing inquiry helps generate ideas, 'answer back' to other authors' writing, adapt and develop conceptual understanding informed through practice. Often this involves blending or juxtaposing theories from different academic and practice realms.

Any potential 'themes' we identify as our research interests are actively disentangled from systemic contexts and this needs due reflexive care, lest we inappropriately isolate and inflate aspects of what is going on, and retrofit labels onto our more subtle experiencing.

Working with ideas and theories can be of value to anyone, but is especially vital in the dissertation research Masters and doctoral students undertake. Critical exploration of theory–practice inter-relationships is then a key requirement, and it is important to be working conceptually with 'themes' relevant to their research, to link up richly and critically with appropriate academic literatures and to be making a theoretical contribution. What constitute relevant ideas and literatures depends on the research topic(s), issues and academic storylines being explored. See APPENDIX B: **Presenting first person inquiry for Masters and doctoral work.**

Threaded through this book are my concerns about environmental sustainability and social justice. Living life as inquiry underpins my attempt to contribute to systemic change in some way, fully aware that holding such an aspiration is a challenge, potentially arrogant, and that I need to be highly flexible and critically reflective about what this might mean in practice.

My attempts to act for sustainability are informed by a range of ideas and associated puzzles – about change, and about how things stay the same. These include theories in the realms of leadership; gender; individual, organisational and social change; careers; systemic thinking; power; and more. It is impossible to generate an adequate listing. During a four-decade academic career I have explored, researched, taught and formally examined a wide range of theories from a range of paradigmatic positions. The ideas used as illustrations in this chapter relate to my quest to contribute to systemic change for sustainability and are set within this broader array.

My intention is always to hold any ideas I use lightly, to adopt them within a frame of inquiry, as cues to rich questioning. For example, as I watch the unfolding dynamics of an initiative, I might draw on notions of systemic thinking and emergent properties, might ponder issues of power in different dimensions such as interpersonal, symbolic and structural, might wonder if enacted differences of some kind are influencing whose views are given what credibility, might wonder about dynamics of inclusion and exclusion, and so on. I will roam around these ideas, seeking interesting angles from which to see what appears to be happening. I will act experimentally, sometimes informed by the possibilities I see. If, say, some people have objected forcefully to a proposal I approve of, I might try out moving towards them rather than band back with people I know support this, as the latter approach might reinforce or open up potential divisions. Notions of systemic dynamics, power and so on are implicated in this. As is an embodied sense that when acting systemically it is often worth noting and avoiding an initial impulse, such as pulling away. See the two sailors image on page 16. See also PART III: **Drawing on the work of Nathalie Sarraute:** Tropisms.

At issue always in seeking to act for change are challenges about whether and how people individually or collectively can influence wider social systems. In what ways do structural and systemic parameters shape and limit what people can do? These questions apply to anyone seeking to 'make a difference', wherever they are positioned in society, including chief executives, corporate responsibility managers, workers in non-governmental organisations, vigilante consumers and direct activists on the streets. I am curious about how people maintain a sense of agency in complex, shifting landscapes, how they can think strategically about change that challenges prevailing systemic patterns, how they conduct their 'responsible' careers (Tams and Marshall, 2011) and how they conduct themselves.

These questions are expressed in institutional theory, for example as the paradox of embedded agency:

> The theoretical puzzle is as follows: if actors are embedded in an institutional field …
> how are they able to envision new practices and then subsequently get others to
> adopt them? Dominant actors in a given field may have the power to force change
> but often lack the motivation; while peripheral players may have the incentive to
> create and champion new practices, but often lack the power to change institutions.
> (Garud et al., 2007: 961)

Associated literatures consider how institutional patterns are established, maintained and changed. Given the challenges of achieving fundamental change,
attention is paid to the role of potential institutional entrepreneurs, people who
create new institutions or help to transform ones that already exist (Hardy and
Maguire, 2008), and whether they can and how they might demonstrate agency.

I find theories of change and leadership from the margins appealing. These have
especially been my heritage given the topics and issues such as gender that I have
explored, and my sensitivity to the political processes of change and resilience/
resistance. In view of the potential disruption envisioned change towards sustainability would require, I assume that people acting for sustainability are necessarily
operating from 'the margins' paradigmatically in some way, even if they look
superficially to be accepted members of the mainstream, and even if they are the
chief executives of their organisations (Marshall, 2007). This is political and risky
work. No one should forget their potential to be seen as 'too revolutionary' if they
'go too far'. Although they must probably also be willing to 'forget' this (at least to
set it aside as it relates to their own safety), if they are to have the combination of
insight, courage and bravado necessary to offer their organisation what it might
not yet know it, and society, needs.

bell hooks, a black feminist, argues that those who consider themselves different can maintain clarity and power by embracing rather than bemoaning their
marginal positioning.

> I am located in the margin. I make a definite distinction between that marginality
> which is imposed by oppressive structures and that marginality one chooses as site
> of resistance – as location of radical openness and possibility … We are transformed,
> individually, collectively, as we make radical creative space which affirms and sus-
> tains our subjectivity, which gives us a new location from which to articulate our
> sense of the world. (hooks, 1990: 153)

Finding such positioning amenable and congruent does not guarantee 'effectiveness' in what a person then seeks to do. It is a location to be worked with, as is
any other.

Also addressing the politics of location, Meyerson and Scully (1995) offer the
notion of the tempered radical, the inside outsider. This has especially caught the
imagination of many people who aspire to contribute to change but have experienced the challenges of trying to do this from outside mainstream organisations,
and are seeking alternative locations for effectiveness (Marshall et al., 2011).

Tempered radicals are 'people who work within mainstream organizations and professions and want also to transform them' (Meyerson and Scully, 1995: 586). They 'identify with and are committed to their organisations, and are also committed to a cause, community, or ideology that is fundamentally different from, and possibly at odds with the dominant culture of their organisations' (Meyerson and Scully, 1995: 586). Tempered radicalism is an inherently systemic notion, as those so designated seek to act for change from within an organisation or professional community, often without official authority for taking up such an extended interpretation of their role (Meyerson and Scully, 1995). They need to be alert to systemic patterns and dynamics, and of how these unfold over time, and aware that their understanding is inevitably incomplete.

In Meyerson and Scully's formulation 'tempered' has multiple meanings.

> In the language of physics … [tempered radicals] have become tougher by being alternately heated up and cooled down … also … they have a temper: they are angered by the incongruities between their own values and beliefs about social justice and … [those] they see enacted in their organisations. (Meyerson and Scully, 1995: 586)

Tempered radicals seek moderation, considering that extremism jeopardises potential change. They criticise both dominant ways of operating and radical change that is un-tempered. This means that they may well be criticised from both, or many, sides and may be seen by others as hypocritical. They thus live with ambivalence that they cannot easily resolve, and so must accept. They cannot dream of becoming accepted as 'mainstream', as full insiders in their organisations. In Meyerson and Scully's view, however, they can also be clear about their identities and attachments. Operating in complex, charged environments they have to manage what impressions they give to different audiences, and to speak multiple languages, although it can be risky if members of diverse groups see this happening.

People taking such an approach risk isolation, and are likely to experience the pressures of potential co-option as they align enough with their organisation to have sufficient credibility to speak for change. Tempered radicals often adopt the strategy of 'small wins', finding key actions that might promote more significant transformation, and judging timing and which battles to fight (Meyerson and Scully, 1995: 595). For example, they reduce large problems to manageable size, treat all actions as experiments which are potentially system diagnostic and therefore learn from what arises. They benefit from being connected to co-learners and to networks of like-minded people, who can affirm their commitments to the issues they hold dear.

Whilst notions such as tempered radicalism can offer a resource, they also present tensions to be experienced and explored. They can be used to fool ourselves that we are living out a radical life when our efforts are more compromised, although not therefore necessarily of no value. Frameworks such as this can be reviewed, scrutinised for their assumptions and heritages, turned in the light, and juxtaposed with other ideas. Tempered radicalism is not, then, an untroubled framework or 'name badge', but a notion to be held reflectively, paying due attention to the politics of change. As this indicates, we need to take a critical approach to any ideas we adopt, however appealing and beguiling they may seem.

DRAWING ON THE WORK OF NATHALIE SARRAUTE

I have been drawn to the work of Nathalie Sarraute for her relevance to inquiry practices and self-reflection. She explores the tendencies and potential pattern-ings we experience and play out in interaction, which living life as inquiry is seeking to glimpse, to open to some, congruent, kind of noticing, review and experimentation in real time. She deliberately eschews notions of ego or the subject. I see her approach as compatible with a somewhat Buddhist notion of mindfulness, a non-egoic noticing of arising mind. She explores these issues through her extended crafts of writing, always questioning what it is possible to know and to say. I appreciate how Sarraute's work is thus permeated with doubt, always tentative. It has offered a language and imagery to contribute to my explorations.

In this chapter, I introduce Sarraute and key notions from her work, making connections to first person inquiry. I have read Sarraute and related literary criticism, but am not a Sarraute scholar and so am drawing on these ideas as catalysts for extending my thinking and practices. This is thus my interpretation and to some extent creation. One contribution to this process was a recorded conversation with Peter Wagstaff, a scholar of French literature in the University of Bath's Department of European Studies and Modern Languages. He affirmed the main themes in my interpretation of Sarraute and offered his perceptions of what she was doing and how she fitted amongst other authors with contrasting and similar agendas in France during the 20th century. This chapter includes some quotations from this conversation and has been checked with Peter.

Encountering Sarraute

I came across Nathalie Sarraute because my husband drew my attention to her obituary (in October 1999), wondering if I might be interested in a novel with no characters (*Les Fruits d'Or*, 1964; *The Golden Fruits*). I was intrigued by her work, as much with the literary criticism about her and her own articulations of what she was exploring, as with reading the fiction itself. (Reading in English, sadly it seems I miss much of the subtlety of what she was doing linguistically.) It also appealed that, according to reviewers, Sarraute's slim first book *Tropisms* (published in France in 1939), contained the kernel of themes that she would continue to explore throughout her 99-year life.

> *Tropismes* already shows the intensity of vision and the poetic dramatisation of sub-terranean psychological movements characteristic of all Nathalie Sarraute's work. (Minogue, 1981: 8)

Sarraute's work is included here because it offers frames for perceiving social life and for considering what it is to act reflectively in the midst of interaction; and she persistently questioned how social life can be depicted in text, what might be appropriately conditional forms. In the next sections, I offer some key ideas in Sarraute's work, with these two themes in mind.

Tropisms

Sarraute explored how interaction takes shape, what can be known, and what can be said. She avoided notions of people as fixed entities, whilst experimenting with depicting how personal experiencing and social process are entangled. Her writing worked from these puzzles. In terms of distinguishing showing and telling, her work is predominantly showing. See PART IV: **Writing as inquiry.** She was a novelist and essayist, and has been associated with the 'new novel' (nouveau roman) movement in France in the 1950s. Whilst she shared their interests in over-throwing the conventions of the standard 19th century psychologically based novel, with its 'conflicts and explicable images' (Wagstaff, 2007), she predates this movement and can be seen as unique (Wagstaff, 2007), independently pursuing her own paths of interest.

A key notion in Sarraute's work is that of tropisms. This especially appeals to me in relation to first person inquiry. It connects to the image of the patterning of behaviour illustrated in two sailors steadying an already steady boat, and aspirations to inquire in the moment. See the two sailors image on page 16. Sarraute identifies tropisms ('the hallmark of her writing', Hewitt, 1990: 59) thus:

> These movements of which we are hardly cognizant, slip through us on the frontiers of consciousness in the form of undefinable, extremely rapid sensations. They hide behind our gestures, beneath the words we speak and the feelings we manifest, all

of which we are aware of experiencing, and able to define. They seemed, and still seem to me to constitute the secret sources of our existence, in what might be called its nascent state. (Sarraute, 1963: 8)

Taking the term from biological sciences, the tendencies for example in plants to grow towards light, Sarraute develops tropisms as a sense of what people are doing, especially in interaction, through which she sees the 'the violent, relentless need for contact with others' (Hewitt, 1990: 215, Note 58). Thus organisms, 'in very profound, but difficult to identify, ways are responding to other organisms and modifying themselves in the process' (Wagstaff, 2007).

Typically a Sarraute text expresses disembodied voices in conversation (Hewitt, 1990: 63), eschewing notions of defined, identifiable characters. Sometimes it is not clear whether the text is private thought or publically uttered, questioning any boundary between the two. What Sarraute is exploring is suffused through the text, often shown in repetitions and repeated phrases. It is therefore a challenge to illustrate briefly. To give some impression, I offer two examples. The first is a full section from *Tropisms* which explores habitual patterning of behaviour, and the repeated phrases which might accompany it. It succinctly gives a sense of people and places in interaction.

Tropisms XVI

Now they were old, they were quite worn out, 'like old furniture that has seen long usage, that has served its time and accomplished its task,' and sometimes (this was coyness on their part) they heaved a sort of short sigh, filled with resignation and relief, that was like something crackling.

On soft spring evenings, they went walking together, 'now that youth was finished, now that the passions were spent,' they went walking quietly, 'to take a breath of fresh air before going to bed,' sit down in a café, spend a few moments chatting.

They chose a well protected corner, taking many precautions ('not here, it's in a draught, not there, it's just beside the lavatory'), they sat down – 'Ah! these old bones, we're getting old. Ah! Ah!' – and they let them be heard cracking.

The place had a cold, dingy glitter, the waiters ran about too fast in a rather rough, indifferent manner, the mirrors gave back harsh reflections of tired faces and blinking eyes.

But they asked for nothing more, this was it, they knew it well, you shouldn't expect anything, you shouldn't demand anything, that's how it was, there was nothing more, this was it, 'life'.

Nothing else, nothing more, here or there, now they knew it.

You should not rebel, dream, hope, make an effort, flee, you had only to choose carefully (the waiter was waiting) whether it was to be a grenadine or a coffee? with milk or black? while accepting unassumingly to live – here or there – and let time go by. (Sarraute, 1963: 44)

Whilst this example might be considered somewhat depressing, it suggests Sarraute's quest to depict the unadorned grain of life, her willingness to say starkly what others might flinch from or seek to dress politely.

As further illustration, 'See you very soon' (Sarraute, 1983: 13–27) is an account of a lunchtime meeting between two friends. The rush of language evokes the 'torrent of words' (Sarraute, 1983: 16) with which one person regales the other. We experience internal and externalised voices. The nature of the relationship and its reciprocity is cast into doubt. But as they stand on the pavement, parting, the person who has spoken most 'experiences something like unappeased hunger … something is still unaccomplished' (1983: 16) and insists that they meet again, soon. A fortnight later the whole scene is repeated.

In her work, Sarraute is determined that though she wants to appreciate and make fleetingly visible these 'darker sides' (Sarraute, 1963: 99) of human interaction, they are 'beyond clear-cut identities, unambiguous situations, and conventional dialogues' (Hewitt, 1990: 59). Sarraute's message is 'the *fluidity* of interpersonal experience against the solidity of appearance' (Hewitt, 1990: 64). So people are not named characters, there is no attempt to build up images of them psychologically, they are voices in interaction, interesting for the situated, patterned but pliable ways in which they engage in conversation and relationship, which is, of course, more than their articulated words.

Seeking to explore such patternings as ongoing fluid processes, leads to Sarraute's interest in subconversations. These are 'what is hidden beneath the interior monologue: an immense profusion of sensations, of images, sentiments, memories, impulses, little larval actions' (Sarraute, 1963: 105). They flow into dialogue, 'so that the insides and outsides are conterminous. Her images of oozing fluids, viscosity, secretions, rhythmic waves … are designed to suggest a hesitant, vacillating, and unnameable experience that underlies and betrays "objective" reality' (Hewitt, 1990: 64–5). The interactivity that arises is intangible, emerging through minimal responses (Wagstaff, 2007). In her writing she is not seeking to illuminate these processes 'but to give hints about how that happens' (Wagstaff, 2007). Amongst other issues, her ideas offer frames for inquiry into the subtle movements of what might be called power.

In the novel *The Golden Fruits*, Sarraute's determination to eschew notions of character is especially strongly shown (Sarraute, 1964). The book tracks the processes through which a newly released novel is initially acclaimed widely in society, then questioned, and later strongly criticised. It does this through voices expressing their views, agreeing with and contradicting the views of others. My image for what Sarraute achieves as form in this work, is the kind of movement sometimes seen in a flock of birds. They turn in one direction, gather mass, seem of accord, and then a few birds take a different tack, seem to be separated from the flock, only for the rest to turn too, swooping together and changing path. Sensitive to patterns of talk in organisations and the ways they shift – how, for example, views that were apparently outliers seem over time to become dominant, perhaps influenced by who expresses them or how they are expressed – I find Sarraute's depiction fascinating. Reading, I experience the movement.

Considering personal and social patterning

In inquiry, I can draw on the notion of tropisms to consider the small preverbal, precognitive, almost imperceptible tendencies with which I and apparently others approach the world. These may appear as habit or ingrained intent we experience and act out. They arise from the interweaving of personal histories with historical and social patterning. I can attempt to glimpse some of these in action, whilst appreciating the challenges of such an aspiration.

When I climb the stairs, for example, I often find I am reaching already for the key to my office door in my pocket. Hypothesis only, but do I tend to prepare ahead, try to be ready for what is about to happen? This could sometimes be valuable anticipation, and at other times a movement, however small, that reaches too far ahead and squashes what else might happen here, before I have any chance of sensing what that might be. Might I eliminate some qualities of 'now' in ordering myself to be ready for what next? In practice I have tried to work with the delicacy of such engagement, finding ways to hold my attention waiting, present and available. Pausing a little before moving forward, opening that move to inquiry, to myself or expressing this overtly. Aspirations again, of course. Sometimes achieved. Paying such attention, I might sometimes notice and shift patterning deliberately, for example moving towards rather than leaning away, might drop the slightly raised shoulder, take a deeper breath.

Casting doubt on autobiographical accounts

Sarraute's work consistently questions our capacities to give life accounts. She did this especially overtly when at 83 she published the nearest thing to an autobiography she would offer, called *Childhood* – not 'my childhood' or even 'a childhood' (Wagstaff, 2007). It involves a pair of voices which try to find a way through to exploring childhood memory. Aligned with her positive disinterest in interpreting gender as significant 'it's written so subtly that she avoids throughout the entire text gender markers on either of these voices' (Wagstaff, 2007). This is a significant challenge writing in French.

There is one slightly more confident voice than the other, and the other is a sort of censor if you like, is constantly questioning the veracity of the first voice. 'How do you know that you know that?' In fact, the opening line of the book is 'Are you sure you want to do this?' There's a constant sense of doubt all the way through it. (Wagstaff, 2007)

This links to tropistic origins, as an exploration of how one recovers memories, decides which are important and so on.

As Sarraute might possibly do, I will leave the voice of this brief chapter sitting alongside other sections of this book.

SELF-REFLECTION AND LIFE NARRATIVE IN THE WORK OF KAZUO ISHIGURO

In this chapter I explore some of the works of Kazuo Ishiguro for the nuanced explorations of memory, self-reflection and constructing life narratives they offer. I have chosen Ishiguro as one author from a range of possibilities, because his writing and quest to explore issues with artistic integrity especially intrigue and delight me. When I tell other people about my interest in novels which explore these issues, they offer their own favourites. *The Sense of an Ending* by Julian Barnes (2012), for example, appears frequently on people's lists. I readily agree. I hope you have your own examples of novels that express ways of being and acting you recognise and that work creatively with the challenges of accounting for these. I suggest that such 'fiction' can enrich our understandings in ways that academic accounts seldom achieve. Issues relating to the qualities of writing and how nuanced accounts can be generated are carried forward in **Writing as inquiry and as representation** in Part IV. Before reviewing Ishiguro's novels, I will outline some issues in working critically with life narrative.

Exploring lives through narrative

Working with notions of living life as inquiry, I am interested in how fragments of life stories come to be told and how they undergo change and reformulation. I see life narratives as provisional constructions of truth which are created through multi-faceted, active processes of interpretation and self-presentation with individual, interpersonal, social and cultural dimensions. In my experiences of working with such material as research data I have found that people's accounts are often multiple, shifting, contradictory and incomplete, and have sought to respect this in how I then portray them.

I am also interested in what reference points people use to generate their narratives, how they deploy personal and social values of what is good or acceptable. In a fascinating collection called *Storied Lives: The Cultural Politics of Self-understanding*

(Rosenwald and Ochberg, 1992), the contributors explore these issues. The editors suggest that people construct their senses of viable lives by drawing on available, and permitted, social and cultural themes.

> We assume that all stories are told and that all self-understanding is realized within the narrative frames each culture provides its members. These frames of intelligibility determine and limit the power of personal narrative. (Rosenwald and Ochberg, 1992: 2)

> Social influence shapes not only public action but also private self-understanding. To the degree that this is true, social control takes on a more ominous aspect. For now it appears that the alternatives one recognizes as possible or moral are constrained in the marrow of individual self-representation. (Rosenwald and Ochberg, 1992: 5)

What stories can be told, and what 'truths' lived, are therefore potentially curtailed, unless people can find ways to live from alternative values:

> Those who would free themselves of their own culture's restrictions must find alternative conceptions of social engagement through which to develop their identities. This too makes liberation difficult. (Rosenwald and Ochberg, 1992: 15)

When we articulate and hear life stories it seems likely that social values, dominant discourses and potential control and self-control are always implicated. They may be tacit or prominent. As researchers we can be alert to these potential intersections of personal and political.

Learning from Kazuo Ishiguro

In this chapter I consider how Kazuo Ishiguro's first three novels resonate with, and potentially complicate, notions of first person inquiry. His later works are also fascinating in this regard, but I will contain my enthusiasm here. Ishiguro has been generous in talking about his work. I have therefore drawn on his voice through published interviews (Shaffer and Wong, 2008) alongside some literary criticism.

Kazuo Ishiguro's first three novels are *A Pale View of Hills* (Ishiguro, 1982 – PVH), *An Artist of the Floating World* (Ishiguro, 1986 – AFW) and *The Remains of the Day* (Ishiguro, 1989 – RTD). They are each concerned with the inherent fallibilities of self-reflection, memory, and the creation of life narratives. Ishiguro puzzles about what happens when people try retrospectively to account for their lives. How do they go about it? What factors might influence, enable and inhibit the stories they can tell and thus the lives they enact? These are issues we encounter in living and speaking from life as inquiry.

None of Ishiguro's novels are what they appear on the surface. With this proviso, I will next briefly outline the ostensible plotlines of these three as a base for considering how they explore self-reflection.

Novel outlines

In all three novels, Ishiguro uses the device of a first person narrator looking back over and seeking to reflect on their life. They take dual roles, both speaking from their experience and taking a reflective position reviewing this. To some extent, they consider alternative perspectives on what they have done and on the notions of integrity that have guided their behaviour. And to the reader it seems these are constrained, with some potentially self-protective limits on where their search for insight might take them. All three narrators also explicitly question their memories and interpretations, and as readers we are soon alerted to potential fallibilities in them accounting for their lives.

A Pale View of Hills (Ishiguro, 1982)

Etsuko is a middle-aged Japanese woman who now lives in England. She looks back to her life in Nagasaki just after the Second World War. She reflects on her brief friendship with a woman called Sachiko in the turmoil and unsettlement of that time. Sachiko was hoping to flee Japan with an American soldier, taking her daughter Mariko with her. At that time Etsuko was married, the couple living with her father-in-law. In the present tense of the novel, she is in England, living alone after the death of her second, English, husband. She is being visited by her second daughter Niki and is haunted by images of the death by suicide of her first daughter, Keiko, who had hanged herself several years before. Etsuko says:

> although we never dwelt long on the subject of Keiko's death, it was never far away, hovering over us whenever we talked. (Ishiguro, 1982: 10)

As the novel proceeds there seem many parallels between Etsuko's life and her memories of Sachiko's, to such an extent that it becomes unclear at times whether Sachiko 'really' existed, and whether Etsuko is talking about Mariko or her own daughter Keiko. In one scene which stands out as ambiguous and is well noted by commentators (for example, Lewis, 2000; Wong, 2000), the elision of characters becomes especially apparent. Etsuko reports how in the later 1940s she followed the child Mariko out along a river-side, concerned for her safety. The child is distressed and Etsuko assures her about leaving Japan:

> 'In any case,' I went on, 'if you don't like it over there, we can always come back.'
>
> This time she looked up at me questioningly.
>
> 'Yes, I promise,' I said. 'If you don't like it over there, we'll come straight back. But we have to try it and see if we like it there. I'm sure we will.' (Ishiguro, 1982: 173)

As commentators repeatedly emphasise, Ishiguro's novels are distinctive for what they do not say, for their style of what is sometimes called understatement.

> A Pale View of Hills is full of silences, omissions and apertures ... What is left out is as important as what is kept in. (Lewis, 2000: 36)

So whilst Etsuko thinks back to her life in Nagasaki in the late 1940s, the effects of the atomic bomb on that city and Japan are mentioned only twice (Lewis, 2000: 37). There are interesting issues, for me, in critics' analyses of this particular silence. In what ways might a character like Etsuko experience a dramatic, landscape- and society-devastating event like an atomic explosion as her life continues? The context for all she remembers carries it. Does she need to mention it separately to create it as figural, when it is inescapable 'background'? As first person inquirers how do we pay appropriate attention to background? See PART II: **Notions of inquiry:** Initiating inquiry: *Scoping the territory of inquiry.*

An Artist of the Floating World (Ishiguro, 1986)

Ono, an ageing artist, is reviewing his career and life. He does this through four diary entries dated between October 1948 and June 1950 and we see subtle shifts as his interpretations develop (Wong, 2000).

Ishiguro says an advantage of using a:

> diary narrative is that each entry can be written from a different emotional position. What [Ono] writes in October 1948 is actually written out of a different set of assumptions than the pieces that are written later on ... so we can actually watch his progress, and... the language itself changes slightly. (Mason, 1989: 334 in Wong, 2000: 38)

Ono has been an acclaimed and successful artist. But he was aligned with the Japanese nationalism of the 1940s, which by the time period of the novel has been publically questioned. Has he aligned his life and creativity with a disreputable cause? Was he indeed creative or overtaken by social forces that he then found himself expressing? How can he now respect himself and his life work? In a parallel story, his position in the family and sense of respect from his children is also opened to question.

The Remains of the Day (Ishiguro 1989)

Stevens is a butler who has especially built his integrity around the notion of dignity and a sense of service (James, 2009; Lewis, 2000). He suggests that serving a great person is an important contribution that someone can make to the world. He looks back from the changing society of 1956 (in which he is serving a new American owner of his stately home) to the time he considered his heyday, serving Lord Darlington in the 1920s and 1930s. The story is potentially blighted, however, by the post-war disparagement of Lord Darlington as a Nazi sympathiser and potentially anti-Semitic (Wong, 2000: 61). Stevens' review extends to his 'personal' life, although separately having a personal life is apparently a somewhat alien concept in his worldview.

In the 1930s Stevens had enjoyed the company of Miss Kenton, a housekeeper at the hall. In 1956 he sets out to visit her (she is now Mrs Benn) on an unaccustomed holiday, borrowing his employer's car, and wondering what clothes are suitable to such an activity. A theme in the novel is whether Stevens denied himself a possible love relationship with Miss Kenton. The priority Stevens has given his career is also shown by the distance he maintained from his father (Wong, 2000), who he identifies as also an exemplary butler, who came to work at Darlington Hall in the 1930s and died there.

As in the other two books, Stevens repeatedly tells the reader that he is unsure of his account of past times, that he realises it may not be reliable. As he reflects, and turns over past memories to consider their meaning, as readers we are aware of how precarious his attempts to identify a viable truth are. Often he seems to be taking certain meanings from events when other interpretations might seem more likely. For example, from reported conversations, his faithfulness to Lord Darlington seems not as reciprocated as Stevens might like to think.

Thematic explorations as inquiry

Ishiguro writes by identifying themes he wants to explore and then finding fertile settings in which he can do this. Whilst ostensible plotlines might suggest that his books are set in post-war Japan (PVH and AFW) or 1930s England (RTD), this is not his intention. He is trying to escape historical specificity, seeing the issues he considers as generic.

Ishiguro sees his first three books as connected novels.

> KI [Kazuo Ishiguro]: In the first three novels, I was rewriting the same thing. I was on the same piece of territory, and each time I was refining what I wanted to say … my second novel was an expansion of the sub-plot of my first novel, but it's about how somebody wasted his life in terms of his career. It's about well-meaning but misguided efforts to lead a good life, but it seems to happen only in the realm of one's career. It seemed to me at the end of writing that book, that if you're talking about wasted lives, you can't just talk about career, you have to talk about the personal arena as well. And so, *The Remains of the Day* is a re-write of *An Artist of the Floating World*, except it's about a man who wasted his life in his career and his personal arena. Each time, I'd think, It's not quite there yet. I've got to do it again but with another dimension. (Wong and Crummett, 2006, in Shaffer and Wong, 2008: 208)

This intention to work with generic, intriguing themes and find fitting settings in which to explore them has been well expressed in relation to Ishiguro's 2015 novel *The Buried Giant* (Kite, 2015). Wanting to explore processes of remembering and forgetting, at both an individual and societal level, he set the book in a somewhat mythical time of 4th century Britain. At that time it seems that, perhaps, a temporary reconciliation had been achieved between people of different faiths and creeds that was about to be lost to such an extent that previous neighbours could consider brutally murdering each other. Ishiguro's puzzles about how this could come about in contemporary society could not, he thought, be explored in specific current or recent locations, lest they be viewed as relevant only to those times and places, subject to scrutiny about factual portrayal. The wider significance of the exploration could be lost. Finding settings for Ishiguro is about potential richness and imaginatively fitting landscapes.

In *The Remains of the Day*, the life of a butler was a fitting device but not the subject Ishiguro was seeking to explore. The Britain he depicts is 'a mythical landscape which is supposed to work at a metaphorical level. *The Remains of the Day* is a kind of parable' (Vorda and Herzinger, 1990, in Shaffer and Wong, 2008: 75). Ishiguro was interested in how we give up our lives to causes and organisations that we might or might not in retrospect consider valuable or deluded. He goes on to suggest that in these terms, 'Most of us are like butlers because we have these small, little tasks that we learn to do, but most of us don't attempt to run the world' (Vorda and Herzinger, 1990, in Shaffer and Wong, 2008: 87). Despite this, 'we just get on with our small lives and hope for the best' (Swaim, 1990, in Shaffer and Wong, 2008: 101). As Wong (2000: 23–4) notes in relation to Ishiguro's first four books (i.e. including *The Unconsoled*, see below):

> Each of his novels supports Ishiguro's contention that, though his characters fail at something essential in their lives, they eventually find the momentum and energy to keep moving forward. The futility of his characters' plights, coupled with their ability to keep forward-looking, adds a poignant dimension to the author's view of the world.

Ishiguro says of the first three novels:

> In those days, I was interested in how people lie to themselves just to make things palatable, to make a sense of yourself bearable. We all dignify our failures a little bit, and make the best of our successes. I was interested in how someone settles on a picture of himself and his life. (Jaggi, 1995, in Shaffer and Wong, 2008: 117)

Associations with first person action research

Drawing clear implications from Ishiguro for first person inquiry is contrary to my intent, and to what I admire in his work. In this section I therefore offer a few associations. I resonate with Ishiguro's puzzles about what happens when people seek retrospectively to account for their lives. His explorations suggest that we tell stories with purposes, and that these purposes and associated assumptions may be fleeting and shift with changing social conditions. We then act with these purposes and associated stories in mind.

In all three cases we might call these depictions of 'unreliable narrators'. But they are also beautifully crafted explorations which cast doubt on notions of 'reliability' as we live with inquiry. Following through the specific twists and turns, complexities and ambiguities (as analyses of these works do admirably – see for example, Lewis, 2000; Wong, 2000) we encounter the paradoxes of authenticity and narrative voices. Potential meanings shift as the stories unfold. Impressions Ishiguro intends are built up, accrued through detailed textual practices.

Considering parallels between *An Artist of the Floating World* and *The Remains of the Day*, Ishiguro says that in the former:

> part of my subject matter really was how parochial people's moral visions tended to be. And this is about an artist who never really saw beyond his small world: he is stuck in this city. The sadness of his fate has all to do with this. He wants very much to give his heart to big causes, but because he is somebody of very limited vision, he can't really see beyond his own circle, he ends up unquestioningly giving his painting, his talent to propaganda purposes in the 1930s as Japanese militarism builds up, and that's the story. (Galliz, 1999, in Shaffer and Wong, 2008: 150)

Ishiguro then gives clues about his craft as writer and how he seeks to show this narrowness of vision. He depicts Ono very much within his own city, assuming in Ono's phrasing that the reader knows the local landmarks he is referring to. 'I wanted to create the effect that the reader … was actually eavesdropping on this rather enclosed narrator talking to somebody … who lives in his neighbourhood' (Galliz, 1999, in Shaffer and Wong, 2008: 150).

Ishiguro has similar intents in relation to Stevens, the butler, who he describes as 'Someone who has such a limited world that he cannot really see the full implications of what he's doing. So Stevens assumes that his "you" is another servant' (Galliz, 1999, in Shaffer and Wong, 2008: 150–1). Ishiguro says he thus 'tried to write the whole book in a kind of "butler-speak"'. He wanted to create the effect of the main character keeping control of his emotions. 'And so, the language itself is of someone who is afraid of the human in him. He always uses these words that keep his opinions and emotions at a distance' (Swaim, 1999, in Shaffer and Wong, 2008: 103).

Having explored people retrospectively ordering their lives in his first three novels, for his next book Ishiguro wanted to write 'from the viewpoint of some-one ... in the midst of chaos, being pulled in different directions at once, and not realizing why'. In *The Unconsoled* (1995), my favourite Ishiguro novel if I single one out, he certainly achieves this. But that is another story.

In my passion for Ishiguro's work I am not saying I wholly agree with his analysis of life and its enactment. Rather my delight is in how he takes themes related to conditionality with which I resonate, and depicts them in fluid, plia-ble, questioning ways, using his crafts as writer. His work is an eloquent reminder to treat issues of self-reflection, memory and life narrative with due caution.

PART IV

WRITING AS INQUIRY AND AS REPRESENTATION

There are myriad ways in which action research can involve writing. Key inquiry practices such as note-taking, journaling, and circulating notes and draft analyses to contribute to cycles in collaborative inquiry are discussed in PART II: **Disciplines of inquiry:** Tracking inquiry processes.

In this part of the book I consider, firstly, how writing can be a process of inquiry and, secondly, some of the issues we encounter as we write in order to represent our work to others. Often pieces of writing have both purposes, and so this is not a clear demarcation, rather it acknowledges that we sometimes give one or other facet primacy as we write.

Working with writing as a process of inquiry is a key strand in first person inquiry as offered here, hence the detailed exploration of its potential processes. The accounts of inquiry in Part V are companion texts.

This Part closes with two illustrations of adopting creative writing approaches, as discussed in **Writing as inquiry.**

WRITING AS INQUIRY

Writing is often a process of discovery, in which the writer learns as they seek to articulate what they want to say to themselves and to others. The phrase 'How can I know what I think till I see what I say' points to this experience and can stand as a motif for both speaking and writing as inquiry. It is cited by Weick (1995: 12) as a 'wonderfully compact account of sensemaking'. He attributes its source through Wallas (1926: 106) to a little girl who had been told to be sure of her meaning before she spoke. I appreciate her alternative notion of how knowing can arise.

Writing as discovery is about process not product. Text is always in or amenable to transition, becoming what it can. At times I will need to keep it to myself. It may arrive at, or pass through, phases when it can be shared with others because it seems to express something of what I hope for it. Later some writing may even appear stale, not now me, a legacy. Although often writing that has had vitality can still evoke the experience and sense of understanding of its origination. And there will always be absences, potentials unexpressed.

One reference point articulation of 'Writing: A method of inquiry' is Richardson's (2000) chapter in *The Sage Handbook of Qualitative Research*, 2nd Edition:

> I consider writing as a *method of inquiry*, a way of finding out about yourself and your topic … Writing is … a way of 'knowing' – a method of discovery and analysis. By writing in different ways, we discover new aspects of our topic and our relationship to it. (Richardson, 2000: 923)

> I write because I want to find something out. I write in order to learn something that I did not know before I wrote it. (Richardson, 2000: 924)

Writing as a method of inquiry then becomes an integral, developmental research process. It is not simply a late stage in which what is already known is 'written up'. 'There is, in the final analysis, no difference between writing and fieldwork' (Clough, 1992: 10).

Advocating writing as discovery can be seen as a political project epistemo-logically, challenging notions of detached, objective researchers studying, interpreting and depicting from a distance. Such conventions are now widely challenged (Denzin and Lincoln, 2011), including in the growing tradition of autoethnography through which researchers explore their experiences appreciat-ing political and cultural insights (Ellis and Bochner, 2000; Sparkes, 2012).

Richardson is very aware of epistemological issues in advocating writing as inquiry. She notes well-established positivist views of what qualitative research writing should be like, and offers her approach 'in the spirit of affectionate irrev-erence' (Richardson, 2000: 923). It appears, however, that she had little choice but to develop writing differently. She admits that for 30 years she had found reading the text of 'numerous supposedly exemplary qualitative studies ... boring'. The writing 'suffered from acute and chronic passivity: passive-voiced author, passive "subjects"' (Richardson, 2000: 924).

Writing is often associated with finding a voice. Inquiry is both personal and political process. For example, since the 1970s many women and feminist schol-ars have sought to gain a sense of voice as they re-vision history and interpretations of the world in which women had largely been omitted or restrictively portrayed. Expressing what might otherwise be censored or cur-tailed has been an important political theme in this work. Issues of voice are relevant to many people, men and women, especially when they respect and wish to articulate multiple forms of knowing. Finding a voice is thus a major challenge for many aspiring writers. Perhaps we are 'fortunate, now, to be work-ing in a postmodernist climate' as Richardson hopes (2000: 928). Styles of writing and creativity are proliferating. But constraints have taken fresh forms, such as the increasing conventionalisation of what are considered acceptable styles for many academic journals. This can constrain voices and what may be researched and expressed. The politics of epistemology and voice thus remain at issue. But it is not my intention to further argue the case for working with multi-dimensional, expressive writing here, as this is well-established, in my view.

In this chapter, I will especially consider practices for writing as inquiry which take us to the edge of exploration and discovery, and will consider how they can be integrated as key dimensions of living life as inquiry and can be incorporated into academic work.

Writing as inquiry is a simple, pliable notion. Any writing can be done reflec-tively. I am interested in writing that contributes to living life as inquiry with its multiple potential purposes as set out so far in this book. A core purpose is that of engaging with integrity in complex, shifting contexts and times, and of track-ing this over days, weeks, months, or years if appropriate. Writing is, then, initially process, although it may later become product.

Such writing is not, for me, primarily about a journey of self-exploration (partly as I do not have a sense of a coherent self to refer to), although it may provide insights and is about ongoing learning. This learning may relate to life patterns, or habitual responses (social as much as for me as person, as explored in PART III: **Drawing on the work of Nathalie Sarraute:** Tropisms) and I can wonder how these are held, what cues them. But I am not interested in tracing them to source; I find this an unhelpfully causative notion.

This book's offering can be set alongside a plethora of texts, with more or less academic intents, that set out approaches for reflexive writing and coach the aspiring researcher writer (for example, Etherington, 2004; Hunt and Sampson, 2006). Some people find the emphasis on writing limiting, and engage in more artful practices, such as drawing as inquiry. *The Artist's Way: A Course in Discovering and Recovering Your Creative Self* (Cameron, 1992) outlines a 12-week, self-help programme, from which a movement of this name has developed.

In my own history I have experienced writing as a process of discovery, and commented reflexively on this in resulting publications (for example, in Marshall, 1984). I have worked with a range of expressive and exploratory writing processes, both as integrated dimensions of living life as inquiry and to help me portray research and ideas. I have also offered such approaches to Masters and doctoral students, and to other people I have worked with, to help them in their own inquiries and writing. These developments have involved grafting different approaches and practices together, and invention.

Writing as inquiry can be used in a variety of ways as an integrated action research practice. These include:

- Providing an ongoing reflective stream in living life as inquiry
- Helping to explore an issue, image or event (past or anticipated) by writing and seeing what comes
- As part of a reflective process of journaling, sometimes having a theme in mind to explore, sometimes starting out with no intent and seeing what arises
- As part of the reflection phase in cycles of action and reflection
- Helping *show* in action to complement what you *tell* about your research and inquiries
- Providing material on 'fieldwork' (whatever form this has taken) that you use as evidence to write up a dissertation
- Writing draft sections of your dissertation, for later development if necessary
- Enabling you to find appropriate emergent form to present any aspects of your work

(Marshall, 2008)

And writing can be an activity you simply enjoy doing for its own sake.

Any form of writing can be developed as inquiry. It is especially compatible with reflective writing and with exploring and generating research stories and accounts. These are demonstrated in Part V of this book. Such approaches can also be applied to working with literature and ideas, and to research analysis, as they involve paying attention to what I am thinking and trying to express, and then finding appropriate forms and voices in which to portray these. Through writing as inquiry I am seeking to make the process and resulting text vital and alive with insight and forthright critical analysis rather than deadened and masked. How we might go about this work is elaborated below.

Welcoming arising thoughts

My respect for the potential richness of emergent writing means that arising thoughts are precious, especially in their potential morning freshness. It is a privilege to sometimes arise to silence and see what appears. This account from the New Zealand novelist Janet Frame's autobiography (Frame, 1999) speaks of nurturing the space in which our writing selves live and unfold, and resonates with my experience.

Frame had been staying with Mr Sargeson who had let her live in the Army Hut at the bottom of his garden. He lived and worked to a strict routine which she adopted. But at first if she had breakfast with him, she would chatter.

> he drew attention to this. 'You babble at breakfast,' he said. I took note of what he said and in future I refrained from 'babbling', but it was not until I had been writing regularly each day that I understood the importance to each of us of forming, holding, maintaining our inner world, and how it was renewed each day on waking, how it even remained during sleep, like an animal outside the door waiting to come in; and how its form and power were protected most by surrounding silence. My hurt at being called a 'babbler' faded as I learned more of the life of a writer. (Frame, 1999: 247)

Over the years I have developed disciplines and practices for working with writing as inquiry. These especially seek to help us notice the critical mind that might censor, amend, reduce, and limit what might otherwise be said; and to find ways to express, respect and work reflectively and critically with our own knowing and voices.

Such approaches do not guarantee that writing flows. But they can help us stick with the task and treat writing as always a process of learning. Often the arising form emergent writing takes is potentially interesting, informative, expressing tacit dimensions of knowing which might well be curtailed if filtered through received or conventional formats. This can help us find appropriate structuring for the writing as later product.

These approaches do not mean that what emerges is inherently 'good' writing, to be shared immediately with others. Although it might be. But having been generated it has the potential to be worked with.

Developing disciplines that help me engage in writing as inquiry, I have found creative writing approaches by some authors appealing and highly congruent. I have drawn on some to extend, enrich and sharpen my practice, seeking also to integrate aspects of them into academic work, as I now review.

Drawing on creative writing approaches

In my development as writer, I have drawn on the work of people who articulate and coach creative and life writing processes, using their work selectively to inform and extend my notions and practices of writing as inquiry in the service of researching. Freefall Writing™ developed by Barbara Turner-Vesselago and depicted well in *Writing without a Parachute: The Art of Freefall* (Turner-Vesselago, 2013), has been a major influence for me. I have had the opportunity to attend two of the week-long courses Barbara offers annually in the UK. Alongside this I set some explanations of how writing can become alive, eloquent and meaningful from Natalie Goldberg whose books *Writing down the Bones* (1986) and *Wild Mind* (1991) I have also found encouraging and practically helpful. Both approaches invite the aspiring writer to take courage and find their own path, rather than be over-shadowed by projected conventions.

Goldberg says 'I want people to be "writing down the bones", the essential, awake speech of their minds' (1986: 8–9):

> The aim is to burn through to first thoughts, to the place where energy is unobstructed by social politeness or the internal censor, to the place where you are writing what your mind actually sees and feels, not what it *thinks* it should see or feel. It's a great opportunity to capture the oddities of your mind. Explore the rugged edge of thought.

In this permissive approach, first thoughts can have tremendous energy. Goldberg suggests that they are 'also unencumbered by ego, by that mechanism in us that tries to be in control, tries to prove the world is permanent and solid, enduring and logical'. Expressing first thoughts, Goldberg claims, allows us to reach beyond ourselves and express 'the truth of the way things are' (Goldberg, 1986: 9).

Whilst I am not comfortable with any notion of 'the truth', I appreciate Goldberg's advice that we listen to first thoughts, whatever we then choose to do with them. A key principle of writing as inquiry is to learn from what you say, and to see where this takes you. It is not simply 'creative', it is alive, vital, for whatever purposes you are following; it can open up what was not pre-formulated, as the little girl told Wallas (1926: 106).

Goldberg and Turner-Vesselago offer 'rules' and 'precepts' respectively, some of which can help people develop their practices of writing as inquiry. These are blunt and directive, useful to contradict the censoring and formality that is expected in much everyday writing activity such as project reports, and to unlearn any early messages that disparaged writing into which people had allowed their own voice expression. (Many people have, for example, learnt not to express themselves as 'I' and find this invitation creates anxiety.)

Goldberg's rules are: 'keep the hand moving'; 'don't cross out'; 'don't worry about spelling, punctuation, grammar'; 'don't think – write' and 'go for the jugular. (If something comes up in your writing that is scary or naked, dive right into it. It probably has lots of energy.)' (Goldberg, 1986: 8). She articulates how working with detail brings writing and its potential for learning and communication alive.

In Freefall Writing, Turner-Vesselago is seeking writing that has 'an aliveness and complexity, a quality of engagement, in short a *believability*, that goes deep enough to make the reader care' (2013: 13). She sees this as underpinned by 'surrender' as a writer to a process you learn to trust. This involves a 'state of absorption' in which

> you are able to let the writing teach you, because the rational, consciously intending aspect of the psyche … has stepped out of the way. You can write with an open heart and allow words that you had not planned to write to surface on the page. (Turner-Vesselago, 2013: 12)

Into this state you can then bring 'conscious thought and intention', the operation of will, to balance with surrender. 'How long it will take to balance the two – to find your own essential balance between will and surrender – you will discover for yourself' (Turner-Vesselago, 2013: 13).

In Freefall Writing, five precepts are offered as 'simple guidelines to make the process of surrender in writing easier and faster' (Turner-Vesselago: 2013: 27–8):

1. 'Write what comes up for you'
2. 'Don't change anything'
3. 'Give all the sensuous detail'
4. 'Go where the energy is, or go fearward' – advocating 'moving toward whatever feels most charged for you'
5. 'The Ten-Year Rule'

Such writing operates from the principle of showing rather than telling (Turner-Vesselago, 2013: 53; also Goldberg, 1986: 68). Incorporating dialogue and direct speech is one approach to giving vitality and sensuous detail to depicted action (Turner-Vesselago, 2013: 139–50). The use of dialogue could attempt to show small movements, which are interactional and social as well as individual, as Sarraute does with tropisms.

Precept 5 in Freefall Writing is a suggestion rather than a prescription (Turner-Vesselago, 2013: 35) and applies when working with autobiographical material. It proposes that older experiences will be both more resonant and less likely to generate reactivity on the part of the writer than more recent experiences might, making them more available as raw material for fiction or other genres of creative writing. Goldberg says such material will be better 'composted' (Goldberg, 1986: 14). It might mean that we will not be seeking to prove or justify a point of view, will not be blocking the reader's access with our own sign-posting (Turner-Vesselago, 2013: 35). Writing as inquiry is, however, often working with contemporary material, as discussed below.

We must learn to trust processes of writing as inquiry, so that they grow, become our own. Frameworks such as those of Goldberg and Turner-Vesselago, and the courses associated with them, encourage this development. The rules and precepts constitute a liberating structure in a way, paradoxical practices that seek to 'cultivate empowerment through development' (Torbert, 1991: 98), which must be followed but then transcended. The practice allows for this potential. Developing the practice requires practice, to let go of the internal censors and write freely, and it requires that you make it your own.

As one form of practice, both Goldberg and Turner-Vesselago suggest using timed exercises in which you can take a topic or start with whatever arises and write for a chosen time (ten minutes, twenty minutes, an hour or longer) and see what emerges. Committing to this development will build up capacity, as physical exercise can. If you have taken a key phrase or notion that you want to explore and started your writing with it, you can see where it takes you. If you pause or lose the thread, you can return to the initial phrase should you choose and start your writing there again.

It is important here to distinguish Barbara Turner-Vesselago's purposes in devising Freefall Writing from those I am outlining for working with writing as a dimension of inquiry. Turner-Vesselago's stated purpose is to show writers 'how to get the thinking mind to step aside, so that writing becomes truly creative – a vulnerable and open-hearted engagement with the moment' (Turner-Vesselago, 2013: book cover). Her belief is that writers need sustained experience of this kind of 'surrender' *before* any specific 'intention' can be brought into the writing process. Nonetheless, I find that some of the powerful practices of Freefall Writing can be adapted *from the outset* to the use of writing as a dimension of inquiry and to presenting research that is alive and rich when writing academically. Anyone interested in Freefall Writing should consult Barbara's own work, especially *Writing without a Parachute: The Art of Freefall* (2013).

Selectively adopting Freefall Writing practices

In my conduct of writing as inquiry I have drawn on Freefall Writing precepts selectively to extend my practice. With my core interest in developing writing as a dimension of living life as inquiry, Precepts 3 and 4 have been especially helpful. These invite me to 'give all the sensuous detail' and 'go where the energy is, or go fearward' (Turner-Vesselago: 2013: 28). These help create vibrant, evocative text. They can also be used to help me reach towards vivid experiencing as inquiry.

I can sometimes, but seldom do, adopt Precept 1, which encourages the writer to 'write what comes up' without any prior agenda. At the outset I often have an initial idea, image, puzzle, issue or phrase I want to start with, from tracking my arising inquiry processes and what presents to be explored. Also, when I intend to write a research account such as those in Part V, I typically know the situation and perhaps some of the potential themes I want to start to depict.

I often write to explore inquiry that is currently in process. I seldom therefore adopt the 'Ten-Year Rule' of Freefall Writing (Precept 5). In living life as inquiry I mainly want to work with what is currently happening, when it is raw and undigested. Writing experimentally about present time issues and experiences – the meeting I just left, the one I am preparing for tomorrow – I am seeking to learn more about how I am thinking, feeling and acting, and so gain perspective and potential to adjust or experiment with any of these in the service of living with integrity in ongoing inquiry. Rather than seek to take myself out of the picture, as the 'Ten-Year Rule' advises, I seek to catch glimpses of myself-in-interaction, through refraction as it were, from different angles of view.

I then selectively incorporate Precepts 2–4 into my process of writing as inquiry. They challenge me to fill out what I am exploring rather than skim its surface or turn it into abstraction. I seek to articulate and tease out sensuous detail, and follow through potential resonances, associations and threads. Exploring a given situation I might, for example, track both inner arcs of attention – what was I thinking, feeling, assuming, trying to achieve and so on – and outer arcs of attention – what I did and said, what others did and said, what I noticed happening (Marshall, 2001), opening more dimensions to potential review. 'Going fearward', I notice potential censors and try to reach beyond them, whilst also treating them with deliberate inquiry. (I can later choose what is too much to say publically.) See PART II: **Disciplines of inquiry:** Scanning inner and outer arcs of attention. Doing all this helps locate me as writer, and open my approach to action to review, and thus contributes to ongoing critically reflective practice.

Working with sensuous detail (even if invented, because it will not come 'from nowhere') presents images and impressions for exploration. This is illustrated and discussed in the story about Inquiry learning groups and working with feedback in Part V. As in co-counselling, I can experimentally amplify the weak signals that arise in expressive writing, act into them, see what then develops. See PART II: **Disciplines of inquiry:** Attentional disciplines. I have opportunities to play and explore.

I find accounts easier to write richly if I start at least by working with the details of people, places and situations that are or were there, in my interpretation rather than 'the truth'. If I try to use pseudonyms initially, for example, the embodied experience is not so fully available to me. So I first write with names or initials. If the created experience is real enough for me I can 'write into the corners', as it were, and find what awaits there. Later I can craft the account, change names, choose whether to disguise, transpose or omit for reasons of confidentiality.

Once I set out, I do not know where the writing will take me, and so I experience the emergent nature of writing as inquiry. Key aspects of the practice are keeping things fluid, moving, and sensing each next step. Such writing means letting images, words and connections appear. The space opens up, and I can be surprised, perhaps shocked. The approach is a route into exploring richly, deeply. It is not simply a stream of consciousness. It is not concrete in a limited way. It may appear as the universal expressed in the particular, but with all its trailing ends, unfinished qualities, changing and being in flux.

If what arises is potentially divergent, I sometimes welcome this. But sometimes I want to keep the writing on track with my initial intentions. These are inquiring choice points. I can take unanticipated directions out of curiosity, and see what learning they offer, especially if it seems I would otherwise be avoiding a difficult issue. But I can then choose whether to include such multiple pathways in the final account, judging whether they might be relevant or digressions. Alongside accounts in Part V then, there was associated exploratory writing that does not appear.

At the end of Part IV I offer two pieces which were written intentionally following Freefall Writing Precepts 2–5, having chosen the topics in advance, during a week-long Freefall Writing workshop offered by Barbara Turner-Vesselago in April 2013.

Sensing each next step in writing as inquiry

There are issues of pace as I engage in writing as inquiry, seeking to follow the emerging threads. If I am rushing at writing, just that little bit ahead of the rhythm with which it is appearing, I lose connection. This may well be anxiety. 'I must finish revising this chapter today!' If I can persuade myself to slow up, or the faltering

(Continued)

(Continued)

writing throws me off and I take the hint and go off to wander for a moment, stretch out my back and return, I can, for a while at least, get into step with the writing, flow with its flow. Then everything I do, going to brew tea, looking out over the blue skied view of Morecambe Bay and the further hills, even popping to the shop for milk, all of that is still writing, still nurturing this diffuse attention inside me that is working on the writing whatever else I am doing. Writing is, then, a whole body, whole person experience. If writing is going well and engaging, I can be quite a fidget when I write, receptively alert. I like to wander off on small errands and come quickly back. Leaving my keyboard does not mean that I have stopped writing, should not be taken as a sign that I am open to conversation. My mind is elsewhere.

Deepening inquiry through working with writing

Reflective writing and living life as inquiry become entangled, and feed each other. Surfacing themes and issues through the writing, I may have the potential to see them differently as I encounter them in experience. Sometimes sources of tension dissolve through writing into them. Sometimes they become clearer, more pliable and amenable to reflection and active experimentation, perhaps in mutual conversation with others. The phrases that appear on the page can seem to name or encode potential tendencies in interpretations, behaviours or emotional reactions. Noticing this allows me to stand back a little, explore them both as self-observer and for their enacted dynamic. I might spot, for example, how behaviour I consider inappropriate becomes triggered, notice the internal and external patterning of how this occurs. This might then open up choices of action, being and attitude.

How can we then work with the material generated through writing as inquiry? Sometimes writing reaches completeness of a kind in its first expression. It then stands as it is. Sometimes it needs clarification and adjustment to help it speak out to a reader. Or we can engage in further phases of writing as inquiry, moving from an initial account, through arising themes to analysis and deeper exploration. Also I can invite feedback from critical friends to deepen my sense of potential issues. See **Inquiry learning groups and working with feedback** in Part V. Resulting notes can become layered text in later writing. At some time I will decide not to develop a specific piece of writing and associated exploration further, and will let emergent inquiry take its course; forever provisional, never completed.

Ways of working with writing can be developed as crafts. But writing is seldom an accomplished, secure activity. In its search for originality, it is not predictable, although having disciplines for engaging in writing can be supportive, as can knowing that whatever the experience on a given day, tomorrow could well be different. I do not assume that writing is or can be easy. Although for some people at some times it is. Rather I see it as a complex process of engagement that we can work with. Apparent 'avoidance' can be part of this work, is worth respecting and exploring as potentially meaningful.

Inviting feedback

Deciding who to invite to give feedback on accounts of inquiry, and on attempts to write these resonantly for dissemination in some way, are, of course, acts of inquiry. Do I look to supportive readers, critical friends, or outsiders for whom even the notion of living life as inquiry might need copious explanation? What can I cope with? I can become swamped, receiving lots of comments from disparate sources, challenged to listen that widely or to integrate what I might learn. Appropriate timing is another factor. In the midst of ongoing action, feedback is potentially highly salient, and yet my unavoidably partial view might slant how I interpret its implications. Working with longer time-frames I might gain more perspective, but learning may seem less impactful, muted by distance. I must treat comments with due regard for all these factors. When I receive feedback on writing, I have choices depending on its framing. Some feedback is about the ongoing inquiry, to be taken into account as this develops. Some is about the depiction of inquiry. My choices with the pieces in this book were whether then to seek to craft the writing given this feedback or to address the issues raised in an additional layer of comments, showing the partiality of any point of view, any basis for action. In this book I have offered a mixture of approaches, as the writing notes accompanying each story in Part V show.

Writing as collective practice

Writing alongside others engaged in writing can offer communal energy, encourage commitment and provide some forms of swift feedback. Over the years, sometimes working with colleagues, and drawing on various experiences and sources, I have developed practices for holding writing spaces, for a few hours, a day or several days at a time. Some have been directed at helping doctoral and Masters students work on learning papers and dissertations.

The format for a writing workshop or retreat is simple, but the experience needs enacting richly and reflectively each time rather than mechanically to formula. It is open to development as participants wish. The core format is:

People come along with some writing they want to do in mind

We agree ground rules and approximate timings

We then work in cycles in which we:

> Go round the group and each person says briefly what they are planning to work on and what issues they see in doing so. We might have some minimal conversation at this stage, but the idea is to voice and then move into doing, not to engage in analytic mind, and certainly not to tell others what they should do
>
> We go our separate ways, find conducive spaces and writing technologies, some favouring handwriting, others working at computers
>
> We write, paying attention to process as we go
>
> At an allotted time – an hour and a half, maybe two hours, or overnight and into the next morning if on a residential writing retreat – those of us who wish return to the base room
>
> We go round the circle saying how the writing has gone. Someone might read out a segment for instant feedback. Again we are wary about becoming too analytic; we are generally seeking to work with processes of writing as discovery rather than impose order. Although we can shift agendas if requested and we agree

We then go through the whole cycle again.

We build in times to go walking, to drink tea and eat cake, to let ourselves be fully embodied in the space. We may well agree times of silence, especially in the mornings. Often writing that arises on waking, after immersion the day before, has a special crystalline quality to it. We do not quickly catch up emails in breaks, we do not expose ourselves to external distraction; if necessary we try to limit these activities to unobtrusive times of the day.

Developing a writing retreat over several days with multiple participants it is helpful to design and hold a space in which people are well taken care of physically, well fed, well supplied with teas and coffees, to be taken as participants wish. At their best such experiences are suffused with mutual qualities of attention and inquiry, and participants can enjoy appropriate autonomy as well as engaging supportively with others.

Typically people are amazed at the evocative qualities of what they and others write when they let this happen. If so much can be well written in an hour, say, surely their thesis does not need to drag on unexpressed for years.

But writing relationships can also be as simple as two people sitting together at a café table, talking, writing, reading out their work, talking and writing again.

Integrating writing as inquiry into academic work

Writing as inquiry especially appeals to students who feel constrained by traditional academic expectations. They welcome practices that help them express and explore their own knowing in the face of assumptions about academic requirements that might stifle their voices and mute their potential contributions. A key question is whether the apparent criteria of acceptability are non-negotiable, as they may seem, or can be challenged. Writing differently is thus political work, seeking to bring academic conventions into question. It can be risky. It requires working with alternative quality criteria that can be legitimated in the institutional contexts in which the aspiring writers present their work. See APPENDIX B: **Presenting first person inquiry for Masters and doctoral work.**

It may be possible, within local conventions, to write a whole thesis as inquiry. But many academic projects adopt a mix of styles, including some which seem more conventional. Adapting writing as inquiry to academic work is more obviously appropriate for certain purposes such as reflection and accounts of action research fieldwork. Pieces written as inquiry may be used in their entirety or extracts taken from them with appropriate framing to illustrate what has been explored – for example, 'at that stage in the project I was analysing issues of xxx, as this dated thought-piece shows'. The dynamics of discovery can also be applied to setting out conceptual, theoretical territory and analyses of literature, with some care and inventiveness. If necessary, writing that started out as inquiry-based can be transposed into other forms, with appropriate framing and commentary, hopefully retaining some of the vitality of its origins.

WRITING AS REPRESENTATION

This chapter focuses on writing as representation. As this is a somewhat contrived distinction, writing is still and continually inquiry. The chapter considers issues of finding form in writing and then some detailed considerations as we prepare writing to share with others.

Finding form

A key aspect of working with writing as inquiry is respect for and curiosity about the form(s) in which it arises. We can then seek to craft these as we move towards text we consider finished enough, for now, to share with others.

By form, I am referring to the pattern, flow and structure of the writing, the shape it comes to take. Distinguishing this from the content, what the work is about, is however false. All content has form of some kind; and form does not appear without content. I especially welcome writing in which content, form and thematic contribution are analogically congruent as this increases potential resonance and enhances the reader's experience, as some fictional writing does. Virginia Woolf's experimental novel *The Waves* (Woolf, 1992; originally published 1931) has these qualities. It explores the nature of identity through the voices of its six main characters, charted from childhood through adulthood in successive waves of expressive text (Briggs, 2005; Marshall, 2008). In Marshall (2008) I explored issues of finding form and sought to learn from Woolf's attempts to trace her writing process.

All writing has form, which communicates. Forms associated with distance, focus, rationality, value neutrality, linearity and so on are favoured in conventional academic scholarship, and we encounter these as subtext when we read. Innovative ideas placed within such structures may well lose their potential. Form can be considered as analogic communication, signalling the status of digital messages

(Watzlawick et al., 1967). We may seek to name and frame what we intend in writing, as in speech (Fisher et al., 2003), but 'form is a meta communication, analogically "framing" that digital attempt at clarification, which may thus be contradicted or rendered meaningless' (Watzlawick et al., 1967) (Marshall, 2008. 684).

Apprehending when form and content are congruent is likely to be as much felt as an intellectual process. For example, a text may appear stilted, careful in its wording and distinctions. I may experience a sense of tussling as the writer tries to pin sense down. But any impression is also only a hypothesis, to be explored as possibility. This reading experience can prompt my curiosity about the nature of the text; send me searching for further clues. In this example, fine-grained distinctions might matter in this field. Or I might interpret a sense of defensiveness, and puzzle about how this arises. I thus see the form of the text as 'informative' in itself, whilst we might experience this tacitly in the main. Interpretation can be influenced but not controlled by the writer.

As writers we can, however, pay attention to form, and consider analogic aspects of communication. Embarking on a piece of writing is a malleable time, during which we can attend to arising form. 'Often we need to "listen" to what form our writing is seeking to take because this may well have congruence, in some way, with the substantive themes we are exploring or with our relationship to them as inquirers' (Marshall, 2008: 683–4). The emerging form may encode our distinctive contribution.

Sometimes we fight and reject arising form because it is not the voice we hoped to use. For example, we may have wanted to sound more academic, or less into advocacy. We may then need to find an alternative voice. Or we can notice and respect what is trying to appear and work with it. Perhaps, the 'non-academic' voice is articulating a form of critique that can be developed. Perhaps the voice of advocacy needs to be expressed, and can be twinned with a more questioning companion to demonstrate reflective richness. Sometimes what we have to say cannot be expressed until we find a suitable form, for us. In my experience, people's writing often starts to flourish, and achieves more intellectual quality, when they address rather than struggle against any problems they experience in finding appropriate form for their work. This often requires both sitting with uncertainty and bold experimentation. We can ask each time why and in what ways arising form is appropriate. We then have the opportunity to work with and craft what is arising, perhaps accentuating what had initially appeared tentatively, finding appropriate structures for representation (Marshall, 2008).

If finding form is a creative endeavour in the way I have outlined, we then face choices about whether to explain forms we have adopted to the potential reader or to let them speak for themselves. Readers may find 'creative' writing formats difficult to access or off-putting. Often such texts have qualities as wholes, arising from flow, repetition, structure as much as content, as Nathalie Sarraute's work does. How we resolve these dilemmas will depend on our purposes and the space within which we are presenting our writing. In situations where being misunderstood can have significant consequences, such as an academic dissertation, some attempts at framing and giving the reader signposting might well be helpful, as long as this does not seem like taming the text or appeasement. Also, readers may need to develop their patience and practices for engagement as they encounter alternative forms of text.

Conventions and the politics of epistemology and form, especially in academic writing, can curtail experimentation in writing, potentially silencing our contributions. If I do not allow the writing to unfold, I have an even more partial understanding than I might. I need to write uncensored, or noticing the censors, to see what emerges. That is why some of the precepts of Freefall Writing (Turner-Vesselago, 2013) have appealed to me. They have contributed to me approaching writing with a formless enough form to let my form emerge through it (Marshall, 2008).

Developing writing

Writing accounts of inquiry to share publicly presents interesting choices and some complications and challenges. It is also a process of development that can refine, enhance and layer the exploration through further stages, and perhaps different forms, of writing. The stories in this book show and explore some of the potential processes involved through specific examples. In this section I will reflect on some generic issues and dilemmas.

How to portray indeterminacy?

Seeing living life as inquiry as ongoing process, I do not think that accounts should be complete, neat, following a notion of beginning-middle-and-end, should ever be finalised. As explained elsewhere I admire writers like Kazuo Ishiguro who depict a sense of shifting meanings in their work. Exploring inter-relationships between form and content, and grounded in experiencing living life as inquiry, I aspire to depicting conditionality – to showing glimpses, provisionality, a simultaneous multiplicity of possibilities, the potential for something else completely to be 'true' next minute – as far as is permissible in the kind of writing I undertake. And I will seek to push boundaries (for example, Allen and Marshall, 2015). I am certainly not intending to offer the reader a 'full view'.

How much to tell?

Transposing the Freefall Writing invitation to write sensuous detail (Precept 3: Turner-Vesselago, 2013: 32–3) into writing as inquiry amplifies challenges that any qualitative researcher faces when they try to give rich, nuanced accounts of fieldwork. When will locating and evocative detail become overload? How can you give sufficient but not too much 'context'? And how to decide what is relevant context, especially when interpreting and attributing 'context' are interactive, co-constructed activities? In what ways is it appropriate to track action research through its twists and turns, weaving in inner and outer arcs of attention, and when might this become too much of a blow-by-blow account or simply descriptive, flat? In what ways can I incorporate theoretical, critical analysis? What warrants do I have for doing so? How much and in what ways do I need to account for interpretive processes? When might this become too much reflexive overload?

I will leave these as challenging questions; they are all issues to be worked with, for discernment. Gaining feedback on draft text can help review options and develop crafts and formats for writing.

What voice to write in?

In first person inquiry it seems perhaps obvious that the voice will be 'I'. With many others I draw back from the over-insistent 'I', but must own my place in the writing. In living life as inquiry my aspiration is not to focus on self, on ego, but to achieve a dynamic sense like a repeated breath or pulsing scanning of attentions, through which I seek to access an extended view or experiencing. There are no easy formulae for depicting this in writing.

Third and second person voices are possible (see Pelias, 2000, for an example of the latter). Sometimes in writing exploratory accounts, I find that a third person voice emerges and I write about someone being inquiring, and that seems fitting. I can take this as emergent form and respect it. For example, this occurs in PART V: **Acting for sustainability: Planning** *Global Futures*: **Meeting vignette**. This expresses me observing myself in inquiring action. As a device a third person voice might also mean I take care to explain to the reader what was going on, and what was on the main character's mind.

Whether to tell one story or several facets?

Reviewing experience as inquiry, there are often multiple stories available to be told, no one truth, multiple potential time-frames intersecting, perhaps some hazy images from which patterned order could be generated. This form needs honouring in the process and depiction. Narrative coherence is not my aspiration, or fitting in my view, especially if it contravenes living with indeterminacy and the spirit of inquiry nested within this.

Any systemic account is limited. Seeking to honour and keep alive multiple connections risks collapsing poly-semic multi-dimensionality. Punctuating an event (Bateson, 1973) to express it makes some aspects potentially figural. Any 'experience' is created artificially from moments in ongoing living, not clearly bounded with its own discrete meanings. The latter leach across lives and encounters. Some novelists create such explorations in text. W.G. Sebald's work, for example, such as *Austerlitz* (2002a) and *The Rings of Saturn* (2002b), interweaves personal, social, historical and political themes as he depicts travels through landscapes, lives and histories. His crafted liminal texts also evoke what is tacit and lost as lingering potentialities in experience.

Boundaries in representing inquiry

See also PART II: **Inquiry in action:** Vulnerability in inquiry. Drawing boundaries in writing applies to ethical and representational issues, both in relation to the inquirer and their responsibilities to other people.

Pieces written as discovery and inquiry are not necessarily appropriate for others to see, especially out of context. Inquiry is generally engaged as life process rather than as production. By no means all inquiries require a public life, are intended for dissemination or publication; living life as inquiry does not require indiscriminate exposure. And yet masking is not a generative first move in writing as inquiry, unless one focuses on the process of masking. But disguise may become appropriate as we move towards writing as representation.

If writing as inquiry is to be incorporated in some way in academic work or a publication, we need to be especially vigilant and thoughtful about boundaries and choices. I can claim my right to tell my story and learning, but this opens up dilemmas. Concern about potential exposure and breaching other people's confidentiality mean that I then need to consider how to do this with integrity. My full version of truth may feel too vulnerable, too revealing to tell. Some inquiry writing is developmental at the time, but is too raw, painful, transitory, too challenging, to be shown to many or any other people. And, typically, it is not a truth to be fixed in place. Sharing such work in its original expression might make me vulnerable. Toning it down sufficiently to share might make it bland and inconsequential.

We can be especially wary about how and where we articulate inquiry that is in process. There can be something special about those raw times when images, feelings and framings are volatile but also malleable. Finding some forms of exploratory expression can be a valuable discipline and a path to critically reflective learning. See PART II: **Disciplines of inquiry:** Speaking inquiry as potentially vital process. But I may need to be cautious about treating any apparent sense-making as meaningful, given its potentially transitory nature. At those times I need to protect the boundaries of inquiry, foster my abilities to keep things open.

If you have been undertaking first person action research for academic purposes, the spectre of what could be termed 'naive humanist realism' might suggest that you should tell the 'whole' truth of your explorations, wherever these have led you. You do not need to offer it all uncensored, taking it to be 'the' truth. You can instead explain *that* and *how* you engaged in quality processes as you explored your knowing, and how you arrived at a suitable representation. These processes might include cycles of action and reflection, sharing writing with others and receiving feedback, and reflecting on arising themes and transposing these into topics you then explored through further cycles of writing. You might choose to explain *the nature* of the inquiries you engaged in rather than explicate these fully. For example, if you have explored a difficult relationship in explicit detail to inform action experiments to improve it, you may want to say *that* you did this, and the *nature* of the outcomes, but not give the specifics. You can delineate and explain the boundaries of disclosure you are drawing.

Also we need to take due care for other people, to be respectful about how telling our stories may intersect with theirs. Speaking out could implicate others, make them vulnerable, be an intrusion and risk breaching confidentiality. I have engaged explicitly with these dilemmas in writing this book, as the introduction to Part V and 'writing notes' attached to stories explain.

When boundaries are at issue, you can pause, consider the choices and their merits, consider who else might need to be consulted and how best to do this, and perhaps discuss these issues with critical friends. Sometimes powerful writing is set aside for a time and reviewed later when dissemination then becomes possible, with appropriate framing and selective use of the original text.

Given the issues of potential exposure, for me and others, I could consider fictionalising accounts. Does what I am trying to express have to be 'true' to a certain situation, or can its qualities be transposed in ways that protect the details but still tell a version of 'truth'? Reviewing such issues in relation to organisational change for sustainability, which might well take inquirers into confidential territory, I experimented with writing a fictionalised account to elaborate inquiry into advocating for corporate social responsibility, drawing imaginatively on stories I have heard from other people. This appears in Appendix C to illustrate this approach.

SELECTIVELY ADOPTING
FREEFALL WRITING PRECEPTS

Learning to Microlight

Writing note

This piece was written as an experiment in following all but the first Freefall Writing precept ('Write what comes up for you', Turner-Vesselago, 2013: 27) at one of Barbara Turner-Vesselago's week-long Freefall Writing courses. The experience was 31 years previously, so certainly satisfied 'The Ten-Year Rule'. It is included here as an example of writing as a developmental practice that we can keep on practising. To explore the crafts of working through sensuous detail, I recalled the event, put fingers to keyboard and wrote what appeared to be said. Writing into the details brought back the events, and information and experiencing I would not know I remembered.

> The first week in June. Down to Cornwall. They spend a week on the airfield, out and about at times, but often in the caravan, drinking mugs of tea and being instructed in air law, principles of flight, cloud types, map notations. There is one other student, then Ian who runs the school and Graham the other instructor. Other people come and go. When the weather permits, not very often, they do tow training on a long blue rope behind a truck, trying to learn how to take off and land, kept below 50 feet and by definition in the maximum danger zone. Sometimes the flying school's one microlight, an American Aerolight's 'Eagle', is damaged in this process. How the undercarriage flexes could be a safety feature, means it can swoop sensingly into the ground, but if it meets at the wrong angle sometimes one of the aluminium tubes gets crumpled or worse. Then activity stops while Ian trudges off to see his friend at the cheese factory where they can work aluminium tubing, it seems. So, it's back to instruction from Graham for a while, including him carrying a door round outside, showing how wind flows or does not across surfaces presented at different angles. Principles of flight and lift.
>
> They watch the weather, especially at dawn and just before dusk, waiting for winds less than 10 miles an hour. In the evening they sometimes go to the Rising Sun for

cider. But in their innocence they had booked a hotel in an interesting-looking market town 10 miles away and further inland. It is not good for knowing the weather on the airfield, and it takes up time going back and forth. If conditions do look promising, the weather can still change as they travel. After several false alarms, they now hold out little hope.

It is their last day. The alarm goes off. It's very early, perhaps they would prefer to stay in bed. She gets up, looks out of the window and it seems still, as forecast, over the town. She goes down to use the phone in the bar. Ian says it looks promising too, although he is up country a bit. They dress and go out. It's chill, the sun still low. They drive over. It does look promising, smoke from chimneys is going straight up, even the tops of trees are still. They cross the moorland, hedges tight at the sides of the road, occasional low cottages, roofs pitched on the outside on top of slates. They turn over the cattle grid and on to the airfield and park up by the hangar. Ian, Graham and a couple of others are already there, busily.

They get out, put on their boiler suits, his blue, hers light brownish, they find their gloves. He takes the shared helmet from the back seat of the car. The air is chill, breath shows, they move around to warm their bodies into their clothes, this space, this morning. She is scared, but this is what they came here to do. She is excited, wanting to complete the promise, to face into what might be possible here.

The inspection. They look the plane over, all joining in, but each needing to be sure. They see that there are no tears in the sail – a rainbow wing, 36 foot wide, panels of blue, mauve, red, stretched over tubing, tip draggers on each end. They check the main wing, and the small canard, out in front with a steeper angle of attack to counter stalling. The clips holding it all together are in place, the small nuts on the small bolts are secure and the tie wires are ok. The control lines work. The triangular undercarriage – one wheel up ahead, held in place between two aluminium tubes, with a footrest strapped across – is all fastened up well.

'Prop clear!' Ian starts the engine, the Robin, 15 horse power, sparks well, sounds sturdy in comparison to the twin Chryslers' lighter note, and has improved on their loosely connected exhausts hanging at angles. Ian taxis the microlight out to a section of main runway. B17s did not fly that easily here in World War 2 because of the height above sea level, and the mists that roll in from the sea cliffs not far away. The concrete is breaking up, with some larger potholes. Dew on the grass; the smell of damp sheep's dung from its moist, stacked, green-grey piles.

It is very still, but they check anyway for wind direction – facing into wind, searching for an even touch on each cheek. Not so vital right now, but it could be if the wind at ground level gets near their limit of 10 miles an hour, because of the wind gradient. Frustrated at the weather all week, they have been learning their lessons, learning what to see and how to see it.

Ian decides she should go first. She sits into the hammock seat, hanging off the wing, and straps the lap belt. The engine is behind her head. She checks that the handle bars control the tip draggers. She takes some deliberate breaths. Last evening, into a dusk sky, Graham, the assistant instructor, ex Auster pilot, did his first solo. In this space where others have flown, he flew. The image of the Eagle doing its left hand circuit is still here, in the field of possibilities in this place.

Under Ian's instruction, listening against the noise of the engine, she lines up, into wind, on the runway. She checks all around, and then she twists the accelerator and heads out, watching the windspeed indicator – the red pea in the Perspex tube strapped to the handlebars. When she reaches about 27 miles an hour, her feet on the front bar, she pushes back in her seat, bracing her legs, and the Eagle takes to the air. The drumming of the wheels on concrete stops, the light sound of just wind, with the wheels rumbling on a few more times before they come to rest and they too are still. Flying! But still need to climb. Her legs are shaking and she braces strongly against the front bar, giving her a steep angle of attack. Later they will say it looked too steep, they were worried for her. But the microlight does not stall, it and she climbs. The wind, the flying, flaps her clothes about her legs, a light rustling.

She levels out, settles into what is happening, breathes deliberately, looks about, sees the world and airfield below. She is flying, all the sensation of being open in the air, light, buoyant, moving freely in three dimensions, groundless and loving it, no upright to try to keep as she hangs off the central main spar, suspended. Time to turn, do the circuit, just one circuit allowed the first time. Her legs are steadier now. She turns, the craft is responsive, connected, it's obvious what to do. She flies on, turning for the circuit, coming back to face into wind again. It has all happened so quickly.

She lines up on the runway, powers off, aims for the 45 degree angle she's been taught, and comes into land elegantly, in her stride, breathing with the buoyancy of the Eagle as they meet the cushion of air just above the runway, parallel out, and the wheels perch down all together onto the concrete. She controls the move along the runway, suddenly having to take the ground and its harsh demands into account again. She brakes, lets the plane slow a bit, puts her feet down as she brings it to a halt. Well. They gather round. She unstraps herself and climbs out of the seat. They put a rope and weight to the craft to secure it. She takes off the helmet. Relief, excitement, having to come out of herself to even hear them. They were concerned for her, lifting off looked too steep. Well, next time.

Have to get on, while the wind is low and before the day heats up. The next student lands hard and the undercarriage buckles. So that is the end of flying for today. And so he does not get his turn, but is generously pleased for her.

They all pack up. He and she go back to their hotel, have breakfast and go home. She knows why the phrase is grinning from ear to ear. Shopping on the high street back home later she thinks that surely everyone should be able to tell, she feels grounded, tall, walking strongly into the ground, all body as one.

They get their own Eagle, get permission to use a farmer's field when the sheep are not in it, away from power cables, rig and unrig the plane watching and misjudging the weather and eventually he takes off by accident when he just intended to taxi, he says. And he grins too.

Reflective comments

Later I realised that a few details in the account were not accurate. I had amalgamated two visits to the airfield into one memory. The first solo happened on the last day of the second visit, by which time we were staying at a bed and breakfast on the edge of the airfield. The year previously, despite a week of careful attention, the weather was never good enough for us to fly.

Barbara Turner-Vesselago's comment on this as a piece of writing:

> So much here is so vivid and memorable … though I still have a mild sense of being hurried forward a bit. When they get up in the morning and go out to test the wind, I don't want to hear about it, I want to be there. Just a beat longer would do.

Walking the River Dart

Writing note

Freefall Writing exercise (following Precepts 2–5) at the same Workshop as the Microlighting story, exploring how to show rather than tell. Minor amendments have been made for clarity. This is included here for the same reasons as Learning to microlight and for its links to action for sustainability.

> Surrender – dropped off by the coach at about 10, after the stuffy atmosphere and talking close up to someone so I could not see their eyes, and them wanting advice on their learning project and to tell me their story, with detail. Fine. It is what I am here for. And also intense. I am in the damp green space, solid ankle supporting boots at the ready. There are plenty of us to shepherd and sheep dog today, and I need to be aware but can also have my breath and story here. We head off, an anomalous rustling line of blue, red, green outdoor gear wanting to encounter deep ecology. A tutor front and rear of the line, we take turns. Shepherd S with staff or crook perhaps, watching, pausing us to hear his evocations of ecological principles, do exercises.
>
> We have suggested that this is not outward bound, or a chatty walk down the river, and that people might like to walk in silence some of the time. And they do. People pause to take in their experience of this place, are together but seem somewhat disconnected from each other too. But attentive, looking out for others with care. Sometimes the streams running into the main river course are high and people help each other across, squelching of boots into water, gasps, smiles.
>
> We stop for lunch, the local company vegetarian pies, the other food made into packs by members of the group, just as some others have cleaned the toilets, swept the floors, washed the plates. Practising sustainability not just talking about it.
>
> It is mid afternoon or later by the time we reach my favourite stretch of the river. I am tired by now, muscles aching a bit, I stumble occasionally on tree roots as we pass. But here I need to be alert. Along the side of the river, down near water level, I pick my way across mossy, fern covered boulders, some big, some small, all rounded by their years of history in that place. The moss and fern, so many varieties, are full and soggy. I move out and back, round bushes, spikey blackthorn, and duck down to avoid the tree branches overhead. I clamber four limbed, breathing well after the day on the move, testing footholds, taking weight on my arms at times, alert, adjusting all of me, taking the shape left by what is around me. I fit in,

am at home. And there is always the chance of slipping into the river or crunching my ankle down between the rocks.

Eventually, we need to leave the river, its dark russet black rush and tumble. We wend up through some oak and beech woodland, the ground sloping, the trees standing upright. Older trees. Tired now, some people talk but most do not. No need for politeness. The coach is waiting in a car park. A quieter journey. Back to tea, and then dinner.

Additional note

Later I tried to evoke that experience as I dedicated a keynote presentation on the gendering of leadership for sustainability to the River Dart and its surrounding woodland. Alongside pictures, provided by members of the Bath MSc in Responsibility and Business Practice course group, the text read:

Fitting into nature, living in context – embodied knowing

Along the River Dart,

clambering four-limbed over mossy slippery boulders,

under low hanging tree branches,

round thorny bushes at the water's edge.

One slip would take me into the strong current.

I experience fitting into nature, and move differently afterwards.

My image of one future for leadership.

As I ponder what is required as any of us take leadership for sustainability and seek to engage in radical co-action, this physical experience of fitting into nature is one touchstone for the kind of process 'integrity' I am seeking.

PART V

STORIES OF INQUIRY

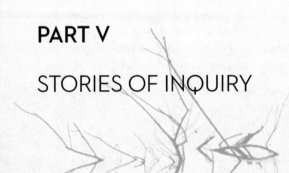

This book is an experiment in representation. The principles and practices of first person inquiry explored earlier are complemented by stories of inquiry brought together here. The chapters in Part IV have outlined some of the writing processes involved.

The stories show writing of different kinds and at different stages of development. Writing generated as inquiry is never fully completed. It can always be developed, layered and reviewed with intentions of one kind or another in mind. Each chapter includes 'writing notes' explaining its provenance. Some include further 'reflective notes', commenting back on the action and processes of writing. Indentation is used to indicate writing generated as inquiry. Much of this has been only lightly edited for clarity, to retain the original voice.

Inquiry learning groups and working with feedback has been through several iterations. It includes a story written as inquiry adopting creative writing approaches. It also demonstrates rounds of working with feedback.

Acting for sustainability is akin to a research journal, following inquiry through several years, seeking to give a sense of some of the processes along the way, including how systemic thinking is an integrated attention in relation to assessing potential for change. It includes a dialogue written as an experiment in portraying micro practices of inquiry in action; and a section beginning the process of thematic analysis based on a piece of writing as inquiry.

Wondering what to do about an elderly relative is the most completed story in the book. As notes explain, it has been told publically a few times, and the written account has been through several cycles of writing and feedback. In a closing section it explicates the principles of living life as inquiry shown through the experience.

Including these accounts in the book has involved extensive conversations with other people involved to invite their feedback and gain their permission to tell the stories here. Key details are given in each chapter. I greatly appreciate people's time, care and generosity in these processes.

Also included in this Part is a poem from Wendell Berry relating to the book's thread of attention to sustainability.

INQUIRY LEARNING GROUPS AND
WORKING WITH FEEDBACK

This chapter has two main intentions. It seeks to show some of the qualities of working in learning groups to support oneself as an inquirer, and then to demonstrate issues in the pursuit of inquiry relating to following through feedback processes. Its material extends sections in PART II: **Dimensions of inquiry**, but it is here in the book because it was written intentionally using several Freefall Writing practices, and so follows **Writing as inquiry** from Part IV. It is an example of working with such material in iterations of inquiry.

The first section of the chapter is an account of working in two learning groups that was intended specifically for this book. It was written in one morning during one of Barbara Turner-Vesselago's Freefall Writing courses. Some minor modifications and additions for clarity have been made to that text. The first mentioned learning group was formed in November 2002 as part of an initiative to enhance quality processes in a wider vital network of action researchers. Our subgroup has not needed a name, but is called 'the southern group' here to distinguish it. The second group formed in July 2008 following a workshop to explore dimensions of the action logics in the Leadership Maturity Framework (Rooke and Torbert, 2005; See PART I: **Action inquiry and action logics**: Action logics). During that experience we often worked in triads as a generative learning format, and so we call this space our 'Triad'. Each group meets every two to three months for a day face to face; with occasional shorter Skype meetings if necessary to maintain contact.

These two are the most recent learning groups in my life. There were others before them. Whilst the framings have varied over time, for example sometimes focusing more on academic writing, the inter-relating of professional and personal lives has always been a theme, as has the intention for the space to be radically developmental. In addition some relationships with colleagues, such as teaching alongside each other on Masters programmes, have incorporated similar learning intents and processes.

Once I had written the original story, there were several cycles of further development showing principles, practices and outcomes of inquiry, and raising questions that have generic relevance. These are shown in outline in the second part of the chapter, and some of their implications for pursuing life as inquiry are reviewed. This chapter thus gives some impression of how engaging in cycles of writing, discussion and feedback, working from an initial specific example, can elaborate and enrich inquiry and ideas, not in the pursuit of clarifying 'facts' but in terms of raising themes and issues for exploration.

One cautionary note: I am writing here about learning group spaces that work well for me. This is not straightforward to achieve, and can sometimes be highly problematic. It is challenging to build up the necessary trust and safe enough space to contain the kind of developmental work which is possible. This involves, for example, navigating issues of sameness and difference. A group in which people are highly similar may appear comfortable but lack challenge; one in which they are quite diverse might struggle to achieve sufficient initial safety to develop but then prove revelatory. Phases of group development need to be lived through, with reflection. Learning spaces are achievements and require continual maintenance. Developing appropriate practices, with integrated review processes, helps towards this.

The sequence of events

The original story was written in April 2013. I used the subtitle *Learning needs friends willing to act as enemies – and as friends* referring to Torbert (1976: 169) and Marshall and Reason (1993: 122) respectively. This can be a simplified depiction of learning group life as discussed in PART II: **Inquiry in action:** Relational work. (The original subtitle is retained here to preserve the integrity of the story as written.)

Feedback on the original stories then took several forms:

Comments from Barbara Turner-Vesselago and other people at the Freefall Writing course:

a) when the first section (relating to the southern learning group) was read out unattributed by Barbara during one of the daily sessions in which she chose pieces for the group to discuss the characteristics and impacts of the writing; and

b) in individual conversations I initiated with two other participants on the course and with Barbara.

There were then several rounds of written and verbal feedback from the four members of the learning groups, accompanied by generative conversations arising from me sharing the original story with them in 2013, and about two years later a draft version of this chapter incorporating discussion of feedback and arising themes.

This wealth of feedback has provided multiple perspectives which I have incorporated in some way into my sense-making and learning. The processes have also shown that writing of this kind can be open and evocative, that people bring their diverse ways of making sense of the world to commenting and that feedback (face to face as well as responding to the writing), can involve processes of sympathetic connection to the person concerned as well as potential insights generated from seeing them and their issues dispassionately.

In the second part of the chapter I reflect on and discuss some of this feedback, selecting (in ways noted) from the wealth of material available.

Permissions

Barbara and the other Freefall Writing Workshop participants have all given their permission for me to draw here on discussions and feedback at the Workshop. The four other people in my learning groups have also all given their consent for this chapter to appear in the book. One person preferred to be referred to by a pseudonym, the others to be named.

The next two sections give the original story from April 2013.

Learning groups in action Section 1: The southern group

Learning needs friends willing to act as enemies – and as friends

I head off a bit later than I wanted, driving south. The arboretum is in autumn colours, some red maples on display near the road; avenues of yellow and russet beech and oak further back. The familiar curves of the road, flowing, going for the apexes. The line of beech along the edge of the estate, amber, some leaves already drifting off in the breeze. I reach towards the escarpment, the view of distant hills, taking its line. The shire horse is in the field, I strain to see.

At the motorway junction carpark I pick up Sara after her trip from the east. She puts her floppy leather bag by her feet. We take the motorway and continue west. 'And how are you?' We dive in – family, health, travel, work, preoccupations – these quickly and deeply; questions. We join the interchange tangle and pick our way through, merging; I crane my neck back right to check, as the motorbike trainer insisted. Multiple lanes, exits, slip roads. Sara helps me keep track of the junctions. Large sheds, distribution warehouses, the back of the shopping mall to our left, factories on the estuary to our right, where once Phil-black used to pack fine black dust into 80 cubic foot corrugated cardboard containers called Octabins. An article about them for a trade journal was my first publication. Another organization from which I had to escape.

Relieved to be off the motorway, another few miles and we reached Jane's, the ample driveway with gravel you have to wade through, making the steering seem sluggish as I park. Jane comes to the door to greet us, we hug lightly. We take off our shoes in the hall, Sara has remembered to bring some warmer socks. I have not. We turn right through the dining area, light wood, large window out to the back garden, to the field and trees beyond, thru to the kitchen. We confirm our usual wishes. A cafetiere of strong coffee for Sara, tea for me. Biscuits – we have each brought some as contribution.

Light floods in; the living room, back through the dining area, is long, with windows at both ends. We each sit where we usually sit, quite spaced out around the copious room. Jane at the driveway end on a sofa, Sara in the middle on a sofa at right angles, me at the garden end in a large armchair. There is an upholstered footrest in between. The furniture has cream and faun upholstery, with worn patches, comfortable, not requiring special care. A slim black ageing tom with a kink in the end of his tail and demeanour which suggests a hint or more of Siamese visits to see who we are. He settles with Jane, purrs loudly and pedals with his feet in appreciation.

We catch up a bit, talk about what has happened in the months since we last met. Sara has been to America to the family cabin in the woods for the summer, and tells of the visitors and how well, or not, they fitted in with the potentially peaceful space and basic living arrangements. Jane's first grandchild is nearly a year old, her other son planning marriage too now, she has been travelling for work a bit. I have been tutoring on two intensive masters workshops in the last few weeks, but the future of the course is under threat and troubling. I ask Sara about the Modernism and the City day school she'd attended and I could not. It was good, she has the handouts for Jane to copy for me, especially for the section on Virginia Woolf. We pass on news about people we have met that we know in common. We agree that the Skype call we had tried as an interim measure had worked better than we expected.

And then we plan the timing for the rest of the day, working back from when Sara needs to reach the carpark and head back home. We have our sort of rules. A turn each of equal length – 45 minutes to an hour depending on the available time. I must not go last, as I drive away and my concentration could be affected by just having taken my space. An hour for lunch. There may be other things we need to check out with each other. We need time at the end to review and to fix a next meeting. That done, we settle again in our seats and someone takes their space.

I go first today.

Despite the trust and comfort, how to be here is also an issue for me. I do not feel that used to people looking me in the eye and being totally accepting of me. When it seems to happen, I feel a slight pull to look away. I know I can be just as I am here, and yet letting down my guard that much feels inarticulate, incoherent, might make them feel unnecessary concern for me if I stumble my way through what I am feeling now, and would say few if any other places. Sometimes, often, it is just such a relief, delight to be here, that my mind and will are blank, waiting to see what arises, and hoping I will not waste the space with trivial chatter. Sometimes I have decided in advance what to work with, although it will then go where it does.

Today I have decided where to start, and dive in straight, deep rather than explaining my way in. I have been reviewing myself and how I operate, partly enriched by working with a close and scrupulously questioning colleague on the masters the week before. It is a process and learning community based course; tutors facilitate not lead; whether to speak and how is as much an issue for us tutors as for participants, and we review such issues as part of the educational model. I have been noticing in this and other contexts my feelings of being responsible and that others are judgemental, reinforcing a need to get things right. I give examples. I have noticed several times recently that I have jumped in to sort something out, and thought afterwards, or been told, that there was no need. This pattern seems confirmed, deep-rooted, and I have worked on it too, 'improved' in allowing myself not to be responsible over the years. As speaking in this space usually does, one thing leads to another. They don't interrupt me, let me sense where I need to go next, unfold the tangled contents of my mind and lay it out a little, let it and myself breathe.

I have noticed how my concern about climate change, bio-diversity destruction and so on affects my behaviour, is on my mind in terms of what I have a right to take (by what right do I take anything that has an un-renewable environmental cost?). Trying not to fly, as I have done for several years, can also seem to tend towards eco-puritanism, self-denial, as time slips away (there have been several deaths and serious illnesses amongst friends and acquaintance lately, reminding how short life can be) – which I am also forcing, in a way, on my partner.

I am not finding time to write, not valuing what I do write, concerned that self-reflective writing is too self-indulgent, not getting on with more traditionally academic writing with a colleague. The current Research Assessment Exercise at work hangs over me, silencing. I know I am not alone in this, could critique the stupidity of creating this much organizational anxiety in a blighted academia at this time – and when there are much more pressing global issues, especially climate change, that need attention. I make defiant choices about how I spend my time, what I think matters, but I also have to fight the sense of failure I then live with.

And, in terms of loss, the course I most care about is not being offered for next year. As people talk about using the 'released resource', will I be asked to teach what I see as relatively trivial? Doing a guest lecture critiquing corporate social responsibility for a colleague lately, and going for teaching with passion threaded with inquiry, I had felt the relief of knowing what I was doing, being back at my centre. But nothing like that will be on offer.

Talking to Jane and Sara, I take brief notes of what I say as I go along, not having known in advance, apart from the first line, what it would be, and track the following conversation. I sit back, look outward more clearly, turning from the inner scanning, take a deep breath, and look to them for comments and questions. There is no hurry; breathing, pausing together.

Sara comments on the huge discomfort I seem to be expressing between self and environment. Asks where exactly I feel under scrutiny. I answer briefly, bringing more potential connections into the felt picture.

Jane identifies with the situation in academia and shares concerns about flying. What do people who see themselves as ecologically committed take as 'just cause' to fly, and how justifiable is that? She reminds me that I did not go to this institution to set up the course which is now stopping. Invites me to reconnect to my major impetus in the world. She suggests that running courses I care about has been a major organizational principle of my life for so long, it will be interesting to see what comes after that.

Our conversation becomes more general, themes that are not unfamiliar to us, but shift shape. When we first came together as a learning group we light-heartedly called ourselves 'women of a certain age', well it is 'women of a certain age plus 10' now. [There are tacit implications here: with many women of our generation, we have wanted to contribute to changing 'the rules of the game' as well as be professionally 'successful' in our own terms.] Seeing each other through transitions, generatively unfolding lives … Today my notes read – 'time, loss, lost dreams, denial, poignancy, life stage, phases of professional being'. I write a question to myself – 'How then to be vital?' We discuss how then to hang on to valuing what we have done and achieved as things change, and how to keep a sense of personal integrity. Typically Sara offers: 'bearing discomfort is another task'.

My time is up. We check if I am ok, if the others are ok to leave it there. We are. I am tired, thoughtful, settled in myself, in my body, not my head. What part do the notes take – an attentional device, a reminder if I ever care to look. But mostly I do not. A trace of our friendship and presence for each other over the years.

We turn around, go to the loo, refresh the coffee and tea. And it is Jane's turn.

I write notes as others speak too. The pattern of centring in, exploring through feeling and speaking, opening to comment and questions, moving towards mutual discussion repeats itself. Other people, especially women of our age or a little older, are threaded through our reflections, present to us, points of reference. We notice what has happened to those already retired, what is happening as our generations (we span about 10 years) retire, or are told they have to wait longer to do so.

It is not mine to speak their issues, but there are many similarities, and not writing what we think we could is a theme for all of us, and later we discuss how that happens – giving our time away, not wanting to be egoic, believing in a relational world which is subtle, nuanced and elusive to depict. And we note that if we do not take the space then others do and they dictate form. By the end of the day we have each recommitted to writing, and have made some practical plans to help with this.

After Jane, we have lunch. Sara and I wander round the kitchen and help a bit while Jane heats up the soup she has made from vegetables from her garden and gets out bread, cheese, salad. We sit at the round table by the patio door with a view of the old apple tree, the birds eating the fallen rotting fruit still, the stillness of a winter [sic] garden. Jane and Sara talk about gardens and allotments. I have nothing to contribute to this conversation, dimly thinking of the tangled mess at home, the overgrown creeper, bushes and tree. My justification for being a faint-hearted pruner – that the family of sparrows hang out there – no longer applies, as it seems the sparrow hawk visiting, braving the enclosed walled space, has seen them off, or worse. We talk about the coming months, what we are each doing, books we have read, movies seen.

After lunch, it is Sara's space. And then we say how the day has been for us as process, if there is anything we want to change for next time. Fix a date. Gently hug each other. Sara and I leave. As we drive back, the thicket of interchanges needs even more care from this direction, we talk on, with Sara's priceless questioning persisting til the end. I drop her at her car, wait to see it starts ok and head back home, radio off, gently.

Learning groups in action Section 2: The Triad

I head off a bit later than I wanted, driving north. I go up over the edge to the escarpment and drop down towards the valley on the twisting road with sharp curves. A lot to see as well as focus on the road – the river is high, I can see its thick brown bulk and contours. The light is slanting on the lower hills, some seem almost to disappear as their wooded mass is flattened back into the valley floor. There is a scattering of snow on the further hill tops. Avoiding the potholes as best I can, over the speed bumps, I make my way to the motorway, go up a junction, then on through the edge of town, on the new road over the water meadow – just soggy today and no birds that I can spot – and head for the hills I saw from the escarpment. As I move away from the town, I look back to see the cathedral, it is picked out in sunlight. After crossing another motorway, and checking that the ancient hollowed oak still clings on at the edge of the lay-by, I drive the curves, lining up on the apexes. There are sheep and lambs in the orchard by the black and white timbered house. This is a landscape of soil, farms, coppices, with views off to further ranges of hills.

Driving through the town, I bring friends who used to live there to mind, enjoy the rich earth on the outskirts, the half timbered houses. Out in the country again, I check my watch, just about in time.

Off the main road, and then right again up a nearly one-track, with caution, I turn into Robin's drive and park at the end of the buildings. Barns, as sheds or converted for holiday homes, a house and a smaller cottage in which Robin now lives. All done with ecological care. Robin is a leading activist in the local Transition movement and more. His buildings, how he manages the stream that runs through the land and the garden too with raised beds are all eco-exemplary. Rob is here already, just, and we hug lightly all round, saying hello. I take off my shoes and leave them by the door.

It is new for us to meet here, we have been in the main house or one of the holiday homes before. Robin has recently moved into the cottage, letting out the house. Etiolated timbers frame and support the internal space. Plenty of evidence of past worm. From the big window in the living area there is a view up a long field to the hills I first saw as I reached the escarpment; I have travelled round their southern edge, so see from the other side.

Coffee for Robin and Rob, tea for me. We find our spaces. I sit in one of the two chairs with my back to the window and view, Rob in the other, and Robin faces us on a sofa. I turn round occasionally not to miss the view of hills, it was easier to see from the conservatory of the house, where we seemed pitched towards the steeply sloping field.

We go round, each in turn telling our news, what is interesting and preoccupying us, taking 10 minutes or so each. Robin offers me advice on low carbon cars, as I need to replace my old A Class after nine and a half years of trundling along together.

And then we plan the timing for the rest of the day, working back from when Rob and I need to leave. We allow 45 minutes each. An hour for lunch. We need time at the end to review and to fix a next meeting. That done, we settle again in our seats and someone takes their space.

Rob goes first today. He is excited by the new and vibrant directions his consulting practice is taking. He is travelling to north America regularly, a nod to Robin, appreciating the carbon consequences of what he is saying, and, but, his work gives him opportunities to raise issues of values with clients. He is also preoccupied with family issues, being a son to an aged father, being a brother. He talks for a while, making associations, offering themes and issues he sees in what is happening to him, wanting to push at edges. 45 minutes is too little. It's longer, over an hour. None of us call time, although I do notice.

Next we have lunch. Rob and I wander round the kitchen and help a bit while Robin heats up soup, it is bought soup today, but often it is home made. We set out oat and rice cakes, cheese, salad. We sit at the table on the yard side of the living space, amongst the beams, Robin's books. We talk about what we are each doing, the coming months, books we have read, movies and plays seen. Robin tells us about hopeful signs in local environmental activities. This is a relief. Things have seemed up-hill for him lately, Rob and I have been concerned for him.

After we all clear away lunch, Robin takes his space. And it is such a much more buoyant story than last time that Rob and I note our relief. Again, the time is too little, extends.

And then it is my turn. I know just where to start today – the workshop I helped organise bringing people from across the Uni campus together about sustainability and what more the Uni might do about this. It is propitious timing for new developments, the new VC and ProVC-R seem receptive. It has been a long, gentle campaign in which several of us have acted together to try to nurture possibilities. And over many meetings Robin and Rob have heard me out on how I try to play my part in this with integrity – both of them pushing that it is a worthwhile cause for me to engage with. The workshop was only 3 days before and went well. But there was also a shadow side, and issues I wondered if I might learn from. I had been dissatisfied with some of the process, torn between stepping in to direct what happened and letting things take their course. I would rather have worked with what was happening – a key image for me was wanting something new to happen and to engage in 'co-action' with others, rather than be directive and simply encounter my own shadow. These are preoccupations of mine. They leave me time to tell my niggles, but eventually Robin asks what had been good about it, as it seemed it was not apparent! And so I give my more rounded views. They seemed not that interested in me looking too searchingly in the corners for potential trouble, but that had not been my intention – rather a telling of nuance to people who I trusted to understand the more rounded picture. Though not if I did not tell them, I suppose. Robin offers the virtues of un-slick process when engaging communities – it does not look so staged and set up, and as if someone else will sort out the consequences. A lovely view.

In this Triad, I am the youngest. And sometimes feel that. Insightfully into systemic thinking and practice as my colleagues are, I sometimes feel on the end of advice and wonder if there is anything more I should know about what is behind that. I take it as straight-forward offering, I think, always valuable and thought-provoking. Sometimes I am not sure I wholly get the frame of assumptions from which the view comes – and I ask. (Surfacing this little edge, I will suggest that we discuss how we see our process these days and what directions we are each pulling in when we next meet. I will send them this write up as a prompt to more review.) In our limited time together, it is fine to have this directness, actually. And I was Rob's PhD supervisor, and was forthright as well as facilitative in my style, so do not have a sense of perverse power dynamics here, just different ways of going on.

Rather quickly we have to finish. We fix a date. Gently hug each other. Rob and I leave. I head back to the hills and round, radio off.

Working with cycles of feedback and development

Working with feedback on the original story has been an unfolding process over several cycles, initially at the Freefall Writing workshop and later in conversations with other learning group members. Two years after the workshop I went through my various notes and others' feedback, and brought together a detailed (3,100 word), account following these twists and turns cycle by cycle, which I shared with the learning group members. The following sections draw on that account but are arranged thematically to limit repetitions.

An evocative tale

People have generally found the story evocative. Some who have experience of learning groups have found it recognisable. In terms of inquiring attention, some people have noted the range of different things I seem to be paying attention to. Comments (about Section 1) at the Freefall Writing course included: *poignant, very sincere, very touching, showing the grain of life.*

The story as an example of writing as inquiry

People at the Freefall Writing course noticed and liked ways in which apparently separate aspects of the story of the southern group resonate with each other, offer interesting juxtapositions and enhance tacit themes. They mentioned:

Navigating complexity – the inner world and the motorway

The shire horse, an image of enduring time.

The sparrows, sparrow hawk and tangled garden.

The story's 'autumnal quality'.

The story seemed to express much more than I had intended. By following the Freefall Writing precept of working with sensuous detail and being specific (Turner-Vesselago, 2013: 32–3), even though this meant creating a fictive specific day, the account incorporated imagery that resonated with themes I could later see as 'tacit' in the experience and thus made these open to reflection and exploration. Setting the story in autumn happened because that is an easier time to note briefly the beauty of the arboretum as I drive by. This then starts to amplify with the age of the women, the later life issues they are exploring and so on. This concatenation of images was unintended but significantly shapes the writing.

Again, following the curl of my recent thinking about the sparrows and sparrow hawk also 'just happened' from the Freefall Writing process. This then resonated well with my concern about feeling responsible, puzzles about whether we can ever intervene for the 'good' in the world, and whether the inevitable unintended consequences could be damaging (with questions about what frame we will adopt to judge them). Writing as inquiry offers disciplines for allowing such amplifications to be expressed, whilst still involving discernment in how to work with them.

Writing course participants thought that including sections of direct speech and dialogue would enable me to show more and tell less (Turner-Vesselago, 2013: 139–49). Barbara considered that one voice had to carry the story for too long. She also mentioned that the story is seen through a 'scrim' of the narrator interpreting. For the purposes of writing as inquiry, I might want to try to see glimpses of the scrim she mentions – of its patterns and preoccupations – as a reflective process. This might become more available if I ask critical friends for feedback on the writing.

Freefall Writing courses incorporate a number of protocols and practices which ensure that whilst the workshops are demanding (as participants engage with developing themselves as writers), they do not make people personally vulnerable. Freefall Writing discourages people from identifying themselves in their writing. The inclusion of the fifth precept ('The Ten-Year Rule') also helps to give writers objectivity about both the material they are using and the feedback they receive. As elaborated in Part IV, writing as inquiry has different purposes and processes, and so the writer might feel exposed if sharing their work. Pieces written as inquiry, when they draw on Freefall Writing precepts, cannot be treated simply as innocent evocative tales, just adding a little richness to our expressions of researching. They should only be shared with due care and review. I have decided to risk the vulnerabilities of offering this account here, having carefully checked consent from my learning group colleagues.

Listening to and processing challenging impressions

That the story of the southern learning group was shared with 'strangers' so soon after it was written and in a context where the nature of the writing was the focus of attention generated feedback I might not otherwise have received. The diverse members of the Freefall Writing course made their own senses of it, refracting different images. Most striking, for me, some people interpreted the women as somewhat disappointed and defensive. Whilst I can see this is a viable impression given some of the words I had used in the story, the feeling tone implied is somewhat disturbing, discordant, and might potentially devalue and reduce our experience. One inquiry question is whether I then welcome this as a fresh view I could not see myself, or whether I discount it, as not my truth. In this case, I have combined these two approaches, as elaborated below.

Comments on the southern group's story from Freefall Writing course participants included:

Women's lives, and lives of women of those times – recognisable.

Not getting recognition in the world comes through. Question of how then do they get it?

Feeling of beleaguered women, of constrained timing, under pressure – imposing these constraints on themselves.

Image of women closing in to form a protective circle.

Greying women wearing themselves out trying to save the planet, look after sparrows etc. But who looks after the women?

A day in a life, a life in a day

Barbara's written feedback included a very helpful image:

One thing I notice and am curious about: when anything emerges that in ordinary parlance would be termed irritation (I think) with other people, there's an immediate stepping back from that, a sort of subduing, or finding a way to get larger than. One thing that this I-character expects from herself, clearly, is enormous patience. Is that something particular to this I-character, or is it a shared value? (That's what I am curious about.) Clearly patience has led her, has led all of them, to some very valuable insights. But possibly also to what I would normally think of as resentment. They're aware of that. They're dealing with it. But my question is, do they feel there's a place for it?

As I am interested in movement, notions of tropisms and so on, this comment especially intrigued me. Over months, I puzzled occasionally at these issues, raising them in inquiring conversation with others, including the learning group members. Whether I am sometimes too patient, what 'stepping back' (an image I certainly recognise) might mean and when it might be generative or degenerative were interesting to consider and track in action.

The gendered aspects to the comments especially took my attention. The impression of 'beleaguered women' was an uncomfortable reminder of the 1970s and 1980s, when some people had seen consciousness-raising activities as women huddling together in adversity – interpretations to be challenged for many reasons. (The heritage and value of consciousness-raising is a strong image for some women of my age.) I therefore sought conversations with three other women at the Workshop, including Barbara, to overtly question this impression of the story. They generally: did not share a sense of the group being beleaguered and protective; affirmed the story's themes from their own organisational and other experiences; had concerns that older professional women should be sharing the legacy of their learning, rather than 'disappearing' as some are doing through early retirement and other means. Barbara did see hints of what she termed 'resentment', 'patience' and 'disappointment', and asked what the women's protocol was for working with such feelings.

This experience of receiving challenging feedback relates to issues of boundaries of disclosure and vulnerability. See PART II: **Inquiry in action:** Vulnerability in inquiry and PART IV: **Writing as representation**. What is interesting to write, and then to explore, can also be vulnerable to discuss, especially when, as tends to be the case in writing as inquiry, the writer chooses to deal with material that is relatively recent.

An incomplete account of learning group processes

One of my questions about the learning groups' story was whether it sufficiently communicates the rich, affirmative experience of learning group membership I had intended. From feedback from learning group colleagues, it does not. It describes the surroundings well, but it does not yet express how we are together, how we live out our strong commitments to the group, to supporting each others' learning, and to bringing ourselves openly to this process. Nor does it depict much of what it is like to occupy the 'spaces' each learning group member takes. Experimenting with dialogue might have helped this elaboration (Turner-Vesselago, 2013: 139–49). In the southern group, we discussed what Jane called the 'immense difficulty of reproducing experience in writing, the gaps and edges that make it impossible'.

There are intriguing issues about writing as inquiry, and as representation of inquiry, here. Any account is likely to be poly-semic, to allow multiple interpretations and to be partial, with omissions and elements of disguise. These are qualities of intrigue I treasure. In **Self-reflection and life narrative in the work of Kazuo Ishiguro:** Associations with first person action research I explained my delight at encountering what might be termed uncontrolled, diffuse, pliable unfolding meaning. These are qualities I am happy to have in my own writing; I am certainly not aspiring to offer the reader a 'full view'.

Wanting, however, in this case to do more justice to the experience of being a member of a learning group, I will complement my depiction so far with Robin's comments from a phone conversation.

He said that what does not come across in the account is:

The delight and joy.

At the end of the day, feeling more centred, more aligned, more accepting of one-self in the current situation and who one is now, feeling more connected to self and others.

The power of being heard within our own frame of reference, and being edged into other frames of reference that illuminate or dissolve what previously seemed impossible situations.

We do not have to keep explicit track of 'learning'; issues that matter come back in later conversations in another form, and as a group we remember for each other and feed this into our questioning, in a collective holding of the space. (From my notes of our phone call, 12 May 2015)

These conversations encouraged me to surface questions I carry:

What rights do I have to be challenging to this person, in this situation, at this time?

Is this a mutual or a unilateral process?

What might be the potential systemic consequences of me being challenging? For example, might I enhance or undermine their abilities to cope with the situation they are in?

Learning experiment prompted through arising questions – the Triad

Writing the learning group story raised many issues that I could then ponder and explore. One was about potential power dynamics in the Triad. In May 2013 I sent my Triad colleagues the full story before our next face to face meeting. In my 'space' that day we discussed it in a wide-ranging spirit of mutually engaged inquiry.

They thought my questioning of potential group dynamics and power issues 'very honest'. Our conversation was fascinating. I learnt that when I talk about 'problems', Rob sometimes feels potentially responsible for taking care of me, and this might influence his tone of commenting. He explained that as the eldest of seven children he has a well-developed style of being a big brother. Also when I take notes during our meetings (of what people have said, to catch their phrasing), rather than responding immediately, they do not know what I am doing, thinking or feeling, and this can break the contact. And Robin's experience of me is: *'Of course, you are always in a hurry'*. Thus the conversation contributed to our ever-evolving group dynamics.

The statement about me always being in a hurry rang in my ears for weeks and months, is there still, a precious piece of direct, unadorned, feedback that I can then work with, pondering my patterning, experimenting with not being hurried and seeing what happens, at times too celebrating whizzing along meta-phorically and physically.

At our meetings I then experimented sometimes with taking fewer notes and timing when I wrote them, sometimes doing so after the sessions. That seemed fine. But scanning my notebooks now I see the pages are quite well covered.

Talking things through in the southern group

The southern group met in May 2013 too, by Skype. The other members had seen the story in advance. We discussed it. We also explored challenges in relation to notions of reflective learning and boundaries of what we are doing together.

Other people's impressions of the women as potentially 'beleaguered' or 'disappointed' had given us strong, potentially emotive, input to reflect on. Whilst we were curious to hear others' reactions, we also allowed ourselves to react against their impressions. The list of words I had noted from our meetings, such as 'loss', were a little shocking to see so starkly written down. In discussion we were clear that we do not see our learning group space as full of regret. It is a space into which we can bring edges of such emotions, alongside a much wider range, and explore their contours and implications. The space we nurture allows us to do this with a directness of encounter we might not often find. But the critical and supportive feedback we give each other encourages us not to amplify such emotions beyond their appropriate domain and proportions. Also, we affirmed the challenging we do, in our own way; wondering if being challenging might take different forms in the glimpses of the Triad process I had given. We talked about whether and in what ways writing evocatively from first person action research is possible, and the potential to feel exposed.

This conversation contributed to our group's ongoing reflections on, and experimentation with, our practice. We decided that at the next meeting we would use cycles of writing as inquiry and reading aloud as part of our process. (We did this once, but then returned to our talking format.) And a year later we organised a three-day writing workshop at a hotel for us each to write on our different projects, a thread of joint activities we have continued.

Ongoing inquiry

The question of whether I might sometimes be too patient (partly initiated by Barbara's question) echoed out of this thread of learning for me. This resonated, as I am often seeking to 'ladder up' into a more encompassing mode, especially when things become difficult; seeking a meta-view of some kind, perhaps to glimpse systemic patterns, including my entanglement, and emerging time phases. But as months went on, I started to pay more attention to the prices I was sometimes paying in time, emotional energy, and intellectual dexterity. As these reflections were percolating through, I noticed how I was repeatedly trying to act with patience amongst contested views on a voluntary subcommittee I belonged to. Holding onto my wish to discern and act 'for the greater good', I tried to keep people connected, to accept and work with fluctuating energies. But I then felt I was placed as tolerant, whilst others expressed their views freely and at length. This was putting me under what seemed undue pressure. Heeding and allowing myself to act from my emotional sense-making gave me a fuller view. I found myself breaking the pattern, letting myself speak more freely, and then resigned from the committee, despite my concerns about withdrawing my contribution to its work, and what might happen next. This move is congruent with a systemic view of life. My change in position meant that others re-positioned, and so the dynamics are unfolding and adjusting, with me as a peripheral player.

In reflection

To close this chapter I will briefly draw together some of the qualities of learning groups depicted here and step back to review some generic issues about inquiry.

In the initial stories and the subsequent cycles of discussion and learning, the chapter illustrates some of the key qualities of working in a learning group, what we can gain and what we then give as members. Whilst groups can have a range of purposes and approaches, they often:

Help members review and inter-relate professional and personal lives

Offer safe enough spaces to support radical developmental work

Open members to multiple perspectives

Provide propitious contexts in which members can identify and work with significant learning edges

Allow uncertainty and vulnerability to be expressed, experienced and worked with

Provide opportunities for members to be heard well, as their stories of self, being and action unfold over time

Allow members to offer feedback and, with due care, to push their questioning of each other, to hold each other to account for their learning and development.

It is delight and privilege to be with people as they engage with deep learning and change, and to work alongside them. Also our own learning is often stimulated as we identify congruence with others' lives and see our potential reflections in their development.

There are issues about working from vulnerability that I want to explore a little further here. Elsewhere I have mentioned some practices and skills I bring to doing this such as co-counselling training. See PART II: **Disciplines of inquiry:** Attentional disciplines. Working in the learning group space and exploring fully could well involve amplifying emotions, expressing fears at the edge of consciousness, and thus working with vulnerability. The space we nurture together allows us to do this with a directness of encounter we might not often find. Feeling unsettled might well be a sign that our exploration is alive rather than habituated. In my experience, my own practices of inquiry and the critical and supportive feedback I receive from learning colleagues encourages me not to amplify emotions I am working with beyond their appropriate domain and proportions. Also I learnt in the early years of engaging in co-counselling that even if we choicefully explore a deep personal 'hurt' in a developmental way, that is not all there is to who we are. And the resourcefulness to undertake the exploration is a meta-layer of being and competence. In learning group dynamics, exploring an issue may well diffuse and transform it, so that the protagonist dissipates the emotions they have temporarily experienced. The images or sense of concern may persist more strongly for other members of the learning group, and they will make their own judgements about how to hold these. It is part of the discipline of such working to encounter next time the full person we know, not to subsume them into the 'difficult issue' they had the courage and resource to explore.

As the initial title for the learning groups' story suggested, this chapter has been an opportunity to explore the textures of what 'friends willing to act as enemies' (Torbert, 1976: 169) and 'friends willing to act as friends' (Marshall and Reason, 1993: 122) might mean. See PART II: **Inquiry in Action:** Relational work. Learning group spaces are achievements and need continual maintenance. These activities require trust of some kind, although this will not necessarily feel 'cosy' and embracing, may be edgy, involve pushing at boundaries, and involve ongoing reflective attention. We enact trust together, it is not a state we achieve.

Some readers of draft versions of this chapter have wondered if the two learning groups portrayed are different in some ways worth mentioning. I do experience them as distinct places, despite the similarity of how our days unfold. But I would not seek to characterise those tones of potential difference, do not see readily identifiable patterns to them. And both groups are continually unfolding, as we as members bring our changing lives in relation to the shifting landscapes in which we operate, and the textures of our conversations develop.

This chapter is a strong advocacy for being in learning relationships of some kind. Can you be an inquirer without being a member of a learning group? Yes. I appreciate that some people may not thrive in group experiences; that, even for those who might, finding suitable learning colleagues can be challenging; and there are practical difficulties about fitting group membership into one's life. From my experience learning relationships of some kind seem vital, and are an inherent dimension to living life as inquiry. Membership of a long-term learning group that works well can bring what you could never imagine, or have reached alone. Other learning relationships, including those with critically reflective teaching colleagues, have played important parts in my life. I doubt if you can develop as an inquirer without good feedback; the orientation of inquiry is being open to and seeking feedback in diverse ways as fitting to context and issues. One generic question I then take from this chapter is how to have congruent practices and ways of extending those practices if inquiry is a life approach.

In this exploration, adopting writing as a practice of inquiry, sharing this with colleagues, and engaging in cycles of further exploration helped focus, extend and deepen the potential learning process. See PART IV: **Writing as Inquiry**. This chapter has illustrated how inquiry can unfold over the longer-term, and that often waves of inquiry do not stop, but transpose into different forms, generating fresh questions. I will therefore close this account here. The mutual development in which I and my colleagues are engaged continues.

ACTING FOR SUSTAINABILITY

SEEKING TO CONTRIBUTE TO SYSTEMIC CHANGE, AS TIME SLIPS BY

The extended story offered in this chapter shows how I partly treat my organisational life as continuing inquiry, working with questions which shift and change, are immediate or longer-term. This account arises from my long-term interest in whether and how to seek to influence institutions I belong to and engage with to pay more attention to sustainability. I think it especially important that educational institutions address issues of climate change and social justice as these relate to their core purposes. In relation to environmental issues, Orr suggests:

> The crisis we face is first and foremost one of mind, perceptions, and values; hence, it is a challenge to those institutions presuming to shape minds, perceptions, and values. It is an educational challenge. More of the same kind of education can only make things worse. (Orr, 1994: 27)

But I do appreciate that if educational institutions stand against prevailing social practices this could challenge their financial viability in current times.

Engaging in the activities depicted here has generated vast streams of action-oriented and reflective notes, inquiry accounts of specific experiences, and notes from meetings with learning group colleagues as I have talked through my intentions, approaches and experiences.

My theories of change have been integrated into and developed through inquiring action and reflection of the kind reported here. The core material of this chapter draws on this array of sources and was written as a deliberate attempt to represent living life as inquiry. Segments written at different times over a few years are integrated into one account. The provenance of different sections and how some illuminate processes of writing as inquiry are discussed as the chapter proceeds. Some 'retrospective inquiry notes', written as I completed this chapter, are also incorporated. Adjustments have been made for flow, clarity, brevity. Some aspects of the story have been filled out to show inquiry processes more clearly.

The chapter format overall is akin to a research journal, written roughly in chronological order, and with some references back or ahead. Indented text indicates the unfolding story, with non-indented text providing commentary, additional material and explanation. A trail of dates and notes on writing formats seeks to help you stay sufficiently located; although the account could also be read as impressionistic rather than as attempting to be clear. Some of the emergent writing linked up different timeframes and moved between ways of knowing, in keeping with my experience. I have tried to tame the material sufficiently to offer it here, but not to wholly purge these qualities.

The main body of the account takes May 2014 as 'now' (the three segments are numbered to help re-orient you after diversions of one kind or another). The chapter is based on a lengthy piece of writing of that date which recapped and reviewed activities during the preceding six years. This integrated some previous writing. Some sections are therefore dated earlier than 2014 to avoid changing the voice in which they were written. The story then continues into 2015, as I remain engaged in sustainability related networks and activities, despite formally retiring from the University at the end of 2014.

This account is told in some detail to show inquiry as an action research practice. But it is not about claiming credit as if I and the people I work alongside are living in a cause-and-effect universe or acting alone. Nor is it about writing an heroic tale. I see working for change as relational practice, and want to develop the crafts of radical co-action, whilst also contributing what uniquely I can. This involves everyday, apparently mundane, activity – I imagine this as 'working the background' – as a stream of vital action.

Working with this chapter, I have considered ethical issues. I have sought to make the story tell-able without breaching confidences. I have asked some specific individuals for consent, which was granted. One person asked for minor adjustments for clarity to the **Planning** *Global Futures*: **Meeting vignette** account, which were made. One person has chosen to be named, one to be referred to by an initial, another for their role to be used. Other names in the chapter are pseudonyms. I have also consulted a senior manager in the organisation about portraying the story as a whole. The account does not intend to criticise the University in any way. By 2015, there is significant activity happening in relation to sustainability throughout the organisation and across its various domains of activity and potential impact.

May 2014 Review 1: Joining a new institution

Writing note

This review was written to show living life as inquiry in action for this book. Undertaking it was still however a process of discovery, throwing up issues which prompted further reflection. Systemic thinking is shown as a significant dimension in my approach to organisational membership, for example informing how I seek to influence the contexts in which I operate and how I pay attention to timing. Whilst the review was originally written in the present tense and this gave it perhaps a certain immediacy, I have changed it into the past tense for clarity of time sequences, as this chapter has become a somewhat complicated patchwork of inquiry fragments. Choices of this kind are typical of the construction processes involved in writing from inquiry.

As will become apparent, when an account is situated influences the view offered. During May 2014 it was not as apparent as it is in August 2015 how much action for sustainability would flourish across the University. The tone of this account might therefore seem less hopeful for significant change than is now justified. But it would be inappropriate to revise the text below. A few brief notes such as this will have to suffice to give added perspective.

A history of seeking to contribute to change

Moving to Lancaster in 2008 was a joy for many reasons. The institution seemed welcoming and open. I might be able to breathe again. Moving after nearly 30 years in one organisation was demanding. But the sense of wider, open spaces was physical as well as intellectual and emotional.

I brought with me a long legacy of trying to make the world a better place. My training goes way back. Trying to do 'good' has been a major theme in my life, which I have explored through various forms of reflective practice and self-development over the years, seeking a kinder relationship to it, for myself and others. How I now carry this impetus in my life is open to ongoing inquiry.

Over the years, trying to play my part in change, I have struggled with what to do and how to do it, and learnt how shouldering tasks alone does not generally contribute to systemic change, although sometimes it can, and how things often show their fragmentation when you stop holding them together and pushing for action. I have tried to develop practices and ideas for being part of change, relationally, systemically. It jars a little to try to speak from them here, as they are about seeking to set ego aside, working through relationships, affirming muted voices and issues, not claiming credit, and often attending to the mundane and everyday rather than what seems prominent. But that is also why I try to speak for them, because otherwise their space is crowded out by more confident tales of actions and apparent consequences. I have tried to live along a different grain, seeing it as political work to affirm and live what might otherwise be discarded or repressed, connected with a network of others with similar intents. This book seeks to express that aspiration.

I feel that time is running out. When I first arrived at Lancaster there seemed the space to work with, the wide horizon. About in the world there seemed some agreement that climate change and sustainability need addressing, radically and urgently. But with the global financial crisis of 2007–8 that clarity has waned, although much is still happening.

How do I then account for my attempts to influence around sustainability? What have I been doing over these recent years? How has it been inquiry? This account offers fragments illustrating this approach, and showing the partial view any one person has.

Locating me and my efforts for change

I joined a small department in a big management school in a University that includes lots of arts, design, critical sociology, an environment centre and more wonderful richness. And people know each other across the campus. I arrived and looked around. There are people interested in corporate responsibility and sustainability widely across the institution. I prefer the latter term, being cynical of much organisational rhetoric and action, a profound problem boxed into organisational response too quickly, turned into often spurious numbers (I watched this take shape from 1995 or so onwards, over a seemingly hurried 10 years, horrified, saddened). We come to value what we can count, and ignore what we cannot. Although there are now many radical change agents working with 'corporate responsibility' as their label too. Many people at Lancaster take a 'critical' view (to which there are many shades).

I travelled across the campus, with an interest in sustainability as my short-hand introduction, and the intention of finding mutual contacts for activities we were developing in the department. I met up with people, one-on-one mainly, often in the Hub, a large, tall atrium space with a cafe, at an intersection in the management school, a mix of seating – the large red easy chairs round low tables; the wooden seated upright chairs and high tables to eat at, close together, sometimes with legs entangled. The background hum of other conversations, chance meetings and opportunities to trade and do deals. I did not want to tread on other people's toes, be the newcomer oblivious to what people were already doing. And, after my last institution and us standing for things against opposition so long, I wanted companions, to be doing this work with other people. One aim of my networking was to find possible speakers for an MA in leadership for sustainability we were developing. I did, aplenty.

People were engaging, diverse in their interests: leadership, small family firms, how social practices are often embedded in systemic patterns not a matter of attitudes–behaviours–choice, carbon footprinting as a way to help companies engage in sustainability change, sustainable marketing … and much much more. I filled up my notebook, was referred on to other people they were sure I would like to meet. It was exciting. Some connections led to mutual activities, all to my sense of being part of a larger network. I told others 'it's such a rich playground'.

And there were various initiatives in this space, across the campus and in the Management School, addressing sustainability and corporate responsibility. But I also learnt that people were busy, some did not have time and legitimacy to develop their interests, that there were impediments to taking things further. I teamed up with other long term advocates of incorporating more corporate responsibility into the curriculum and into the school's activities generally. Much had been achieved, but there was so much more we could envisage. One person told me that it was an open field, that I should get on and do things, I would not be treading on people's toes. I was not so sure. Hesitant. Interested in testing where energy was, what might be possible, how to dovetail my efforts with those of other people. A couple of us raised sustainability and corporate responsibility as a formal agenda item at a cross-school meeting to see if there was interest in developing these themes further, given their appearance across the School's work. Plenty of perceptive comment, and evidence of what was already going on. But not really an appetite for more, it seemed at the time.

My inquiry purposes at that time were: seeking to understand the dynamics and interplays, the moods within which current activities were happening; wanting not to cut across others' activities, even unawares; wanting to develop my own identity in that space; connecting up, widely, richly; seeking a sense of 'what is possible here?'; and not taking on too much and overloading myself, as I had often done previously.

Several of us set up an informal network called Sustainability, Responsibility, Plus (SR+ for short). We could not agree on one common title and did not want to waste energies trying or to lose people or facets of important issues by inappropriate naming. SR+ met monthly initially, with people sharing what they were doing and some guest sessions. The network faltered early on, too reliant on me to organise dates and speakers. A committed doctoral student noticed and offered to help, and SR+ survived. We invited speakers from across the campus, supporting cross-institutional links. Contributing to such networking became one of our key intentions.

Whether and how to follow things through was difficult to decide. Despite the Dean's encouragement, I did not pursue possible membership of an international network on corporate responsibility in management education. I noticed my fatigue at the prospect (given my activities at my previous institution), the sense that energy was not yet full enough across the School for there to be widespread engagement, that I might have to lead it largely alone. (And it would involve the kind of bureaucratic work my dreamer self has only learnt to do as necessity, and was/is trying to escape.) I let it slip, explaining why to the Dean, gently suggesting other possibilities for action closer to where energy seemed to be. I watched, took on some activities, including being contact and judge for our regional leadership for sustainability prize, but tried not to do too much. Timing was not right, in my view, despite some other people's encouragement. Was this a missed opportunity? I will not know.

Telling this now [in 2014] as a story could make it seem too intentional. It was not. The interest and fun of meeting people dominated, expanding my thinking and senses, connecting me diffusely to the new organisation. Are academics ever that corporate? Connecting me too with how I stay alive in my work, by pursuing things that seem to matter to a wider world as well as me, are infused with values. I have been lucky to be 'allowed' to do this, generally, over the years. Rather than intention, for me, it is working with possibilities. The possibilities for connection were obvious and reasonably immediate. I connected other people up as well as myself. The possibilities that more might happen were more tenuous, ephemeral; should not, cannot be stalked, manipulated.

Links that have developed with people at the University and locally in the town and region who are values-oriented and into sustainability and social justice are important to me; give a sense of wider connectivity, validation, alignment. I feel part of a dispersed network of kindred spirits, acting for social change and reflecting on what this might mean. I recognise them, am recognised by them. This is in some ways purpose enough for what I do, grounding for other possibilities to arise.

Interlude: Seeking to portray myself in action

As I tell this story, my aspirations for my conduct are relevant to how I then operate from inquiry in practice. To give impressions of me in action, I therefore insert this brief segment from reflective notes written in February 2013 following another venture. I had worked alongside people from Occupy Lancaster (the original initiators), the Economics Department, the students' Economics Society and members of the MA in Leadership for Sustainability to arrange a half-day open workshop in which four speakers offered contrasting perspectives on growth and inequality in economics, and participants (students, local people, academics) engaged in round-table discussions and questioned the speakers.

Afterwards I reflected in writing on the roles I had taken, my approach and the generic points of inquiry I typically have in mind when involved in such activities. Rather than offer these as uncorroborated claims, I have checked this insert back with two co-organisers from Occupy Lancaster.

In my review, I depicted my inquiry intentions in action as:

- Working alongside, offering ideas;
- Proposing initiatives, but explicitly opening these to question, not wanting to take over;
- Working with and through connections;
- Fostering network development as a long-term intention, through specifics of current action;
- Being aware how multiple paths of agency operate across the same space and wanting to find my place amongst them elegantly rather than compete, overtly or covertly;
- Being cautious if I find myself offering what seems an habitual approach.

I also identified commitments I bring to any venture, especially to devising formats and processes (which often matter as much as 'topics'). These are: equality, active learning, dialogue, mutual discussion (rather than polarising debate), suspicion of expert authority (including mine) taking over; and being of service. Engaged in practice, I openly question whether this kind of collaborative approach is what is appropriate at this time in this situation, and am interested in other points of view. Perhaps, at times, I and we need to be more forceful, less into seeking dialogue. I am sometimes. And, whilst it has its shadow sides, I think a participative, sensing, systemic approach is something I have trained and believe in, and is what I can contribute. Living life as inquiry is at its heart. (Although not all living life as inquiry is in this style.)

Feedback: The two allies from Occupy Lancaster thought I had summarised my role well, and offered further feedback and reflection. They suggested that I had acted as an intermediary, a 'key link person between the different parties', and that the initiative 'would not have happened without [this] facilitation'. They thought that everyone on the planning group had been able to contribute, and to question each other.

May 2014 Review 2: Linking up attempts to influence

Early on in my time at the University, I met with Mike. He is the director of an associate company of Lancaster Environment Centre which specialises in organisational responses to climate change, and is an author on carbon footprinting and emissions. He is a bundle of energy, keen to see change and to push the Uni to do More. We share lots of interests. And in his physical style he is often racing on, impatient. I keep pace sometimes, matching him, pause to be more reflective at others, and he respects that. We have developed a pattern of checking both ways, using each other to sound things out. We talk change approaches. His are perhaps a little more directive than mine, although we share concerns about readiness, who to influence to encourage change and so on. In an early meeting in his office, we sketched who we knew across the Uni with interests in sustainability, wondering if we could engage them in some joint action. We did not follow through in that way at that time. Partly I was recognising, as I had already seen in other settings, that prompting possible change is diffuse and difficult work, and that despite people's enthusiasm, action is often not followed through, usually because of other pressures and lack of time, but also for 'good reasons', that important, counter-vailing, factors are in play. So we worked in our different ways, meeting every so often for coffee and talking about how we were each getting on, what might be next.

Retrospective inquiry note

This relates to the theme of inclusion and thus potential exclusion that arises in action research initiatives of this kind, Mike and I have debated this often. Does the urgent need for change in relation to climate change mean we should get on, engaging with a small band of like-minded people, but risk excluding or offending others, perhaps even breaking relationship? Is the radical inclusivity I aspire to impractical? Or do initiatives need to be widely participative to have systemic potential? Of course these are not such stark choices, and in different circumstances we can work with them flexibly.

With our different energies, perceptions and styles, Mike and I complement each other. We have worked well together in the main, and appreciate having each other as allies. We have affirmed this again recently in emails discussing this draft chapter.

Opportunities opened out in March 2011, when a senior manager, the Pro Vice-Chancellor for Research (PVC-R) organised a Uni-wide symposium on sustainability, inviting six speakers, Mike and I among them. By then I was occasionally invited to meetings about sustainability in other areas of the University. This was interesting, affirming and somewhat strange given my short-ish time in the institution and the other people around who might like to have been considered. I tried to keep information flowing back and forth, to play my part as conduit. The symposium was interesting, with attendees from across the campus. I met new contacts. There could have been more general conversation though; the speaker format rather took over.

The following summer the PVC-R funded six student internships to take the sustainability agenda forward in some way, perhaps by working with each of the symposium speakers. Mike and I conferred and proposed that the interns review the University's research, teaching and own practice related to sustainability. The other speakers agreed to our suggestion, and Mike and I helped the interns shape their work and identify initial people to talk to. My cross-campus networking was proving invaluable. The interns then snow-ball sampled, reaching a wide and diverse range of people.

The students' report was exciting, giving a rich picture of lots of activity and commitment related to sustainability across the University, although showing too how people have their own terminologies which need respecting. The findings were partly represented in a large map of who was doing what, showing links and connections. Even more encouraging was how the interns threw themselves into the venture, cared, asked challenging questions and wanted the Uni to give sustainability an even higher priority. They made proposals about what the University could do next, including the idea of becoming a 'Living Laboratory', integrating and linking up between our research, teaching and practice. The rationale, as Mike and I came to tell it, was that 'really' implementing sustainability is a challenge very few organisations have achieved (and they cannot ultimately as no organisation can do so alone), that learning how we can improve on what we already do would reveal typical issues of attempting change, and that we could do this reflectively through processes of action research.

It is interesting how much of an anchor for future work the Interns' Report and the mapping have become. Seeing with a long view, the review was a valuable intervention, although we could not predict that at the time.

This story has a lot of lulls in it, where little apparently significant seems to happen. In terms of cross-campus activities there next came one of those. The Interns' Report was presented to a small group of us, and people were allowed to give it wider distribution. The SR+ network had an animated session discussing it and possible next steps. But nothing much new appeared to happen for a while.

Retrospective inquiry note

I could pause and review the attribution 'little apparently significant'. Of course it is not easy to tell what is happening and if it might prove significant. Reaching mid 2015, it appears that a latent, wide-spread groundswell has been building all this time. Informal and formal meetings are helping this coalesce; there are clear signs of institutional engagement. People are generating opportunities to act and show solidarity. But there were plenty of times in between when we thought nothing much was happening.

I had called the SR+ meeting about the Interns' Report but avoided taking on the arising ideas as an action list, although I bore them in mind as possibilities. I did type up the notes and circulated them to all those involved, a systemic approach of connecting up feedback loops wherever possible, potentially helping information reach nodes in networks where it has not been before. But was lack of any action at that point a fault? I do not think so.

Looking back to autumn 2011, we were awaiting the new Vice-Chancellor (VC) and once he arrived we wondered how he would conduct himself and what his concerns and priorities would be. So some organisational processes seemed to slow up. About a year went by. Mike and I met and talked occasionally. In our different sectors of the University we took, and generated, opportunities to promote attention to sustainability and made connections, between people, ideas and talk of possibilities. The SR+ network continued meeting. Across the campus different groups developed their sustainability related activities. But the potential to join these up, to make them more prominent, did not seem amenable to realisation. I judged it not a good time to push agendas. Meantime I carried on meeting people, criss-crossing the campus, engaging in some joint activities, contributing to keeping conversations going. I checked with other people how they saw potentials for change across the institution. 'Slow' would be a summary of their views; another sign that perhaps I should not be trying too hard. There were important developments happening in various places, but did not seem (from my inevitably incomplete view) to be a rising tide of cross-campus energy commensurate with the interns' aspirations, at that time.

Ongoing action Part 1: Sustainability in my own activities

During those several years, in what might be termed my own 'jurisdiction' I was busy developing a range of initiatives, with colleagues and an external partner, taking 'leadership for sustainability' as a guiding motif. I could see how these all supported each other and that as an array they could generate momentum. I articulated this framing for internal and external consumption. This stream of overtly experimental activities went well for quite some time, securing some funding, building connections.

There were also several more speculative activities, potentially promising conversations with both internal and external contacts which eventually did not generate the concrete proposal we needed to help us work together.

As we went along, colleagues and I would repeatedly check: 'is there more we should be doing just now?' Mostly we thought we were doing enough to gather potential energies, and give possibilities a chance to flourish. Sometimes we would identify further opportunities and set off on new lines of inquiring action.

Being invited to join networks outside the institution led to stimulating engagements, for example gaining perspective on the changing world of corporate responsibility, and meeting committed people in the region who were making their contributions to change for sustainability.

One strand of external activity was accepting invitations to give presentations on taking leadership for sustainability. As inquiry, I would try each time to push the boundaries in that space: to speak forthrightly about climate change and associated issues, work openly with multiple ways of knowing, ask provocative questions, and seek to align sufficiently for at least some people to hear me and respond. With these agendas, speaking to an audience is always a challenge, always feels risky, potentially vulnerable, on an edge – has always to be experimental. But I try to use the space and access I have been offered with integrity, aware of the paradoxes in the format of 'keynote speaker', and the potential replication of unhelpful social patterns.

Whilst much of this work was fascinating and fun, at times, set alongside other teaching, admin and research, it seemed voluminous and rather uphill. I enjoyed the agility of holding it all in mind, but this could also be challenging. At times it all required more valiant trying than I wanted to engage in. And over time things shifted. The Masters in leadership for sustainability we developed worked educationally, but then did not recruit well. There were other disappointments. Energies, and people, moved on. I became increasingly wary about how I spent my time; the time that is running out. After some years in this situation, the balancing of whether to persist or desist began to shift. See PART II: **Disciplines of inquiry:** Finding resonant phrasing.

As time went by, and some activities waned, this decline in meaningful work threw up significant life review questions for me, which I took into reflective writing and conversations. These were threaded alongside action, mutually informing each other. As I moved into 2014, with the prospect of formal retirement at the end of that year, I especially pondered what I have done during my career, what activities and potential contributions I value, and what people and networks I feel aligned with. I was also noticing when what I termed 'probably the last ever' of some activities I treasured (such as a week-long Masters workshop) was occurring. Reviewing my life and learning journey was interesting, emotionally toned, taking a longer-term view on unfolding action. Despite anticipating it, the time for formal retirement seemed then to come suddenly, although given the never-ending nature of many academic lives, it was not clear-cut, and thus not easily explained to other people.

Whatever was happening in my immediate activities, staying connected and active across the University still enticed me. It felt interesting, potentially strategic, to be imagining sustainability and its enhancement across the whole institution, and seeking to influence its contours. I appreciated occasional signs that I was recognised as having something to contribute in this sense.

Also, from the viewpoint of potential change, it was helpful when external bodies, such as those accrediting Management Schools, attributed importance to corporate responsibility and sustainability, and wanted our organisation to account in these terms. My colleagues and I could show how our efforts contributed to the School's profile on such issues, we could tell this story well. This gave our local activities more legitimacy.

Ongoing action Part 2: Meeting on the path

Writing note

This brief reflective note was written on 26 April 2013 articulating a core image of inquiring action I had held for some time. This had been exemplified in intense experiences over the previous few days. Encounters of the kind described happen spontaneously and frequently. Their potential seems built into the physicality, flow and collegiality of the University. Names given are pseudonyms.

> Meeting people in passing, on the path, seems to be my way, my form, at the moment. The pleasure and connection of moments and contacts, the sense of mutual support. Like seeing Jenny last week and finding out what is happening about the possible centre funding. So I could link what the funders are seeking to the proposal for an eco-hub that arose from another group discussion. (Fitting in comments at any opportunity, linking up ideas, people, images of possible futures.) Like seeing Ruth in the Hub just now, her enduring enthusiasm and change insight. Meeting Dave on the path in the morning, talking up possibilities for integrating more attention to responsible leadership into courses. The spontaneity of calling Roy to see if some environmental champions might come on Friday, his response and action. Pausing in the Hub to process my reflections on last week's keynote with Clive, wondering if I had been provocative enough, knowing he would understand my questions. This feels like thinking on the go. Not that I want to tell a causal tale.
>
> These experiences have a sense of playfulness. The joy of being in movement and seeking the just-enough-ness of it all. Mutual space and influencing. This contrasts to times when I have been involved in making representations to senior figures, appealing to already overloaded people who are valiantly doing their best in complex roles. Although keeping everyone informed is a bit demanding. Inclusion, but inevitable exclusion, and the difficulties of that, because of who I do not then meet in passing. And all the time it is shifting, including some groups around the University leaving, their energies lost from the interactive picture.
>
> Over the years I have debated the perversities of trying to influence senior people. Whilst this seems a necessary approach, it risks replicating patterns of hierarchy, of accepting that some people are 'in charge', and thus spending energy on what shape arguments have to be to reach and energise them. Recently, I have been happy enough to leave this work to colleagues; it is all part of the matrix of movement for change.

May 2014 Review 3: Taking some next steps

And then, in autumn 2012, Mike pushed again, and met with the PVC-R and the new VC. Mike with his PowerPoint presentation, exhortation for the Uni to step up and make more of its potential. And the VC agreed to fund a next step activity. Mike and I debated. I am wary of adrenalin-rich workshops, a good time had by all, and little happening as a result. Or a small group of people struggling to make something happen and wondering if they are wasting their time. I favoured also working through the organisational processes that are there, but under-used, like supporting the departmental environmental champions in their potential as organisational change agents. But, and, we decided to organise an event, a workshop to bring people across the campus together, inviting them to connect up more and envisage and request next steps for the Uni. My image of this way of working is of strengthening the metaphorical wildlife corridors that already exist across the Uni, it is an aspect of what I term 'working the background'. One participant in the resulting workshop was more literal; he suggests we smash up the campus concrete and let nature back in.

By then, Mike and I had been joined by a colleague from another Faculty, S. He is an expert on design for sustainability and brought a lot of energy to the venture, and another view on choices.

Developing *Global Futures*: seeking a bigger vision

In the sections which follow, I show glimpses of my critically reflective practice as this venture proceeded. We arrived at the title of *Global Futures* for the workshop. We invited an external facilitator to join us and arranged several events spanning two days for him to contribute to:

A seminar for a specialised doctoral group

A Keynote presentation on developing sustainability in communities, attended by about 50 to 60 people, including the VC

A drinks reception

Dinner with the VC and a small group of people, and

The one-day workshop for 24 people

I brought some clear purposes to this venture, especially that of including other voices, such as those of Students' Union officers, whose insightful work on systemic change for sustainability I greatly appreciated, and the departmental environmental champions, and helping to bring people into conversation. For example, I thought certain people from the Management School would benefit from meeting people from other Faculties, and would find ready connecting points in current projects.

Planning *Global Futures*: Meeting vignette

Writing note

This section was intentionally written as an experiment in using direct speech and dialogue as a form of representation to show rather than tell. It was written in April 2013 to illustrate how our organising team of three had operated as we planned the *Global Futures* events, and to inquire into and reflect upon our relationship. It depicts a typical meeting. The writing flowed, as I could see and recall the situation so fully, a meeting with specific content but a typical pattern. Not that I am saying this is an 'accurate' account. The inquiry in writing was how to portray the qualities of being there, and the sensibilities and behaviours of living life as inquiry that the character who is me in disguise was operating from. Writing the account in the third person just happened as I started out, and so I followed this through. It was written from the main character's point of view rather than as if an observer, to give access to her reflecting and purposes, and to help situate the reader in this perspective.

   In the account, I have attempted to show examples of micro level inquiry in my approach to our work together. For example, my strong intention of working with others so that all contribute creatively means I pay attention to how to mesh with others' ways of being, allowing them space, but ensuring I have space too. I am aware that small moves can sometimes seem defining to others, and am wary of doing this unawares, or of acquiescing when this seems to be happening round me. I pay a lot of attention to framing, inviting discussion of framing and re-framing (Fisher et al., 2003). Sometimes I sit well back, interested to see what might arise. Sometimes I move back and forth, into advocacy perhaps, but then opening up what I have said to inquiry, lest this proves dominating (in relation to others) or a partial view that needs expanding. I might then adjust, or re-affirm my view, seeking dialogue.

Working with Mike and S on organising the *Global Futures* activities was demanding because of all we were trying to do, but also engaging and a pleasure. We were still new as a team, and so potentially a little hesitant with each other. It seemed to me that we were all willing to be inquiring in how we interacted, and yet we were task-focused, keeping up a pace, not spending a lot of overt energy on how we related. Both of them questioned a lot and could and did spot potential inequality dynamics, which contributes well to robust, reflective relationships. We thus worked alongside each other, openly and with agility; checking sideways when looking for sufficient accord to move on. This gives a sense, perhaps, that all three of us like action and getting on with things. It was delicate, fascinating work. So in conversations such as that below I think we were all engaged in some forms of first and second person inquiry, as we sought to shape an inviting workshop space in which third person, collaborative, inquiry would become possible. The congruence of this mirroring between our process and the engagement we were seeking to encourage was promising.

Our organising involved repeated meetings, usually in the Hub café, but with some elsewhere on campus, typically an hour of intense activity, accompanied by a lot of busy email traffic.

A typical meeting of the *Global Futures* team

When she reaches the Hub cafe, S is already there, setting up his laptop on one of the small round tables in the eating area. He looks up and grins in greeting.

'And how are you today?'

'Oh, fine, a lot on, you know; and you?'

'Same here' he nods assent.

She puts her papers down on the table, the jumble she was able to find today, not sure she has the latest versions of them all. Hangs her shoulder bag off the back of the chair.

Mike appears round the corner, hurrying, clothes slightly askew. He will probably have cycled in, but, whatever, shirts seldom seem to stay secure in trouser tops for him, not that he minds or it matters. He puts his notebook and pen down on the remaining space on the table.

Mike: 'Yesterday I saw TW from Engineering, I think we should invite him to the workshop too, don't think he was on the list.'

'Yes, fine, I don't think so, but we can check. But first, can we just check what we have to do today, I think we just have an hour?' she says.

'Yeah'

'Yeah, me too'

They all throw in topics: who to invite to the workshop, working on the draft invitation, the draft flyers for the keynote and other seminar, room bookings, catering, briefing the external facilitator … S types, she takes hand-written notes. They stop, are flagging but know that is not all.

'That's enough for today!' S says, 'By the way, I've asked Rebecca in my department to help us with the admin, nothing else seemed to be happening on that. Is that ok?'

'Great'

'Well yes, we did talk about central admin providing some help, but no one has asked yet.'

'So, back to who we've invited, Mike – shall we look at the spreadsheet we started?'

'I don't have that with me' says Mike. They all look over the copy she has brought, Mike reading out the names. 'Yes', to some. To others, 'Not sure, their work seems very focused and specific.'

'We only have limited spaces, 20? 25 at most? We have to select people who are willing to learn together, to advocate other peoples' points of view', S reminds them of an earlier principle they agreed. 'I don't know most of these people' he says, 'but that's ok, we've got a spread across the Uni. There is A in my department; I think she would be good.'

Without much discussion, she is added in.

'Are there any economists?' he continues.

They all laugh. They don't think so. If only there were prominent economists into environmental issues on the campus.

'Ok, then' Mike returns to scanning 'if we're worried about numbers, let's leave out X, Y and Z this time, and hope they won't be offended', pulling a slightly worried face.

'Ok, agree', she says, 'but we can afford to invite more people initially than 25, some won't be able to come, people will drop out at the last minute.' Totalling up, 'I make that about 35, shall we stick with that for now? I can update the spreadsheet and send it to you both. Can you then check it? And I will do a final version for Rebecca.'

'So, what's next, the invitation?' S moves them on. 'This version looks ok.'

'Which one is that?', Mike asks. S turns his laptop so Mike can see the screen. She moves round behind them to see too, checking it's the latest version. A colleague goes by on his way to get coffee, rests his hand on S's shoulder, western edge, north American tones still 'and what are you three all doing together then?' This is her patch, but S has come from the other side of the campus, Mike from half way between. They answer briefly, their eyes still glancing towards the screen.

'I can see you want to get on', he says and waves as he moves on.

'*Global Futures* Workshop', S reads out, slowly, checking each word, a gentle Welsh lilt shows through now …

'Dear … As many of you know, during the last couple of years this University has been seeking to increase the impact of its work around environmental and social responsibilities – "sustainability" for short.

The VC is now supporting a next-step activity, a *Global Futures* workshop that brings together people from across the campus to make further connections between our activities and arrive at proposals for the University to take its interests in sustainability forward …' He glances up, eyebrows questioning.

'Ok so far' they both say.

'In framing this event, we suggest that a wider vision is needed to address the multiple challenges facing the world today.' 'Is that right "a wider vision"?'

'We thought about putting in a lot more there', she says. 'What Mike was summarising last week: people's answers to climate change so far are within paradigm, more efficient uses of energy and resources mean lots of rebound effects that cancel the "savings" out, apparent effort but upward curves continue, this Uni and readiness for more cross-disciplinary working, lots of potential, need really radical blue skies thinking and so on. I made some notes on it, tried to fit them in. Then took most of it out, seemed to go on too long, looked as if it was telling people what to think, and we want something new to arise. It's a bit flat, but we could just say "bigger" instead of "wider"? We did think of "more encompassing", "working in different modalities", "different ways of thinking", but that sounds a bit, well …' The word does not come.

'Might put the scientists off you mean?' S fills in. 'Let's go for "bigger"', checking eye contact with Mike. S corrects the text.

And so they move on through, line by line. At the end, S says 'That looks pretty good then, I'll send it round for a final check off.'

'I revised the text for the notices about the keynote and doctoral seminar to line up with the workshop invitation', she says, 'I'll amend to "bigger" where it applies and send them round too for final checking. Need to talk about how we get the keynote one sent out but can do that next time, perhaps.'

'Did you hear on the Today Programme this morning, a piece on Brazil and smog in the cities', S asks, 'I'm doing a seminar in Sao Paulo next month, will be interesting to see what is happening.' Judi had heard – 'There's a doctoral student in our department, researching what is happening to people in favelas [heavily populated informal urban settlements] because of construction and preparations for the World Cup and 2016 Olympics … Disturbing. Fascinating. Let me know if you want to contact them.'

Checking their watches …

'So, food then, shall I just ask Rebecca to sort that?' scanning the to-do list, S offers, unaware that this will be a significant issue.

'If it's all about sustainability we need catering to match', Mike is clear.

'Could you, we, come up with some guidelines for what we need, so Rebecca can talk to catering? They have done some great local food buffets before. I think they have some idea, but probably need us to be clear with them. And please can we have malt loaf or something else with body to it with tea and so on when we arrive, not just sickly pastries?' She contributes, from her more limited experience of achieving eco-aware catering at the Uni.

'Well, it's quite simple really: food in season, local if possible, but that is not the only factor, reduce waste as much as possible, food and otherwise. I could go with Rebecca to talk to catering.'

'What's happening with the evening dinner with the VC, facilitator and so on?' S asks.

They are still a relatively new combination. This will be two connected events with profile, spending money directly assigned by the VC. More importantly, it's a great opportunity, the kind Mike and she have been trying to prompt for some time. How it is done will be important, reflective of potential change and practice for sustainability, or could replicate more limited ways of operating if they do not think things through. And this is all additional, voluntary work they are fitting into already busy lives.

'I did some checking out. I invited the VC to the keynote and to dinner after, thought I needed to get it in his diary, trust that is ok with you?' she scans. It's ok. 'We need to decide who else to invite, what are we trying to achieve through the dinner? And by the way the VC is keen to keep catering spend on campus, so it needs to be in the Uni dining room, not at the hotel.'

S 'Oh', pause, 'what's the food like there? Will it be ok?'

'Yes, it's good these days. And there is no choice if we want the VC there. We could ask the same principles as for the other catering.'

'Yeah, I can talk to them about that too', volunteers Mike. 'What kinds of things do we have in mind?'

He opens his notebook, pen at the ready, writes down the list he has already started – food in season and so on … looks up.

This is now too much for S.

'I'm not good at talking about food this much, I don't really care. We could do Kentucky Fried Chicken for simplicity?' His charming, playful grin seems to reach well to the eyes, and not knowing him so well yet, she wonders about his apparent frequent good humour, unusual amongst her colleagues these days.

'So, can we leave the food for now, leave it to you and Rebecca, Mike? But can we have beer from the local brewery for after the keynote, that would fit wouldn't it?'

A slightly conciliatory air about the last bit, she thinks, though good idea, and yes, she wanted to get out of food detail by now, although keen that catering too should exemplify their topic, purpose. A little ripple in their relating, an adjustment, all parties fine it seems, and so they move on. She is noticing the dynamics, the small movements, fascinated by how they are all coordinating their actions, moods, tones.

'What next?' She asks. She and S scan their lists. 'How to brief the facilitator? Have you heard from him lately S?'

'No. Not since he agreed to do it. He is travelling a lot, hard to reach. Well … When we have the invitations and flyers, we can send them to him. There was some brief-ing in our initial email.' He finds this (she is impressed with his filing), and reads out some key words.

'Yeah, they fit with the workshop invite still.'

'And then he sent back some ideas', she reminds. 'But in the workshop invite we adjusted his list of possible issues the bigger vision needs to address, slimmed it down, and made it "could" not "should" – energy, production and consumption, law, trust, governance. We don't know yet what will come up. I think it would be good to all have a Skype with him, fill in the background, what's already done, what we hope from this action.'

S, already typing the email to the facilitator: 'So, we want to leave things open to emerge, but we definitely want plans from the day, not lots of hot air?'

'Yes, and the reason we wanted someone from outside rather than to run it our-selves was our concern that people go to these things, get high, and nothing happens as a result. So we wanted more impact from having someone with their own ideas and reputation about communities designing for sustainability coming in, more impetus, but also for him to help our next moves arise, rather than offer templates for what we should do.'

She touches back to key intentions, not to fix them but to keep on track, and check if they need re-framing. And she notices that S, as the recent addition to the team, does not have the years of talking this activity up that Mike and she have, and sometimes she feels it is ok to be explicit about some of the backstory, the charac-ters, how this fits into the University space. But she is also wary of therefore assuming anything that fixes things. It can all move on.

'That's right, isn't it?'

Mike and S agree.

[In the Skype that results, which Mike cannot make, she initially holds back a bit, wanting to hear the facilitator's fresh ideas. But then finds she has a lot to say about the kind of process and event they want and why, what the context and history is. She is wary lest she over-rides what the facilitator might bring. But S would not have been able to say these more historical pieces. She weighs up whether she is being too definitional and decides the danger is more in not offering enough fram-ing to cue the outsider in to the setting he will enter. She is pretty sure he will not remember it all, but that will probably be fine.]

'When are you two free then, for this Skype?' S offers the facilitator some dates and times. 'Right, that's sent then.'

'I've got to go soon', Mike says, 'what haven't we covered?'

'Time for a next meeting? Who we invite to dinner with the VC?' she says.

'Who's coming so far then?' Mike asks.

'Us three, the facilitator, the VC that's 5', she says 'we thought a max of 8'.

'What about the PVC-R, he started this all off with his seminar?' Mike asks.

'Can't come, on holiday that week, sadly', she has checked it out.

'Not a very good gender balance', says S, 'or age range'.

They are amused at the image of them evening up the balance by inviting young women, a shared gender amusement she enjoys, but they scan nonetheless for who they might consider.

'We need to spread across the Faculties too', Mike notes 'are there some younger women in science?'

She comes up with one name; her travels around the Uni mean she has contributed quite a lot to the list of potential attendees. They agree to email other ideas.

Half standing up already, S's laptop closed and crooked in his elbow, they agree another hour, next week.

'That's all good then ...'

S heads for the door near reception, Mike and she for the back entrance.

'Do you think it's going ok?' she checks in with their earlier conversations, the gently held 'project' of promoting more attention to sustainability at the Uni that has brought them together.

'Yeah, yeah, it's good, yeah, I think it's good', he smiles and dashes away.

She returns to her building, up the stairs two flights, her office, puts the papers on top of others unfiled, and checks her diary for what next.

Note: This marks the end of the March 2014 account. Remaining sections were written as dated and drawn together to create this chapter.

Ongoing watchful preparation for the *Global Futures* events
Writing note

The following (dated) sections draw on reflective writing I did as the activities progressed. Engaging in this way helped me review and potentially adjust how I was seeing things, feeling and acting.

My main focus of attention was on the one-day workshop, wanting development to come from it. The other activities were important, but would largely take care of themselves. We hoped they would affirm the importance of sustainability in the wider community and provide another space for people, including the VC, to meet and connect around this. We were also curious to learn more about where sustainability fitted in the VC's perception of important issues.

Some sections of that contemporaneous writing are, in my view, too revealing about self or others to offer here. This will be indicated as an example of working with such text. But saying things frankly to myself was valuable inquiry which helped me, inter alia, to let go of concerns I then considered unnecessary, and led me to find inquiring ways to act with others.

See PART IV: **Writing as representation** for discussion of boundaries of disclosure in first person action research.

Below, I also give some information on what did happen to show action, and inquiry in action.

In the run-up to the workshop, I scanned what was happening with issues I thought especially important for success, keeping a watchful eye. I especially monitored attendance. Inevitably in the week beforehand there were dropouts. I worked at filling the spaces to keep the numbers up, using my knowledge of networks to widen participation. Apart from a perfunctory 'I'm sure you will be ok with me doing this' email, I did not ask Mike and S's permission but just got on with it. *Working the background* in such ways attends to the ground from which other action springs, or does not, or in which ideas will flourish, or will not.

Anticipating the 1st March 2013 *Global Futures* workshop

Writing note

A few days before the workshop amidst my other busyness I was a little nervous and so wanted to reflect on how I was approaching the event. I wrote this as inquiry (on 26th February 2013), in the present tense, which is retained here. Indentation shows a direct quote from the original. Some has been omitted as being too personally revealing or long-winded. This is marked with square brackets and 'Omitted', and explained to some extent. The reflective writing showed how I was aware of carrying forward questions, potential orientations and previous feedback from one experience into another, and reviewed whether I needed to heed or review their potential implications for the forthcoming events.

> And so today where am I with all this? Quite nervous really about Thursday and Friday, and yet willing to see what arises. In the *Action Research Handbook* chapter (Marshall, 2001) I said about setting up or engaging with rich contexts for inquiry. This will certainly be one. There are: the practicalities of getting it all to work; how to bring a sense of possibilities and be also open to what arises; how to work alongside the others, given my sense already of our different interpretations of what it is about and different ways of conducting ourselves. I have pre-set, or tried to (will they all turn up?) some space for potential connections to emerge by who has been invited.

In briefing others about the forthcoming events, I'm realising how germane the Interns' Report is, that this workshop would be a follow-on. I have a sense of responsibility for carrying forward the intention and the specifics of what they have done and suggested, alongside Mike.

Questions I am carrying:

How to be present enough and not trample on my colleagues' toes, and ensure they do not trample on mine?

How to engage with the VC? I have very limited notions of who he is, how he operates. But he'll be visiting my department the day before which would be helpful for gaining some impressions. Although I am wary of seeming to try to attract his attention in some way, of contributing to the kind of 'waves' that happen around people with perceived power.

[Omitted: reflection on a recent reception at which I had not tried to attract a prestigious figure's attention, but seen others doing so successfully. Late in the proceedings, I had spoken for one brief sentence with him. Later I felt dissatisfied about what had happened, despite my avowed approach of indifference.]

What are my intentions entering these events? Inquiry?!

Yes, I will be attempting to help LU do more around issues of sustainability, form more connections and develop more joint and overarching activities. And I would love us to make this more of our overt offering to the world. And I know how dangerous that might be. Just now environmental issues seem to have gone down people's list of priorities, pushed out because of economic crisis [as if they are disconnected?!], and with any solutions people can imagine framed in terms of growth and regenerating economies – so old, environment-depleting strategies. So it might be unwise for LU to market itself as sustainability. Another Management School I know did that years ago and last I heard it was not going so well. I should contact them for an update.

And so, I can be there in inquiry, continuing my interest in what enables and disables potential change. And I can listen well to what is on people's minds as they consider doing more or differently, and what they are already doing of course. I am very aware that much is happening elsewhere on the campus, not needing me and my advocacies.

In fact it is my/our activities that are now not going so well, in the Dept. The MA is good as education, but there is not a market for it, it seems.

[Omitted: reflection on how activities had developed and not developed in my Department since I had arrived, raising questions for me about the roles I had taken, and what might have been good and not so good uses of my energies, despite having looked promising at the time. This moved into some reflections on life patterns, which linked back to what I might be carrying into the forthcoming events. I pondered how to take them into consideration in how I approached the workshop.]

And Thurs, Fri?? Themes of needing to be organised, feeling responsible to others.

My mind slips to the Economics event [this had happened four months previously]. How afterwards some of the Occupy people thought I had let the speakers off the hook about the participants' challenging questions. Although someone else thought I had handled chairing that part of the conversation well, not pushing for confrontation inappropriately. In retrospect I can see both points of view, and that I might also have pushed the questions harder somehow. At the time it felt enough pressure on me to make the intentions of the assembled people realised enough. And I do not believe that pushing challenges on people is often effective to encourage them to open up to learning and doing things differently. The questions I always carry relate: What is possible here? Might maintaining relationships be more important than other goals, in this moment?

Writing these notes proved a helpful review, helped me scan, disentangle and notice some emotionally toned reactions that I might otherwise have carried unawarely into the activities.

Global Futures events, March 2013

Day 1

I did not write many process notes from Day 1. It was a day for keeping moving, doing what was needed practically, pulling back to enjoy the activities once other people seemed settled. A description would not enhance this inquiry story, in my view. However, one image sticks in my mind as an example of the connecting we had wanted to enable. At the drinks reception after the evening keynote, the VC and two people from Occupy Lancaster were deep in mutual conversation about sustainability issues and the relationship between the University and the town.

Day 2: The *Global Futures* workshop

Twenty-four people attended from across the campus, including us three organisers, many not initially knowing each other. There was a simple timetable for the workshop, with activities, group discussions, much mapping of ideas in large print, report backs and discussion. The activities were interspersed with refreshments, including the vegetarian lasagne lunch (to minimise waste) and malt loaf, which was well received.

The Workshop started with introductions to:

- The history and framing for the event.

- The 'big questions' on which we were suggesting a 'bigger vision' was required. A speedy PowerPoint presentation from Mike on: climate change, escalating emissions despite attempts to moderate them, rebound effects, the richness of work going on at Lancaster, and the potential to develop it further.

- The invited facilitator.
- The working space, a lab area in the Design department, offering plenty of creative work spaces and formats. Available: large whiteboards, coloured paper, big marker pens, sticky notes – to capture discussion and display it for others to see.

Prominently on one board was a large-scale print of the Interns' map of sustainability related activities across the campus in research, teaching and the University's own practice, with the invitation for people to write on more connections.

Cycles of activity:

- Speed meeting: four rounds of people introducing themselves to people they did not know, exchanging interests and passions, and noticing cross-cutting themes
- Whole group: a round of names and locations in the University, and cross-cutting themes people had heard so far
- Subgroups: people identifying and discussing their passions in relation to sustainability and mapping emerging themes
- Report back
- Subgroups: people envisaging their ideal activity and a workplan to help realise it. Debating and mapping ideas for the future
- Report back
- Plenary discussion of what next
- Conclusions and Close

One image from the Workshop: I arrive, join in the melée of greetings. We are called to order by Mike and take our seats. Initially I sit back, take a few deeper breaths. I am sure it will be a stimulating day. But just for those first moments it was enough to have helped it happen, for these people to be in the room. I had no doubt that we would engage with each other and the issues.

Reviewing the *Global Futures* workshop: Debrief 1

Immediately after the *Global Futures* events I was happy to pause, celebrate that it had all happened, and take a rest. Three days later (4th March), I reviewed the initiative using writing as inquiry. This is Debrief 1 in this section. Twelve days later, Mike, S and I met and my notes from that gathering are the base for Debrief 2 below.

Writing note

The 4th March 2013 review was a lengthy piece of writing as inquiry (1,806 words) completed in one session. It was a way for me to debrief the experience, check what I was thinking and feeling, scan for learning and ideas for next possible action, and critically review all of these. Rather than offer all this writing to show it fully, I have chosen to 'ladder up' and consider what themes and issues it incorporates. This illustrates the initial stages of thematic analysis as another form of working with inquiry accounts. Quotations from the original text are indented (kept in original sequencing as this may be relevant). Whether to show in full or step into telling is a choice when trying to portray writing as inquiry of this sort. Influencing factors include readers' anticipated tolerance for lengthy text, confidentiality, vulnerability, skilful writing practice, balancing different sorts of text in a total piece, and wordcount.

Themes in 4th March 2013 review were:

Recapping the background to this event, how it had arisen

I noted the step forward it seemed to represent in connecting to the VC and the PVC-R, and how the door might now be open for further developments.

'It's there to be played for', the text said hopefully.

Pondering dynamics of relational practice in the service of change

Inquiry questions: What is on my mind? on my emotions? puzzling me?

Being inclusive. Working alongside Mike and trying to hear his ideas that seem different from mine at times, and allow them to take their own form fully rather than be skimped and trimmed by my different views. Learning what it is like to work with S, how he operates in a bigger group. And I have therefore engaged openly with some things that I would not initially have devised – wanting above all else to see and act beyond my own patterns but also therefore beyond my own shadow. Systemic change does not, I assert, come from any of us acting individualistically, using conscious purpose to carve out our straight lines of intent through the world. So what are alternatives? The gently phrased 'relational practice'? Well yes, and I have long been suspicious of the over-harmonious projections onto this. I note, then, how much we bring to every attempt at a present moment.

Reviewing the role I had played

Integrated tracks of inquiry for me throughout the *Global Futures* initiative were how to dovetail my activities suitably with those of others, and how not to over-impose my shape on the events, wanting them to be co-created and novel experiences for me, from which I would learn. I could have offered to facilitate the workshop, but decided early on not to do this, for these reasons and the overload it risked. Inviting in an outside facilitator brought fresh energy to the initiative. One consequence for me, was ambiguity at times about whether to advocate for ways of running the workshop, or let things take their course.

My reflective notes passed back and forth over these issues. I recapped when I had and had not offered views and shaped what was happening, and whether these actions were appropriate. Whilst I might have done things differently, I judged my actions appropriate enough in the circumstances.

> Did I take too much of a back seat? Don't think so. With Mike, S and the facilitator doing their things, no need for more framings, that might have seemed competitive. And I had certainly had my say, including in who was in the room, including the last minute additions. And what was said on the invites.

> So am I satisfied about working alongside what emerged and not telling people what to do more? Well yes. How can we each participate in truly emergent process? How can we contribute to creating enabling conditions for more emergence? What kinds of persistence do we then enact?

I pondered if I too often avoid advocacy, a voice that jars for me unless twinned with inquiry. But decided that I do advocate, by one means or another.

I also explored how I had stepped more into an organising role than I had intended, as this seemed necessary to complement what others were doing and to support the administrator. I had been wary of taking that role, because of the potential stereotyping and the poor use of my time. Willing as I am to be 'of service', I do not think this is always recognised by others as a choice and as a thought-through intervention. Often I will do it to ensure an activity's form is sufficiently congruent with its purposes, and so does not undermine them. (I realise that some people might see such attention as trivial, but I see it as political choice.)

Reviewing dynamics of organisational change

> My concerns that an event might build energy and then be disappointing afterwards. In a way I set these aside to engage again in experiment, once the activity was sanctioned and funded, to give it a try. We did include people who might take things forward, provide the slower waves of change initiatives, in the attendees list. So the event fitted into the bigger picture of action for change at the Uni which I hold. Shows too how my networking ever since Feb 2008 is part of my contribution.

I had pursued the event whole-heartedly, setting aside my reservations about whether showpiece events generally contribute to systemic change. Thus the workshop and its aftermath became an action research experiment in these terms. I could be curious about what happened, including my parts in it, rather than pursue it as a prescribed action plan. Emergent action accrues in some way. We might well be too agentic and focused if we look for recognisable and immediate impacts.

> What then does not get shown in any account? Me wondering if it is all futile? My despair that it is all too late [in relation to climate change, loss of biodiversity and more ...], that the means we are using to address these issues are wrong, framed by the mindset through which we got here. That we need to do and say less ...

I scanned across other activities that I cared about, which were meeting opposition at the time. Noted how I might be transferring tiredness and low expectations of effects from those battles into my appraisal of the *Global Futures* initiative. I ranted briefly on the pressures some people express (in the media and publications) to make action for social and environmental change fun, as 'negativity' puts people off.

> They threaten that if we get the message wrong we could put people off, and the tentative small things people might have considered, even those, will not happen. Well! It would probably not have amounted to anything much anyway. So why make me so cautious about expressing my stark views on all this? Not that I have things right in my own life …

(This seemed a necessary letting off of steam.)

Reflecting on reflective writing

There was a closing reflection on whether any retrospective reservations I had felt about the workshop were being 'churlish'. I had been tired over the weekend, needed just to let things be. This tiredness (a reasonable aftermath to a long-anticipated significant event) might have slanted my later impressions of the day, which had been energetic, engaged and generative in so many ways.

This is an important reminder that whilst review and evaluation are potentially helpful, we need to take care in these processes. If they are over-hasty, simplify complex situations into simple outcomes, transpose emotional tones into reactions to other situations, they can be unhelpful, potentially degenerative. And this is not always that clear to discern. It is not about 'getting it right'. We need a lexicon for self-reflective inquiry that is not self-punishing, but does have a prospective edge, without swinging from one extreme of behaviour to another. And this is reflection not excavation. 'It was what it was.'

Timescales of reflection are significant. Reviewing the workshop two years later (in 2015), I am fine about not having shaped the day more myself, about not having pushed for outcomes and thus felt more duty to carry things forward. Because the context for doing so was not propitious, at that time, we later came to realise. But slower acting waves of change would work through. See below.

Reviewing the *Global Futures* workshop: Debrief 2

Mike, S and I met on 13th March 2013 in the Design Building for a change. We reviewed what had happened, the workshop especially; agreed what tidying up and admin we would each do; and considered what next. I made notes, as usual, mostly action lists of different kinds. These inform this brief summary.

Our debrief about the workshop was direct and business-like, typical of our style of interacting. We agreed that the event could have been better but that it was good enough, and at least we had made a start. It was interesting and a relief that we agreed with each other so readily, given our different stakes and roles in the planning, preparation and event itself.

We also agreed that the vision of what could happen next would have to come from us, and that the workshop had conferred on us the right to put that forward. Other people had volunteered to become involved, if we could get something moving. We agreed it was time for our group to change shape, become more inclusive. In our summarised proposals, we assigned ourselves to a potential advisory board, alongside other members.

We had invited one attendee to the workshop with the agreement that they would produce a report of the day, and we then worked with them on the draft text and how the event was depicted. The resulting 16-page report evocatively captured the energy and engagement of the event, the analyses and ideas generated, and the proposals made through photographs and accompanying text. Copies were distributed to attendees, interested people who could not attend, the VC and PVC-R.

Next steps and reflecting on systemic change

Combining our learning from the *Global Futures* workshop and the Interns' Report we generated proposals for potential cross-campus coordination, taking an action research approach, to help further develop action on sustainability in terms of teaching, research and the University's own practice. Our next inquiry questions were how to promote these proposals in the University – who to address them to and how, given that responsibilities were spread across a range of people, offices and functions. In the following weeks, we each had conversations with a range of people who advised on how we might take things forward. They were opportunities both to contribute to thinking and to gain perspective on how others saw things, on what was on people's agendas. We fed this information back to each other.

Despite initially promising signs we could not secure sponsorship or funding for our ideas at that time. A small budget was found to run some open, cross-campus seminars and networking events. This kept the pulse ticking, at least.

Looking back, it was not a great time to make our proposals. The VC was initiating a new consultative, organisation-wide planning process, to help decide on organisational priorities. Our initiative could be seen as separate, seeking to bypass this. In time, impetus for more action related to sustainability has developed through this and other consultative processes, and from a range of independent initiatives, coming from multiple directions.

Biding our time, and playing our parts in prompting and joining arising discussions, the outputs from the Interns' Report and the *Global Futures* event became key resources we drew on, which seemed to have potential validity given the wide range of people consulted in their formation. Whenever an apparent opportunity to take sustainability related activities further presents, we draw on this material, amongst other ideas. We hold the history, know something about where the energy and potential might be, know some of who is doing what. The interns' map has been a resource and exemplar. I have kept showing it to people, for its impressive scope as much as any detail, and have occasionally given someone a copy. This approach to action seeks to contribute, alongside others, to potential systemic change. And living the process through inquiry helps identify possible organisational and other impediments to pushing action for sustainability even further. Through these months, my sense was of keeping committed as a gently held purpose, wanting to be along in some of the unfolding of what was happening, but not seeking to push issues too hard, inappropriately or in unpropitious circumstances.

Along the way there have been many choices about what to put energy into. In some cases, I have experimented in action, pushing forward, seeing what might become possible, persisting at least for a time. In other situations, especially if other people are involved and pursuing issues well, in my view, I engage tentatively, support their efforts, and play 'wait and see'. Between the broad choices of persisting and desisting are shades of engagement which mean not withdrawing when something might be promising, otherwise I could help to undermine it, but not investing more energy than is reasonable either.

As I complete this book, there are now multiple continuing and new initiatives across the University which have sustainability at their heart, and a significant sense of people and activities connecting up, partly through new formal and partly through informal processes. From the apparent lull two or so years ago, it was hard to imagine the current situation as possible. But much was becoming ready, in various ways and across a range of people, that is now coming to fruition. Without claiming too much, I am sure that Mike, S and I have, jointly and separately, played some parts in this, have helped things along.

'WORK SONG' BY WENDELL BERRY

2 A Vision

If we will have the wisdom to survive,
to stand like slow-growing trees
on a ruined place, renewing, enriching it,
if we will make our seasons welcome here,
asking not too much of earth or heaven,
then a long time after we are dead
the lives our lives prepare will live
here, their houses strongly placed
upon the valley sides, fields and gardens
rich in the windows. The river will run
clear, as we will never know it,
and over it, birdsong like a canopy.
On the levels of the hills will be
green meadows, stock bells in noon shade.
On the steeps where greed and ignorance cut down
the old forest, an old forest will stand,
its rich leaf-fall drifting on its roots.
The veins of forgotten springs will have opened.
Families will be singing in the fields.
In their voices they will hear a music

risen out of the ground. They will take

nothing from the ground they will not return,

whatever the grief at parting. Memory,

native to this valley, will spread over it

like a grove, and memory will grow

into legend, legend into song, song

into sacrament. The abundance of this place,

the songs of its people and its birds,

will be health and wisdom and indwelling

light. This is no paradisal dream.

Its hardship is its possibility.

Wendell Berry (2012: 217–18)

WONDERING WHAT TO DO ABOUT AN ELDERLY RELATIVE

In this chapter I tell and review a story of sustained inquiry from a typical (home) life to illustrate the everydayness and potential multi-dimensionality of approaching life in this way. We were wondering what to do about an elderly relative, and came after a while and much discussion, to treat this explicitly as inquiry, as a project. This changed how we conducted ourselves, how we made sense of what happened and how we acted. Living through this experience involved articulating some general principles of inquiry as frames to anchor us. A review of how these were played out appears at the end of the story.

Throughout the experience we took notes of: what was happening, conversations with other people involved, practical information, actions we were taking and our reflections and ongoing sense-making. We exchanged emails with others involved, and talked things through with them and with a wider network of friends and family.

Writing note

I told an early version of this story whilst it was still in process (and I was highly emotionally engaged in it), as an invited speaker at a conference on work-based learning, intentionally transposing the principles and practices of inquiry between worlds. I had checked confidentiality and permission to tell the story with two other key people involved at that time, but was unable to check with the elderly person himself. Immediately after that conference session I felt quite uncomfortable. The experience with the elderly relative was highly salient in my life at the time. I was determined to express inquiry from it, rather than hide it away as too alive. But doing so made me feel exposed, vulnerable. This was not helped by the circumstances. I had to leave soon after my contribution to catch a train home. I felt emptied out from giving my talk, had a strong visual image of someone I know dozing in the front row during it, and had little sense of what people had thought, although there had been a couple of quick comments of appreciation. Another keynote speaker who left when I did noted on the journey that the story showed how I made myself vulnerable, seeming to confirm that my contribution had not been conventional for that space. I felt slightly embarrassed, needed to take myself gently home.

The story was told again three times a few years later at a conference and two seminars on action research as an explicit example of the practices of living life as inquiry. Those experiences were not as intense as the first, but each time my feelings became exposed, and once I had stepped into the story-telling it was not easy to step across into the role of running the session within which it was set. Working with a co-facilitator on one of the occasions helped with this.

For the third re-telling, I wrote an integrated account starting with my original PowerPoint presentation and incorporating previous side-notes. This provided initial material and storyline for this chapter. At a Freefall Writing workshop in April 2013 I unintentionally wrote a parallel version one morning. This emerged in the third person. This expressed evocative images of living the experience, so I integrated the two accounts. I settled on a first person voice to be able to express my experiencing more fully. Here I use the past tense. Some sections of the earlier version were in the present, but that could seem contrived now as time and life have moved on. The account has been checked and discussed with a key actor and their consent for publication re-affirmed. The story has been elaborated at times to make the situation clearer, to offer a more externally facing rendition. Occasional notes reflect on choices in telling the story here.

One question of any account that has been significantly reworked as this has is whether it still sufficiently shows the tensions and ripples of the lived experience and its emotionality. To me it does when I read it, even now. I have not therefore sought to fill out such dimensions further. (If I wanted to, I could use writing as inquiry to take myself back to specific moments and write from inside recalled experience, but allowing that what emerged might well be congruently inventive rather than a factually 'true' account.)

Cast and situation

The situation involved an 89 year old, called Jo here, who was living alone apart from a beloved cat, in a house which he had shared with his now-dead spouse, Esme, whose ashes were scattered in the garden. He was resistant to even discussing moving, but had become less able to cope, showing signs of not remembering well. One very engaged neighbour was concerned about Jo's ability to continue to live alone and mentioned this to family members when they visited.

The people initially involved, in addition to Jo and me, were:

My partner, Morris, a chartered engineer with his own language of inquiry and process, partly developed from a quality perspective

A few other relatives who were in active touch and visited occasionally

A friend of Jo's, Margaret, with whom he exchanged three- or four-day visits every few months

Neighbours, one prominently, others in the background

(All names are pseudonyms.)

Living with concern

He had been a cause for concern for several years, the elderly relative. Some people living further away than us had been saying for some time that he should be in a care home as he could not cope. We had resisted, deflected, knowing that Jo wanted to stay in the house, with the cat, had no plans beyond that. Self-willed, selective in his hearing, overly polite face to face. Were these signs of age or a hardening of the patterns he had always been? Certainly recognisable.

Our low rumbling concern showed through in debates, debriefings of visits, occasional conversations with other family members, a sense of upset and uncertainty. It was strongly in our attention sometimes, and then set aside.

The situation was continually unclear. Sometimes a relative would make the case – that Jo needed taking in hand and helping to move into sheltered housing of some kind, to a place where he would receive more care and protection. They could cite signs of difficulty they had noticed. But Morris and I were wary of potentially violating Jo's patterns of life and expressed choices, and wary of a general approach that we came to call 'tidying up the elderly'.

Jo's familiar situation, including routinely allowing himself to be woken in the middle of the night to let the beloved cat in or out, was his choice, it seemed. He wished to stay where he was. We did not feel a right or wish to intervene. And so we and others provided what support we could, but did not generally take over the practicalities of life, apart from some routine bill-paying. When we visited we ensured Jo ate well, and took him supplies. After ten years of living alone, he had strong preferences and habits. He kept the house clean, and the garden tidied quite well.

In this phase we debated a lot, Morris and I, especially as we came and went to visit Jo. The emotionality, spontaneity. I would be working at home in my study, and Morris would call by, something on his mind, inviting my attention. We would fall into a discussion of Jo and his situation, what we should do, what rights we did and did not have to intervene. Our feelings, a sense of mourning, of loss, whilst still actively engaged with the legacy. Tearful, tired afterwards, needing a cup of tea.

The two of us also discussed what to do with other family members through phone and email conversations. Our inquiry practices involved sharing information, reflecting, asking questions. 'This is what happened when I/we visited.' 'This is where I think we are. What do others think?' 'What else should we be paying attention to?' There would be flurries of ongoing review over a week or so. These exchanges were partly about giving each other support, partly about gaining perspective, partly aligning views with others. Then we would reach a temporary sense of resolution, arrive at views we could articulate, for that time, and these informed action. We would rest back for a few weeks, as other issues in life took the foreground.

There were some differences amongst us at times about whether to push forward or hold back, in general terms. We two had questioned and resisted people's calls for forceful action. But we came to realise that other people's accounts suggested that Jo was less coherent, more dependent when with them, so we appreciated that they were quite likely forming different impressions. It was interesting that Jo might be behaving differently with different people, more dependent with some, more capable of independence with others, so interpretations varied with this different data. Was this flexibility a sign of capacity of a sort, a further deterrent to underestimating Jo and his right to live as he said he wished?

In parallel we talked with friends and family about Jo, and about how they were coping with elderly relatives in similar situations. Many were living similar dilemmas.

Engaging in inner arcs of attention and inquiry

This long-time concern and debate about whether to intervene included continually questioning ourselves, wondering, for example, 'what is my, or our, stuff in all this?' 'Whose agenda is this?' We were wary of taking control, treating the situation as a management problem to 'solve', as we saw some others do in similar circumstances. But we wanted also to be appropriately caring. Discussing what was an appropriate blend of engagement and distance necessarily pulled in our personal and joint patterns of response.

Reflective note

At any point in telling this story, multiple potential windows could be opened to show the inquiry we were doing. For example, here we considered what were we protecting, avoiding, seeking. Who were the potential 'audiences' for our attempted displays of 'integrity'? (If that is what we were seeking.) When we told our stories to others, did we adjust what we said to how we thought they might see and judge us? If so, in what ways? For example, when speaking with people we knew had been highly committed carers for their elderly relatives, we wondered if they might think us negligent.

This story cannot tell all the pathways of inquiry we explored, individually and in mutual conversation.

Noticing signs of change

Then our perception of the situation changed. Over only a few visits we began to think that things were now becoming more confusing for Jo, repetitions more frequent;

there were more times when he seemed very unclear about what was happening. When we visited and took him out to lunch he would often be confused initially, might not have remembered we were coming, and then became more alert, lucid and engaged after eating. We tried to discuss how he might take better care of himself, eat nutritionally better food. He parried our attempts.

Alongside this, we felt that the close neighbour, similar age and situation, was a little more insistent, and starting to put gentle pressure on us, saying that some-thing needed to be done. They reported a situation a year or more before when Jo had been potentially in danger from an uninvited visitor to the house, and they had called the police to intervene. We felt bad at not knowing about this before, at not having been able to help, and grateful for what they had done. We were also con-cerned about the burden on them, sympathetic to them not wanting to continue to be so responsible.

Some more distant relatives expressed concern, asked if we had noticed deteriora-tion, implied, we thought, that we should be taking action, as they had done in a clearer situation with another person. But we were hesitant about just doing what others, however well meaning, thought we should.

Our debates intensified. Talk and more talk; tiring, emotional talk, back and forth. Our reservations about intervening continued, we did not want to interfere, take over, upset the patterns of his world, take away his liberty, become responsible for consequences. But we decided it was time to pay more attention.

Consolidating our inquiry approach

We decided we would visit more often, share our impressions and thoughts with other relatives more frequently, see if we could be more helpful. This was one December, from which further time scales are now tracked.

As we continued our extensive debating, I suggested we declare our intent and processes of inquiry more explicitly, explaining the notions of potential first and second person action research practice I was coming from. My partner agreed with this, readily amplifying from his own notions of quality processes. This more explicit inquiry approach meant that we intervened more deliberately, and framed what we were doing as experiments, agreeing to treat whatever happened with curiosity and as potentially valid information, rather than seeking to get things 'right'.

The sense of agreement was a palpable relief, and our committed practices of itera-tive inquiry, using our different languages, amounted to much the same thing – cycles of action and reflection, continually questioning purposes. We also involved other people in a question-posing approach, opening ourselves to more information, and to alternative interpretive frames on our experiences.

We were busy. I contacted Jo's general medical practitioner (GP), wanting to involve him both for his professional expertise, and for the credibility he held with Jo, informed by long-term family connections. We asked how the GP saw Jo's situation, especially whether he thought Jo safe to live alone and drive his car. The GP's initial answer was 'leave him in his home'. He talked about how he was addressing similar issues with his father. We asked the GP to visit, and he conducted a mental health check and thought Jo alright. By now we were experiencing how plausible Jo could seem with visitors, how he rose to the occasion, especially when engaging them in conversation on his terms. We thought this might misrepresent his everyday functioning. But who were we to say? We were impressed and puzzled, but not looking for one 'true' measure. I wrote to the GP querying their confident-seeming interpretations and offering alternative data. They responded thoughtfully, and with more conditional advice.

I contacted the local social services to see what possibilities of support and alternative residence there were. A gem, the social worker Jeffrey met with me to talk the situation through. I felt some confidence and professional curiosity about approaching the social worker. But I do not always cope well with people working from normative professional codes. Jeffrey did not do this. He offered what I would call a systemic sensibility, blending professional knowledges with his own experiences of running a care home for the elderly and looking after his own father. He spoke thoughtfully with me about how I was approaching things, what I was trying to do, my concerns. He led me through an exploration of what choices there were and some potential consequences, for example that whilst the disorientation of moving can curtail some people's lives, moving in time to create new connections and patterns can enhance life for others. I appreciated his open questioning approach, how he acted as a thoughtful sounding board, and that there were no clear answers.

By then we were into spring. Returning from such meetings I would report back to Morris and talk things through, send emails to other family members. We would live in a sea of questioning conversation.

And all this time we drove back and forth, through red earth and rolling hills, seeing the sunlight strike the cathedral in the valley as we passed, familiar miles travelled in better times. We caught the lost smile and compassion of Esme, Jo's late wife, the original master gardener, as we pulled up at the house.

Experimenting with possibilities

What we did that spring could be described as a campaign, but was more emergent, step by step than that. One major experiment was wondering if we could help Jo to eat better and so improve his overall condition and mental processes. We had repeated conversations that went: 'Jo, we think maybe you aren't eating as well as you could and it would be better for you if you did.' 'Oh, really, do you think so?' Apparently cup-a-soups were popular for his lunch and we tried to discuss their (low) nutritional value with him, scientist as he proudly was. Blank looks. After protracted discussion, he might appear to agree with us, and show a little interest in our ideas for improvement. Each time the conversation started afresh.

Through the social worker we contacted a (privately funded) home care agency. There was a meeting in February at Jo's home, with Jo, Jeffrey, the home care representative and me. I arrived a bit ahead of time. Jo had set out a coffee tray, as he liked to do when expecting visitors. (So he was expecting visitors ...) He had put out six cups for 'all those people coming' and moved his car onto the grass to make space for them parking on the drive. I thought I might well be learning about his sense of invasion.

Politeness and coffees delivered on a tray in the sitting room, the furniture arranged as ever, green upholstery on green carpet, home sewn arm covers, the old oak chest, the tracery sided table from India. Familiar patterns, material and in behaviour.

During the meeting Jo seemed plausible about what meals he cooked, how well he managed. I thought I knew differently, but chose not to contradict him. Through the seemingly somewhat random conversation, Jo asserted that he looked after himself and the house 'rather well, thank you'. Jo's potential plausibility with an audience was by then amusing as well as frustrating. As he often did during conversations those days, he also said he wanted to stay as and where he was.

I sat on the familiar sofa in the familiar green room, with so many traces of Esme, keeping myself relatively small in the situation, but also present and gently but persistently pushing for a trial of some help, however modest, for a different way of operating. My proposal, representing the family's concern about Jo not eating well enough, was for a service that would cook him lunches two or three times a week. I pushed this, against Jo's resistance, aware that I was doing so, but wanting, now we had hesitantly reached that point, to try for a shift in pattern, an opening up of possibilities. The initial agreement was for two days a week for meal preparation at lunchtime. Days and times were agreed with Jo, food preferences clarified and notified. The care person patiently took notes, seemed to understand my attempts to enlist her in the experiment.

As the weeks went on, Jo's visiting carers completed a Log Book at the house. We learnt a little from Jo himself, but he could not tell us much. So we looked at the Log Book when we visited. The arrangement soon shifted to cleaning rather than cooking, with Jo cleaning alongside the carer sometimes. He had previously seemed to have cleaning well in hand. Increasingly the visits moved to coffee and chats. This fed our impression that Jo lacked company as much as food. The Log also showed that he was sometimes out when they called. After a while, the arrangement became one day a week. Jo sacked them sometime in November. The Agency had sent a letter with Christmas charges. We wondered if he had misunderstood it as applying to him. He was money sensitive (but comfortably off), and this seemed an important operating pattern. Jo wrote a clear, lucid, polite letter terminating the arrangement. The care company's contract was with Jo, and so it had always been difficult to find out from them what was going on. We only learnt about this weeks later. We were impressed in a way, amused that he had 'repelled boarders'. But now this possibility of expanding support with its weekly visiting had been curtailed, another safety check had gone, leaving Jo slightly more exposed, we felt.

In a parallel experiment, also initiated in February, we tried to encourage Jo to go to lunches at a local care home which was a short walk, bus or car ride away in the town centre. Non-residents had to book a week in advance. We wrote big clear notes with instructions, but could see prior booking was not that easy to achieve for someone with memory issues. A two course hot lunch was only £2.50, and this pricing appealed to Jo. I booked us in and took him along once, ate with him and introduced him to people. A few weeks later Morris took him there, and the staff knew Jo. So he must have found his way there on his own, at least once. But it did not persist, and asked later about that home he could not recall.

Alongside these activities, we continued trying to talk through with Jo what was happening and why we were concerned for his well-being and trying to 'help'. These conversations started each time in much the same place. Whilst they seemed somewhat disconnected, his comments had an apparent clarity. 'I like my independence' he would say, 'I want to stay here', answering us indirectly perhaps, but directly enough.

During this time Jo was still exchanging visits every few months with his friend Margaret. These seemed to go well enough, from the limited accounts we heard. We suspected that he ate more regularly during them, and so would be at his best. We hardly knew Margaret and so did not try to contact her separately. Jo had invoked her as on his side, resistant to any change. At one of the meetings with care workers at the house, she was present, in the background. I asked her directly but gently what she thought of Jo's situation. She was cautious, but could see how Jo was not coping, appreciating our concerns and the potential to improve things. Her affirmation for our attempts to ease Jo into a more viable situation was helpful.

Trying to relieve some of the pressures on Jo, we heeded his continuous complaints about the gardening taking up his time, that there was always some 'cutting back' or lawn-mowing to be done. It was an extensive plot, the maturing garden created through Esme's skills, yet more traces of her presence. Morris lined up potential gardeners, had them visit, got quotations. But Jo did not want to commit, was reluctant to spend the money, said he would look at the quotes himself and do something. He did not.

Whenever we visited, I would call round to see the close neighbour, to keep them informed, appreciate what they were doing to keep an eye out for Jo, and hear how their life was. We occasionally took them a bunch of flowers or a cake. As the summer and autumn went on they increasingly expressed concerns. I would hear, respect and appreciate them and their vigilance, report back to Morris and other family members, discuss what they had said. And we did not want to be overtaken by their sense of responsibility. I would suggest to the neighbour that they were not either, whilst realising this was difficult for them. Later, knowing they wanted this burden lifted became a potential pressure of responsibility on us, which we discussed and actively reviewed.

This could seem a hard, uncaring approach on our parts. We were very aware that we might appear negligent to others, especially to the more distant relations and to friends who had intervened more and so supportively in their elderly relatives' lives. We debated this too.

Identifying what especially concerned us

From our ongoing 'chatter' we realised that Jo continuing to drive his car was a major concern to us. What if he had an accident? What if this involved other people? We had raised this with the GP. In time he would have to revalidate Jo's driving license, but that was not for a while. He suggested that 'little accidents' are a warning sign, the occasional scraped bumper and so on. Jo seemed not to be suffering from these, and so I worried but we did not interfere. If he became unable to drive so many of the other things he did would become impossible. It would be a major intervention to curtail him in this way, we could anticipate the likely decline; we did not think we had the right.

Resting in inquiry, agreeing to 'play wait and see' (in a vigilant sort of way)

By autumn, Jo had successfully repelled all our interventions, all our attempts to 'help' him. We respected that, were amused and impressed. This seemed to show a level of systemic organisation in how he was choosing to live his life. We continued to be highly concerned, but decided to rest back into vigilant inquiry rather than attempt any new action initiatives. We did not want any interventions we might make to compensate for and so to mask emergent, systemic properties of the current situation. We decided to comply with his voiced wishes, as long as he came to no harm it was alright.

Talking and talking again, we were seeking a way to summarise and frame what we were doing for ourselves and others. Framing would make it easier to hold, but also more open to re-framing. We found a way of saying where we were: that we were awaiting either a direct request for help or an obvious emergency as a 'sign' that we should intervene. We decided that unless these conditions were met any further action would be invasive. We tested this 'formulation' out on other relatives, the neighbour, the social worker, family and friends. It was not refuted, countered. So we settled to living by it, still highly concerned, preoccupied, but not finding anything more organised to do. We were also aware that other people might be seeing us as negligent but could not find a way to say this to us. Whilst we tried to invite feedback, one could wonder if we were too assertive in our 'framing', whether we showed sufficient signs of openness to challenge.

Recognising shifting patterns

From the December onwards we noticed significant signs of deterioration. When we visited we often found food we had taken on a previous visit still in the refrigerator uneaten. Fridge and freezer had become confused too, as soggy packets of oven chips in the former showed. Attempts to explain the difference would be met by blank looks, avoided eye contact as we were obviously being more than a little tiresome. But we then would be curious, that the chips had been bought, about whether they were ever cooked. Asking questions received fewer and fewer apparently lucid answers. Asked about house insurance, Jo looked away slightly and said 'there's been no call for it', for example. And we realised how much we were living in different worlds.

Christmas was very unclear. Jo's short-term memory was very poor. We visited. Other relatives stayed over for several days, during which Jo treated them as kindly carers, but did not appear to know them. Looking ahead, it would be Jo's 90th birthday in early February. We decided we would have a family gathering and the more distant relatives were keen to attend. We booked a table in a favourite public house where we had eaten together over many years, and in easier times. In the week before the party, Morris went over to see Jo several times to feed him meals, trying to help him be at his best for the occasion. On the day some of us went to the house to join him for mid morning coffee and collect him. He knew we were coming, but too many people around at one time was a bit overwhelming.

Sitting in the restaurant area, at a long table decked out in festive trappings for twelve people we ate and talked. Jo sat in the centre of one long side, looking out of the building toward the carpark and fields beyond. We signed the menu in his honour. He was with and amongst us jovially, as was his way. And he was confused and disoriented at times. Despite our clear messages, 'happy birthday!' '90 today!' Jo did not share our view of what was happening. He moved between interpretations, having plenty of ceremonial experiences to choose from, it seemed, for example was it some sort of society reunion, might people be about to plant a tree, he wondered, as we came toward the end of our meal.

After the party we all returned to the house, milled about, had tea, served birthday cake despite our repleteness. Jo's attachment to the tea trolley and associated rituals of sitting patiently round the living room were a long-standing family tradition, and fond joke. Some relatives stayed on to be with Jo once the rest of us had gone, to ease the change. Whilst we were all concerned about Jo, it seemed from our side conversations during the day, we were still not clear that it was time to act.

Receiving a clear warning sign

On Tuesday 14th February I was away tutoring on an intensive workshop for a week, enough on my mind. The sign we had been awaiting came. Jo had been found wandering in the town, petrol can in hand, disoriented, thinking that his car had been stolen. The police returned him home, phoned Morris and advised that this should not happen again. The car was parked in town, in one of Jo's usual places. Morris went over, retrieved the car, put it safely away in the garage and confiscated the keys.

So, in consultation with other relatives, we decided to take permission, that the time had come.

Where to look for a suitable care home was an early question we debated, whether to move Jo nearer to a member of the family perhaps, or near his childhood home. After reviewing options, we favoured looking for somewhere in the landscape he then knew, where he could be taken out to familiar places, although this meant more travelling for people to visit. Other family members agreed to this.

Focusing inquiry

We swung into action. I got back from the workshop on Friday afternoon. On Saturday we spent hours online looking at potential care homes, reading reports on institutional inspection visits and what these had found. In this unfamiliar world how to judge the comparative importance of a frayed carpet or a missing care plan?

On Sunday, we set out to visit five care homes, printed table in hand on which we had summarised key information, with a list of questions we wanted to ask, including about availability of rooms. We took sandwiches and supplies. We took notes as we went along, tracking our impressions; sat in the car between visits eating and talking.

We travelled back home, tired, emotionally exhausted, bombarded by images, sights and smells; shocked by some of the stages of ageing we had seen, spying our own mortality; confronted by our grief at losing the Jo we had known. We were impressed by the compassion of some of the care workers, noted the exhausted faces of others. One had looked especially tired, doing their paperwork after the busyness of Sunday lunch. We typed notes into our table: what we had seen, factors for and against. We realised how fleeting impressions affected our views: a resident in one home trying to gain the carer's attention but receiving no response; the uniform furniture in the home where residents were not allowed to take their own. Having to share our impressions, as another cycle of experimenting, encouraged us to set things out more fully. If we could articulate and share our sense-making we could also review it critically. We found we could identify first and second choice quite easily and rule two out completely. We emailed the table to other relatives for their opinions. Other people agreed; one visited the first choice to form their own view and agreed again.

Robbed of his mobility, Jo became increasingly housebound. Visiting mid afternoon one day we found him cowering in the hallway in his pyjamas, a vacant, suspicious look. We thought that his eating was even more limited than before, that he was quite likely no longer cleaning the house. We still occasionally wondered if we should intervene, but did not tarry long on such questioning. We were focused instead on how to do 'well' what we felt we had to, discussing what that might mean in the circumstances.

And so we stepped into the next phase: on Monday the 20th Morris took Jo to see the care home ('I am *not* coming here' he said, sitting in their lounge, drinking tea). We secured a place, on a month's probation. Washing and mending favourite clothes and cautiously buying some new ones, name-tagging; selecting the furniture to take.

Three weeks later, a last lunch with other relatives at the house, on the weekend marked for Jo's departure, at the dining table Esme and Jo had had made for them, and had so well provided with excellent home cooked food and hospitality over the years. The story now, two weeks of 'Rest and Recuperation' to give him a break. It was not clear what he knew, thought.

After lunch, Jo paused in the doorway between kitchen and dining room and said 'It's the end of an era'. And we all paused and opened to him, but did not quite know what to say, except to affirm, 'my goodness, yes it is!' Our tears on his behalf, but also on our own. It seemed a moment of unconscious lucidity. How immensely practical we then had to be, as well as living how it felt.

We all went to the care home, moved in familiar furniture, ornaments, framed pho-tographs, books. Tried to settle Jo, ply him with cups of tea. We felt the softness of the net around us. We smiled hesitantly in passing at other residents, not knowing how or if to connect.

That evening, we enlisted the help of the neighbour to catch the freedom loving tomcat in the house, so he could go to the cattery for four weeks, and could be returned if Jo's probation did not work out. We went down town for a pint of only so-so cider but keen to sit somewhere else amidst the bustle, emptied a bit, full of impressions, before the tasks of the next day.

Supporters in inquiry

Living each next step takes an open kind of threaded attention, seeking a sense of the grain of what is happening, and being questioning and challenging about what seems to be going on, or implied. Along the way we especially appreciated people who were also into inquiry in their own distinctive ways. Jeffrey the social worker had been. The care home manager was too, in a relaxed way, offering timely non-intrusive comments. Some weeks later, when Jo was still unsure where he was – or rather he was sure at any given time that he was back at school or about to be drafted to a new billet (and would go there by bike), or was concerned that he had not recently had a letter from his parent – I asked the manager whether she thought it would help to show him on the map where he was and explain. The manager asked 'Can I be cheeky?' and kindly suggested that there were plenty of cues – lots of elderly people around, nurses in uniform – that he could decipher as being in a care home, should he choose, and that I could leave him to his views of the world.

How do we know if inquiry of this kind is successful? This is always a testing question. But when Jo said how much he loved the view of the hills from his new room, it seemed some small affirmation for keeping him in that landscape rather than transplanting him.

After a few weeks, some of Jo's clothes and possessions were missing. This was partly the laundry service, but also he had wandered round leaving books and other items where he wished, with no sense of boundaries about his allocated space. We were initially upset, especially about the new clothes, which he would not therefore recognise as his anyway. We wondered if it was really a safe enough space. We asked this openly amongst ourselves as family, hearing back the answer 'yes' in different forms as people shared their experiences. The expertise and caring of the home's staff and management had especially impressed people. We decided we had to let go some notions about possessions, but we also found safer places for those with sentimental meanings we did not want to become mislaid. Now we knew the local conditions of life we could act accordingly. Most of Jo's possessions reappeared, although he was not consistently dressed in his own clothes.

After a month the care home manager reviewed Jo's 'probation' and said that they were willing to accept him as a permanent resident. Morris asked again 'is this what we think we should do?' This was a discomforting and fundamental question to raise then. We had been following a path, and it felt too far down the line and unsettling to review it. A few of us did try to pause and reflect, briefly. By then we could see no alternative; we thought that returning Jo to his house was clearly not a viable option. We moved the cat on to a friendly foster home.

Once we thought Jo safe, we could be more curious about how the world looked to him, and about whether we could puzzle some of that out from what he said.

What happened?

Jo lived for several years in the care home. He seemed to feel safe and contained there; he connected with some of the other residents. After a short while we stopped trying to take him out for trips, as that did not seem important to him. The staff were always friendly and caring when we visited, engaging with any questions we had. Jo died after a short illness at the home, in his own bed.

Reviewing principles and practices of living life as inquiry

Some themes emerged through our conversations and had phrasing we could hold on to as 'guidelines' in living this experience as explicit, shared inquiry. These are listed below and connect to the Dimensions of inquiry explored in Part II and other material in the book. We found that what we were doing as inquiry was:

Taking initiatives and treating what happened as information. We tried to be appropriate in what we did, but did not have to be right. We were interested, impressed, for example, in Jo's capacity to return his life to the shape he preferred, despite our valiant attempts to 'help' him.

Taking an attitude of inquiry. This was our primary motif for what we were doing, and we often reaffirmed this approach in how we framed our actions and questioning to other people. This seemed to make sense to some people, but not perhaps to others. We had then to live with being misunderstood, considered a little strange.

Putting information into systems and watching sense-making unfold. For example, in our ongoing 'reviews' we wrote up notes and circulated these to other members of the family with questions and ideas for potential implications. Others reciprocated, answering back to what we had sent, or starting their own string of inquiry.

Working through feedback loops: using those already available or connecting up new loops. For example, with the GP, we 'answered back' to them in a letter, rather than verbally, so that the exchange would become more formal, and needed a written answer.

Paying attention to where 'system' boundaries were being drawn or enacted. We were thus testing for inclusion in the circle of those willing to be inquiring together and in the circle of those involved in, caring about, the action. For example, we sought to work alongside the neighbour rather than draw a boundary around us as family. We also engaged with the GP for their long-term connection with Jo rather than purely in a current medical capacity. We initially thought of Margaret as a guardian of the current situation, as Jo had depicted her. When we tested this we found that she was more open to inquiry, and so we invited her too into our questioning.

Living and respecting multiple ways of knowing. We took this approach ourselves and framed our questioning to elicit this kind of engagement in others, especially paying attention to emotions – and allowing for how they affect sense-making and potential action.

Following and respecting shifts in energy. This was often very demanding, for example when a day would become overwhelmed by our feelings of grief about what was happening to Jo and our puzzlement about how to act with integrity, and we would need to take extra care of ourselves, recognise our vulnerabilities.

Questioning and inviting views. This might have seemed strange to other people involved. The home care agency were not adept at working in this way, it seemed. But the social worker and care home manager were.

Considering how overt it is valuable or possible to be. I realised as we went along that an approach such as Torbert's 'frame, advocate, illustrate, inquire' can sometimes seem too challenging and clarity-seeking in murky, unclear circumstances which have to be lived with as they are. We noticed Jo had his somewhat indirect ways of replying to the issues we were raising. These were not, however, framings we could open to mutual discussion.

Often playing wait and see. Despite our urgent sense of concern, we soon realised that we could not hurry what we were doing. At times it was difficult to sit with uncertainty, for example when we were concerned about Jo driving, but we felt we had to do this. We learnt that if you sit with a situation long enough, it moves on, and finds its own path for doing so, which is then 'instructive' in some way. Working in this way involved allowing time, paying attention to pacing, considering what is 'timely'. And more speedy action could then arise, be considered appropriate.

Paying attention to who contains and how to contain ongoing inquiry. We encountered the issues of who holds the field when focal actors are inquiring. Doing it ourselves created challenges sometimes, especially when one of us was off alone with professional staff who did not seem that respectful of multiple questioning. How inquiring might be seen by others was a continuing issue. When both of us were there we could shift roles to engage in mutual containing, a heterarchic approach. See PART II: **Inquiry in action: Creating and protecting spaces for inquiry.**

We were seeking conditions in which anyone could ask questions of purpose and strategy. When the care home manager asked me 'Can I be cheeky?', in response to my wish to explain to Jo where he was geographically, this seemed a generative sign of us negotiating the space for inquiry at that time.

Writer's footnote – life patterns link

In an inquiry of this kind, I have a sense of what might be termed potential traces, as patterns of engagement unfold with their histories of previous relationships between those involved, alongside their current impulses, tendencies, concerns. Given the long-term family, and neighbourly, relationships in this story, the potential for our histories together to influence inquiries is obvious. As an embedded inquirer, I am seeking to pay attention to these potential traces in how I see, think, feel and act. I am especially interested in whether I am unreflectively replicating traces and historic patterns, when I might be able to respond afresh to the situation, and might then be able to act more 'appropriately', reviewing how I might judge this. Of course I might not be able to respond afresh, and wonder if I can at least notice this.

Such issues are especially obvious in terms of differing views about whether, and if so how, we should intervene in Jo's life, and how we then interpret what different people say, perhaps assigning them motivations, or taking an habitual stance in relation to their views. Between my partner and myself there is a long history, with all its foibles, of working alongside each other on emotionally charged and practically demanding issues. For example, was there an element of me being action-woman in relation to Morris, taking things on, seeking out possibilities for what we could *do* as systemic tests?

There are probably glimpses in this account of these issues and potentialities. I have chosen not to amplify them, partly for reasons of confidentiality, but also because doing so might fix what were only fleeting glimpses and possibilities in the experience itself.

PART VI

CODA

This part of the book contains two loosely connected pieces. The first is an example of ongoing writing as inquiry. The second offers some brief closing reflections.

ONGOING INQUIRY: WELL, I WON'T BE DOING THAT AGAIN

Writing note

This piece was written early autumn 2014 at a writing retreat with two learning group colleagues to explore a resonant phrase I had found myself saying repeatedly during previous weeks, treating this as a gateway into inquiry. This is an example of embarking on a piece of reflective writing to check my pulse in a way, to hear myself speak and see whether there are issues that need further consideration. The piece also captures some of the everyday ways in which my life at that time was adjusting, taking new tones, and how I was engaging in this with curiosity and inquiry.

As I started writing I wondered whether this example might have some place in this book. So I avoided giving much 'sensuous detail' (in Freefall Writing terms) as that might go beyond my right to tell my own story and trespass into revealing the stories of others. Being somewhat generic is therefore a writing choice I made.

The version presented here is slightly changed from the original for clarity, and two paragraphs that I now think 'too much information' have been omitted. In effect 'retirement' has been even less clear-cut than I anticipated. One emerging theme from the writing contributed to my shifting perspective. My strong attachment to sustainability related networks and colleagues was clearly expressed. I have stayed actively engaged with these, even accepting a second invitation to join the subcommittee that I mention below I had previously declined.

Transitional inquiry: autumn 2014

A key channel of inquiry in my life right now is how to conduct myself with integrity in the closing months of my formal academic career. I have been well aware of this inquiry for the last 6 months or so, and now, with 3 months to go, it has become more figural, an integrated aspect of every day.

I find myself thinking, and sometimes saying 'well, I won't be doing that again', so far always with a sense of relief and amusement. I notice and am curious about this letting go, watching the process. Does it devalue what I have previously treasured, or remedially reassign some things that have always been trivial and tiresome, but which I had treated with too much deference? I also notice its implications for how I conduct myself with colleagues, who will be doing 'that' again. My jubilation is not intended as a slur on their need to maintain future commitment. Although I do find people's envy reassuring that I do not have to be too bereft.

For example, at the end of last academic year, our tutor team of six reviewed the undergraduates' feedback on our management consulting course. It is a pedagogically thoughtful module: two terms, compulsory. Plenty of learning opportunities, but challenging real life clients, assignments that track the learning, no exams, group dynamics issues to engage with to make good-enough consulting teams. And each year, whilst we can see students' development and most of the clients are extremely happy, the students' feedback is mixed. They tell us what we should have done differently, like drop the lectures that seemed to them irrelevant (well …) and each year some of the students who did not get the grades they hoped for criticise the course strongly (aided by an online feedback system which allows extensive commenting). And we, the tutor team, feel somewhat mis-represented and deflated, and vow to try even harder again next year. Well, I won't be doing that again.

And as I mark and double mark 10 Masters dissertations at 15,000 words each (mindful of the relationships I have with some of the students, developed over four months in a learning set, coaching their development), and I engage with colleagues to arrive at final grades, a collegial and thoughtful process as usual – well, I won't be doing that again.

I say it with especial heart about the sense-less admin, the form-filling, the hoops to be gone through, the demands already to know publications building towards another UK Research Assessment scrutiny in 2020; the signs of how academic life has become constrained, and often trivialised.

A key dimension of this inquiry is how I now am in the everyday life of the Department. For example, I can see that some things that seemed important until only recently, tensions and difficulties that plague our lives, feel less important to me. I find it hard to muster engagement with them, whilst appreciating keenly that my colleagues are concerned. I notice and adjust my stance, lean in a little to where they are placed, listen to their views, but also see if my new-found distance has anything to offer. In meetings I am even more watchful than I used to be about whether some younger colleagues want to speak, not wanting to inadvertently step in front of them. I can still be strong in debating with more senior colleagues though too.

Just the other day we had a monthly Departmental Meeting. I still feel part enough of the Department to go, pleased to welcome new colleagues, interested to join in discussions about strategic developments. And how much to speak, when and how to offer a view, seem even more questions than they always have been. I noticed that I was saying 'we', but had a pause of reserve in my mind, especially when we were projecting into the future, what 'we' might become. I had little to say in conversations about what courses the Department might develop. Some of the possible futures would not be my choice, but there will yet be protracted discussions, and people will work their ways into what they might want, the potentialities and pitfalls. I mentioned a couple of potential unanticipated consequences that it would seem negligent not to say, trying to avoid the whiff of 'we tried that before, and it did not work', which is so deadening.

I am leaving at a time when cross-campus efforts to promote sustainability in research, teaching and the University's own practice are coming to a new stage of flourishing. Trying to play some part in this has been passionate work for me. I have already had to decline membership of a new cross-Uni committee that only a year ago I would have jumped at. Losing that 'playground' and contact with the people who I feel alongside is a loss to the richness of my life, to connection to meaningful work. And one I do feel.

Sometimes I am struck by sudden emotions. I do not know now when something will strike me as sad or a potential loss. It happens most around the cross-campus sustainability networks and other specific colleagues with whom I feel a sense of collegial alignment. When emotions bubble through, I usually pause to notice them, and take stock of what they imply. But they are typically not so specific that they need expressing at that moment in that place, in my view. They seem to me webbed into a wider sense of how I have shaped my life, found some significant meaning through what can be termed 'work' (a complex notion in an academic life) and the networks of people I therefore engage with. And I do notice that some sorts of relationship will stop being possible as this life of employment ends.

There is another side to this that I mention briefly to show the often both/and qualities of living life as inquiry. My academic role puts me often in the position of facilitator and helper, especially of people's learning and more general develop-ment. I have filled out this aspect of the role possibilities, wanting to be 'of service', to contribute, as mentioned elsewhere, to the world being a better place. I notice in terms of tendencies, that this wish to be helpful and encourage people to be their fuller selves is one I adopt more generally in life, and have to treat with caution. I imagine my potential to be a roving 'helper', and might need to watch this as my work role provides fewer such requirements, possibilities. Systemically I do not think an over-eagerness to be helpful 'wise' for me or others.

Given the cycles of the academic year, I am not now responsible for passing on many activities to other people. It is a great delight and relief that three colleagues are taking on the Sustainability Responsibility Plus network that some of us started on my arrival in February 2008, so its contribution to cross-campus networking for sustainability will continue.

And some relationships will continue. I cannot yet imagine not being in touch with some of my colleagues and what we next do, whether our future relationship relates to their work, will need to unfold. I think I might make an unconvincing col-league when I am not interested in the challenges they encounter every day. And I might not want to 'wind myself up' by staying engaged with ongoing plot-lines which I can see are energising for them, but look more distorted or misguided from my more distanced viewpoint. I anticipate that 'you should not take that so seri-ously' could be both a well-intended offering and seem lacking in empathy.

One of the most open aspects of this inquiry is that I do not know what to say to people. It has taken me some time to say 'I am retiring at the end of December'. Whilst it has been 'true' for months now, I have had to speak myself into saying it with conviction and without qualification. And I may well have some continuing role with the School. And when people ask what I will do, I am at even more of a loss. 'I want not to be so busy, to have life arise more', I say. 'I don't want to get involved in organising things, in having to be goal-directed'. I am so looking forward to having space in which interests could arise and I could have the chance to follow them through a little. I have glimpses of possible interests: literature courses, immersion learning French, writing what engages me rather than in voices I think I should adopt, spending more time with family and friends. But I do not want to turn these into projects, plans and targets. I want to escape that energy of following projects through, that I am told I can be so good at. Letting possibilities surface, take shape, gain energy, have their own momentum, rather than needing pushing along, is the next phase of inquiry. And I don't want to be pushing other people along either. I can feel a phase of wilful un-responsibility (in the service of systemic responsibility) coming on.

And so this might seem a rather incoherent leave-taking. And what previously seemed important is fragmenting, so criteria of what is worthwhile are on the move. Including those criteria to apply to this book and what voices it takes, and how it is positioned, in what worlds it is positioned even. Do I try to hold things steady? Or accept that migration is life, and live through and with the shifts I am experiencing? I have to choose the latter, with curiosity.

IN REFLECTION

As I have worked on this book, I have expected that perhaps ideas for a closing Reflection might arise. In this final week before I send the book to the publisher it seems that few have done so. That is fine. I will, then, be brief. I will work with the principles of speaking just so much and no more outlined in PART II: **Disciplines of inquiry:** Speaking inquiry as potentially vital process.

I do know what I do **not** want to do here.

I do not want to summarise key messages and lessons for first person action research and living life as inquiry. That is not how I hold these approaches. My attempts to communicate images, principles and practices of inquiry have already appeared. I trust that you will have created your own sense from engaging with the various sorts of material in the book, and from taking this into conversation with your own ideas and practices. Just as you will leave a city, such as Paris, having explored with guidebook alongside you, you will have found your distinctive way through.

I do not want to extol the virtues of living life as inquiry. I hope I have given a more conditional picture.

I do not want to explain and clarify how the principles and practices of inquiry outlined in the earlier sections of the book are shown in the stories in Part V. The stories offer a more diffuse sensibility of inquiry in action. Further clarification would be antithetical.

I do not want to expand on my concerns about climate change and social inequality, and the challenges of how to pay these due attention. These are threaded through the book, as they are through my life. Living at this time calls us to have some response which goes beyond 'business as usual'. I could reflect on whether living life as inquiry is an adequate response. How we would know is open to critical questioning. Current times call me, us, to live with courage, to question compulsive action that might become 'more of the same' and ask us to develop our capacities to discern this. In my view first person action research and living life as inquiry have a part to play. But they also incorporate challenges and complexities.

I do not want to highlight a few aspects of the collage of offerings here, as that would bring those into focus and risk losing a sense of the wider, somewhat diffuse, array.

One image for a closing reflection has however arisen repeatedly, encouraging me to trust it. It is of this book bringing together into one place so much aspiration for living an inquiring life that it has a density and intensity that might become unbalanced, might lose the pliability, playfulness and choice this notion is also seeking. I therefore offer a slight counter-movement. It is impossible to live fully as this collected work might seem to suggest. There will always be shadow sides in seeking to do so, although these too are part of the richness of life we have to engage. I want to advocate yet again that we should hold bold intentions for living life as inquiry lightly, work with them dynamically, let ourselves be surprised. And, whatever first person inquiry means for each of us, we need also to take care of ourselves.

APPENDIX A

SCANNING ARENAS OF ACTION IN CHANGE

Combining inquiry, systemic thinking and attention to issues of power, and paying attention to ideas such as tempered radicalism (Meyerson and Scully, 1995), as we seek to contribute to change we can consider the range of arenas of activity in which we might be involved. See PART III: **Working with academic literatures**

People can become very focused on doing the core 'work' for which they have passion and commitment – that of sustainability or diversity, for example. Whilst this is vitally important, it could be helpful to attend to other dimensions of the potential for change. Unless this happens the core work can become unsupported, more difficult to influence, and can in extreme cases contribute to exhaustion or burnout. Scanning other arenas of potential activity and reviewing what might be possible can perhaps help to balance out this tendency.

The framework below is offered as a base for inquiry into ongoing action. It is not a formula for success. Acting for change is a gritty process. There are shadow sides to any initiative, and quite likely unintended consequences which we later encounter and have to work with. So this approach comes with a significant health warning. I apply ideas of this kind to my own activities. I sometimes find myself in trouble; you may do too.

Arenas to consider as ongoing inquiry include:

- Engaging with your core interests and activities – strategically as well as tactically. For example, judging timing, whether to use informal or formal processes, whether to seek 'small wins' that then help future change attempts

- Maintaining your own role, position, organisational credibility and access to diverse sources of power

- Building relationships, widely

- Communicating about your interests and activities, and as inquiry; engaging in dialogue – with those who are like-minded and those who take different views. Considering how overt to be. You may not need to seek permission, but the rule of 'no surprises' may apply

- Building organisational capacities to consider the kinds of issues you want to challenge or introduce. For example, offering frames and languages relating to sustainability so that these later become resources people can use

- Helping to create the conditions for emergence and change. For example, linking up feedback loops so that information reaches places it has not done before. If capacities for inquiry flourish, you will need to accept that other people may well then take initiatives too, and you might not be included

- Influencing fresh articulations of organisational strategy, policy and accounting; laying down rubrics that can become future resources or metrics to invoke for change

- Using your organisational base to work beyond organisational boundaries. For example, becoming a member of a standard-setting initiative

- Working outside the organisation to build credibility that transfers inside. For example, winning awards and recognition for your organisation for its equality related activities

- Finding support and mentoring; this might well include peer mentoring given who is active in promoting change

- Paying attention to your own identity issues and sanity – allowing yourself space to network with like-minded people, refresh your energies, find new ways to articulate what you are doing, rest and refresh

- Engaging in 'inner work' such as reflecting on your purposes and approaches to change, aided by critical friends; giving yourself space to remember who you are and what matters to you

You can consider:

- How you are working across the range of potential activities

- If there are any arenas you are ignoring and why

- Whether there are personal, institutional and other patterns that encourage you to address or not to address some activities – for example, not to take time for yourself – and whether you want to make different choices

You may seek to position yourself appropriately, for now, to draw on your talents and history and have what you consider scope for impact. This might be inside 'mainstream' organisations and professions, or outside, or on the boundaries as inside-outsider. There are also choices about how overt or covert to be in your views and agendas.

Dunphy et al.'s summary evokes the conditionality and challenges involved:

> As change agents and change leaders, we are only one source of influence in a complex changing reality. Nevertheless let us not underestimate the potential transformative power that we represent … Change leadership involves owning our own power and using it responsively and responsibly. (Dunphy et al., 2007: 322)

Whilst acting as self-appointed change agents to our organisations, society, and the planet it is also advisable for us to consider how to conduct ourselves with humility, curiosity, craft, courage and care for self as significant ancillary dimensions of inquiry.

Might Herb Shepard's classic 1st 'Rule of Thumb for Change Agents' apply?

'Stay alive' unless you want this 'cause to be your last'. (Shepard, 1975: 1)

Or might it be too late for this luxury?

APPENDIX B

PRESENTING FIRST PERSON INQUIRY FOR MASTERS AND DOCTORAL WORK

Whilst first person inquiry approaches integrate quality processes, if you are presenting your researching for an academic qualification, it is especially important to be able to demonstrate that you have paid attention to quality in appropriate ways. Given the politics surrounding epistemological and methodological choices, and the vigour with which these can be played out, this brief chapter addresses some key concerns for those undertaking first person inquiries for Masters and doctoral research. (This could apply to some undertaking undergraduate studies, with due consideration of course framings, formats and published quality criteria.) Other relevant material is threaded throughout this book.

Living life as inquiry challenges some prevailing conventions of scholarship, as do other action-oriented methodologies (Raelin, 2009), and thus may encounter political boundaries and shifting landscapes of acceptability. If you are adopting an action research approach for your Masters or doctoral research, framing and positioning your work is vitally important, in relation to the wider landscape, and taking account of your own local institutional circumstances. The politics of epistemology can be highly contentious.

Framing your research involves exploring epistemology and methodology to affirm the kind of space you want to think and work in. It is an active approach, identifying, generating and addressing quality criteria of your own choosing. If you do not, tacit conventions and fantasies of inappropriate notions of validity (such as objectivity, avoidance of 'bias', reliability) might well appear largely unbidden, for you and those who assess your work, but put the research venture somehow on the defensive. There is now a wealth of resource to help. This includes Sage Handbooks which are key signposting and boundary expanding publications: for example, Denzin and Lincoln (1994, 2000, 2005b, 2011) for qualitative research, and Bradbury (2015), Cooke and Wolfram Cox (2005) and Reason and Bradbury (2001, 2008) for action research. Autoethnography is also a related discipline for first person inquiry, with its own literatures (Ellis and Bochner, 2000; Holman Jones et al., 2013; Learmonth and Humphreys, 2012; Sparkes, 2002, 2012).

Sometimes people are ashamed of their inquiry processes, and think it best to keep quiet about them. When discussing and writing their Masters or doctoral dissertations, they will pretend more objectivity, linearity, rationality and prior knowledge of what 'it' was all about than they were actually working with. But this can reduce to convention what might otherwise be nuanced, interesting richness, and evades inherent complexities about seeking to know, which might be highly relevant to the subjects being explored. Disguise and falling between paradigms are dangerous possibilities that compromise people's chances of making the 'contribution' that a thesis needs to develop, and of reaching appropriate quality standards.

The quality criteria for Masters and doctoral research can be engaged with assertively and innovatively, as students frame and place their work. From my experience, key generic criteria are that the work should be:

- conceptually rich
- well located in understandings of appropriate literature(s) and theories
- aware in relation to research paradigms and appropriately located
- methodologically well-grounded
- grounded in sustained 'fieldwork' of some appropriate kind
- critically reflective in relation to all aspects
- making theoretical and methodological contributions

It is, however, very important to check local articulations of criteria and consider, and state explicitly, how your work addresses these. In theoretical terms, for example, action research dissertations often occur at intersections rather than being bounded by only one clearly specified 'field of knowledge', and this positioning, the choices involved, and what conceptual depth therefore means will need explicating.

Those developing action research dissertations also need to consider what they take to be 'data' and ensure that this relates to any claims they are making for their work. For example, many first person action researchers think that they have improved their practice in some way through their inquiries. It is weak just to say this, as an assertion of learning, and stronger to have 'data' of some congruent kind to support it. This could include thoughtful self-referring criteria of judgement, such as evidence of their increased capacity to operate and express their views in a given situation. But it is helpful to include other people's feedback in some ways, although this is not objective, given different perspectives, and may too require critically reflective commentary. See PART II: **Inquiry in action:** Quality processes: working with feedback.

Addressing issues of quality requires, again, active scoping, choice, creation and articulation. Resources for considering potential criteria of quality include the Handbooks mentioned above, articles in compatible journals and the works of innovators in their fields such as Lather (1993).

I hope that you will have choices, taking account of but not being subservient to the context you are operating in. You also have the potential to contribute to re-framing scholarship.

But in some contexts pretending you took a more conventional approach *is* a better kind of story to tell, politically, and your sense that this is required might well be right. It is wise to check this out through active questioning of those shaping and holding the space, such as research supervisors and programme directors, and through experimentation in the ongoing processes of dissertation writing. If, for example, a research supervisor is not familiar with action research and suspicious of first person inquiry, developing explanations which convince them of validity can be a constructive and educative process.

Working with first person action research and affirming this paradigmatically, there are still many choices of boundaries in seeking to represent inquiry in scholarly contexts.

If you have experienced inquiry that has lots of texture and learning that seems deep and meaningful, a belief in some form of 'authenticity' might suggest that this is the truth of the inquiry and that you should report it all, and literally, as your data and evidence, no matter that you may well be espousing an inter-pretivist or social constructionist epistemology. But full disclosure could be termed 'naive humanist realism', an apparent injunction to tell 'everything' in order to be 'honest'. This can be daunting, and unsettling, threatening your sense of voice. There are important issues here, but there are also potential legacies of positivist thinking, which warrant critical review.

You have the right to keep your boundaries, and to say this and the nature of the choices being made. Often it is the *nature* of what happened and the quality processes engaged in that are more relevant to the quality of inquiry and sense-making than what 'actually' happened. You do not have to tell it all, but you can use your inquiry journey material as a source for the way you then write. You can then point to other sources of data, and keep them private. This is especially relevant to those writing Masters and doctoral theses, but applies to any form of inquiry and the need to 'account', including to the kind of story you choose to tell family and friends.

In my own writing there are sometimes succinct phrases that signal this pro-cess of drawing boundaries. For example, in the first chapter of *Women Managers: Travellers in a Male World* (Marshall, 1984), I noted how welcome but also unset-tling it had been to engage with radical (rather than reform) feminist ideas, as I developed my sense of a feminist perspective. The text is not that specific in illustrating what this meant. People who have had similar experiences might well fill out its cryptic phrases. I thus sought to do some brief justice to how fundamentally disturbing that time had been and how all my ways of relating to others had been affected.

Core concerns are what notions of quality, rigour and validity can be applied to first person inquiry. In some institutions there is a long track record of accrediting such work. But also times change, and departments and schools in which this work has been developed wane. I have lived the issues of what it means to play this edge between inquiry as a lifetime practice and seeking to bring it into the academy, opening the latter to review. The wider landscape has shifted too. Right now, space for innovation feels curtailed. Academics in the UK are under extreme pressure to publish in 'highly rated international' (mostly USA) journals, with their, more positivist, rules for writing and for social science. The spaces for experimentation, action accounts, multiple ways of knowing, and experimental text seem to have contracted. This is a source of regret for me, and many colleagues. These are issues in the backcloth against which I am writing this book. See PART IV: **Writing as representation**.

APPENDIX C

FICTIONALISING INQUIRY ACCOUNTS: AN EXAMPLE

Advocating for corporate responsibility as systemic intervention

As discussed in PART IV: **Writing as representation:** Developing writing, sometimes there are significant ethical or confidentiality challenges which curtail what can be reported. One possible strategy is to invent accounts that do 'justice' in chosen ways to the research. This piece is an example of trying out this approach. I started writing with themes relating to acting for change for sustainability in mind, and wanted to show some micro practices of undertaking this as inquiry. I had an image for the opening scene and then let the story unfold imaginatively. The main text was written in one sitting, with a final paragraph added later to round off the vignette.

In this vignette I intended to show:

- Multiple layers of attention open to inquiry simultaneously

- That control-oriented behaviour is not appropriate (but that those acting for change do need some other forms of forcefulness)

- Being in inquiry with sustainability agendas involves wilful vulnerability

- Nothing is ever 'done' or achieved, and 'finished'

Another meeting and maybe another opportunity. She collected her copious papers, now neatly ordered from the work she had done on them the night before, and headed for the board room on level 4. Ahead of time. Outside, set out on trays, the flasks of coffee and hot water, the random assortment of teabags, and the short, slightly stingy, white cups. But she had taken her green tea already, had not wanted to arrive there needy.

People filed into the room, well known and not so known. Andy smiled encouragement across to her, but it was too late by then for them to check any details. She chose her place, half way down the table, with a view out across the woods, and with key players in easy sight-line.

Apologies, Minutes, Matters Arising. Slowly it seemed, rehearsing what had already taken ample enough time. And so to today's agenda. An update from the Chair about meetings they had attended, a financial update, some uncertainties, but not cause for concern. And then to their item. Corporate social responsibility. Andy opened, Anne watched round the room for potential reactions.

Andy: Anne and I have been reviewing our situation in relation to corporate social responsibility commitments, and looking at what our competitors are now doing. Whilst we have a lot of activity, and quite a lot of commitment in different areas of the organisation, we do not make CSR part of our core message of who we are, as an organisation, as a brand. We wanted to discuss this, to test out whether people are willing to make more overt commitment, to develop our activities. If there is interest there are various ways we could consider doing this. Anne has been doing some analyses.

She passes round a summary one-page spreadsheet, listing organisations they think of as competitors and what they are currently doing in the name of CSR. Triple Bottom Line reporting, new product design minimising materials, maximising potential re-use, supply chain initiatives, fair trade, volunteering projects and so on. Set out like this it does seem rather a mish-mash. She does not want to lose the message in the detail.

Anne: So that is a summary of key activities companies like us are engaging in. In the top row of the table we have shown what we are doing. We got an award for our volunteering scheme last year, so that was good publicity. But many people are now looking for sustainability initiatives that are strategically integrated into core business. And we can't say that we do that that well, or that we join up what we are doing.

In considering what to say they have paid a lot of attention to framing. Now it is more tricky. Ideally they would now inquire, open discussion up to people's information and views. Hope that these work their way through and arrive somewhere close enough to commitment to do more, even generate ideas about what 'more' might be in these circumstances. But their previous experiences of this space make them wary. There are a couple of clear spoken senior staff who think CSR an unnecessary added extra, at best a 'nice to have' in their language, that the company cannot afford. And the 10–15 minutes they have for this agenda item curtails the space. So should they move straight to advocacy, they have debated. But it is also uncomfortably cold pushing ahead without knowing how their opening pitch has gone down today. And in this slight pause …

'Well you know my views. We have discussed this before and nothing has materially changed. A lot of activities listed on this spreadsheet are green-wash at best, costing them a bomb in PR budget. Or they won't outlast the people currently pushing them. For example, XX overstretched themselves with CSR reporting and generating ambitious improvement targets.'

An example oft repeated. Best not to respond, that would be picking a fight and on narrow ground.

Another speaker picks up the thread: 'I hear they are going to tone the whole process down this year, subsume CSR into their main report, play down targets. People will fill in surveys saying that they are green consumers but it doesn't affect their buying behaviour that much, actually. I think we are fine as we are. No evidence that we should panic.'

Some nods around the room. Some faces close in a little. Will any of the people who they've lobbied in advance and who seemed supportive speak up? Would it be politic to ask them or put them uncomfortably on the spot? Another pause ...

'Well, I agree with Andy and Anne that the time has come to take more of a stand on sustainability. We've been looking at climate data and projections. It is negligent to carry on with business as usual. And interviewing for the graduate scheme last week, I was impressed with how many students asked us what we are doing, said they want to work for an organisation that is doing its bit on CSR.'

A ripple of adjustment around the room. This was from a former ally of the first commentator. Something seems to have shifted, just a little. Will it be enough?

The Chair allows another few people to speak. Views seem fairly evenly spread ...

Then the Chair asks: 'Well, did you say you had some proposals for us to consider?'

Time is passing, have they left it late to introduce another spreadsheet with a table of possible actions? They hand it round anyway, mentally adjusting what they will say – the two minute rather than five minute version. They have given pros and cons: of joining YYYY, of signing up to the Global Compact, of inviting the design department to attend a cradle-to-cradle workshop and consider their product range in these terms ... and so on ...

Inquiry ...

How to proceed? Review at next meeting? If they push for agreement now, will it be minimal, for the easily chosen options? If bolder moves are suggested will they fall apart within a week because wider agreement has not been reached, underpinned? Can they keep on waiting patiently and presenting options without feeling compromised, tired, and that they should look for new employment?

They have briefed the Chair, that if there is sufficient interest at the meeting, it would help to have outcomes for moving forward that take the form of experiments, consultation, learning processes, that can be bold enough, but keep on adapting and unfolding as they go. Did the Chair understand what they meant, the systemic view of the world from which they were coming?

It seems they have, enough ...

The Chair: 'Well, it seems we are not all in agreement, but there seems to me sufficient interest too for us to consider some of these options. Rather than throw it back to Anne and Andy I think a wider group should take a look and come back to us with some proposals, costed of course. Can I have some volunteers?'

And there are some volunteers. Timescales are set, a first meeting planned.

And so on to the next Agenda item.

Anne sits back, temporarily tired now. It's difficult to concentrate for a while, as she replays the last 15 minutes in her head. Next it will be interesting to see where the energies are, what ideas people have, how commitment can be opened up. She is sure the potential is there, and equally sure that it cannot be hurried, that she and

Andy need to work at opening up spaces for discussion and learning rather than to swing into action with 'and this is one [a CSR plan] we made earlier'. Perhaps, though, it is time for a celebratory walk round outside the building, a view of the hills.

And later in the day, she and Andy will check in, review their approach, talk inquiring process for the next steps, as ever holding alongside their broader horizon of concern about the significance of climate change, the yawning gap between what companies think bold and what is needed.

The experimental account stops there. There is no spurious sense of achievement. It illustrates how any next step is unpredictable, open to multiple influences ...

REFERENCES

Acker, J. (2004) 'Gender, capitalism and globalization', *Critical Sociology*, 30(1): 17–41.

Allen, S. and Marshall, J. (2015) 'Metalogue: Trying to talk about (un)sustainability – a reflection on experience', *Tamara: Journal for Critical Organization Inquiry*, 13(1–2): 1–13.

Allen, S., Marshall, J. and Easterby-Smith, M. (2015) 'Living with contradictions: The dynamics of senior managers' identity tensions in relation to sustainability', *Organization & Environment*, 28(3): 328–48.

Alvesson, M. and Deetz, S. (2000) *Doing Critical Management Research*. London: Sage Publications.

Argyris, C. and Schön, D.A. (1974) *Theory in Practice: Increasing Professional Effectiveness*. San Francisco, CA: Jossey-Bass.

Argyris, C. and Schön, D.A. (1996) *Organizational Learning II: Theory, Method, and Practice*. Reading, MA: Addison-Wesley.

Argyris, C., Putnam, R. and Smith, D. (1985) *Action Science*. San Francisco, CA: Jossey-Bass.

Bakan, D. (1966) *The Duality of Human Existence*. Boston: Beacon Press.

Banerjee, S.B. (2008) 'Corporate social responsibility: The good, the bad and the ugly', *Critical Sociology*, 34: 51–79.

Banerjee, S.B. (2012) 'A climate for change? Critical reflections on the Durban United Nations Climate Change Conference', *Organization Studies*, 33(12): 1761–86.

Barnes, J. (2012) *The Sense of an Ending*. London: Vintage Books.

Bateson, G. (1973) *Steps to an Ecology of Mind*. London: Paladin Books.

Bateson, G. (1979) *Mind and Nature: A Necessary Unity*. London: Wildwood House.

Bateson, G. (2000) *Steps to an Ecology of Mind*. Chicago: University of Chicago Press.

Bateson, G. and Bateson, M.C. (1987) *Angels Fear: An Investigation into the Nature and Meaning of the Sacred*. London: Rider.

Belenky, M.F., Clinchy, B.M., Goldberger, N.R. and Tarule, J.M. (1986) *Women's Ways of Knowing: The Development of Self, Voice, and Mind*. New York: Basic Books.

Berman, M. (1981) *The Reenchantment of the World: Secular Magic in a Rational Age*. London: Cornell University Press.

Berman, M. (1990) *Coming to Our Senses: Body and Spirit in the Hidden History of the West*. London: Unwin.

Berners-Lee, M. and Clark, D. (2013) *The Burning Question: We can't Burn Half the World's Oil, Coal and Gas, so How do we Quit?* London: Profile Books.

Berry, W. (2012) *New Collected Poems*. Berkeley, CA: Counterpoint.

Bradbury, H. (ed.) (2015) *The Sage Handbook of Action Research*, 3rd Edition. London: Sage Publications.

Briggs, J. (2005) *Virginia Woolf: An Inner Life*. London: Allen Lane.

Calás, M.B. and Smircich, L. (2004) 'Revisiting "dangerous liaisons" or does the "feminine-in-management" still meet "globalization"?', in P.J. Frost, W.R. Nord and L.A. Krefting (eds), *Managerial and Organizational Reality*. New Jersey: Pearson Prentice Hall. pp. 467–81.

Calás, M.B. and Smircich, L. (2006) 'From the "woman's point of view" ten years later: Towards a feminist organization studies', in S.R. Clegg, C. Hardy, T.B. Lawrence and W.R. Nord (eds), *The Sage Handbook of Organization Studies*, 2nd Edition. Thousand Oaks, CA: Sage. pp. 284–345.

Cameron, J. (1992) *The Artist's Way: A Course in Discovering and Recovering Your Creative Self*. New York: Penguin.

Capra, F. (1982) *The Turning Point: Science, Society and the Rising Culture*. London: Wildwood House.

Capra, F. (1996) *The Web of Life: A New Synthesis of Mind and Matter*. London: HarperCollins.

Cassell, C. and Johnson, P. (2006) 'Action research: Explaining the diversity', *Human Relations*, 59(6): 783–814.

Chandler, D. and Torbert, B. (2003) 'Transforming inquiry and action: Interweaving 27 flavors of action research', *Action Research*, 1(2): 133–52.

Charlton, N.G. (2008) *Understanding Gregory Bateson: Mind, Beauty, and the Sacred Earth*. Albany, NY: SUNY Press.

Charmaz, K. (2005) 'Grounded theory in the 21st Century: Applications for advancing social justice studies', in N.K. Denzin and Y.S Lincoln (eds), *The Sage Handbook of Qualitative Research*, 4th Edition. Thousand Oaks, CA: Sage Publications. pp. 507–36.

Clinchy, B.M. (1996) 'Connected and separated knowing: Toward a marriage of two minds', in N.R. Goldberger, J.M. Tarule, B.M. Clinchy and M.F. Belenky (eds), *Knowledge, Difference, and Power: Essays Inspired by Women's Ways of Knowing*. New York: Basic Books. pp. 205–47.

Clough, P. T. (1992) *The End(s) of Ethnography: From Realism to Social Criticism*. Newbury Park, CA: Sage Publications.

Co-Counselling International (UK) (2014) http://www.co-counselling.org.uk/

Coghlan, D. and Brannick, T. (2014) *Doing Action Research in your own Organization*, 4th Edition. London: Sage Publications.

Cook-Greuter, S. (1999) *Postautonomous Ego Development: A Study of Its Nature and Measurement*. Unpublished Harvard University doctoral dissertation, Cambridge MA.

Cooke, B. and Wolfram Cox, J. (eds) (2005) *The Fundamentals of Action Research, Volumes 1 to 4*. London: Sage Publications.

Cunliffe, A.L. and Easterby-Smith, M. (2004) 'From reflection to practical reflexivity: Experiential learning as lived experience', in M. Reynolds and R. Vince (eds), *Organizing Reflection*. Aldershot: Ashgate. pp. 30–46.

Dar, S. and Cooke, B. (2008) *The New Development Management*. London: Zed Books.

Denzin, N.K. and Lincoln, Y.S. (eds) (1994) *The Sage Handbook of Qualitative Research*. Thousand Oaks, CA: Sage Publications.

Denzin, N.K. and Lincoln, Y.S. (eds) (2000) *The Sage Handbook of Qualitative Research*, 2nd Edition. Thousand Oaks, CA: Sage Publications.

Denzin, N.K. and Lincoln, Y.S. (2005a) 'Introduction: The discipline and practice of qualitative research', in N.K. Denzin and Y.S. Lincoln (eds), *The Sage Handbook of Qualitative Research*, 3rd Edition. Thousand Oaks, CA: Sage Publications. pp. 1–32.

Denzin, N.K. and Lincoln, Y.S. (eds) (2005b) *The Sage Handbook of Qualitative Research*, 3rd Edition. Thousand Oaks, CA: Sage Publications.

Denzin, N.K. and Lincoln, Y.S. (eds) (2011) *The Sage Handbook of Qualitative Research*, 4th Edition. Thousand Oaks, CA: Sage Publications.

Doppelt, B. (2003) *Leading Change toward Sustainability: A Change-management Guide for Business, Government and Civil Society*. Sheffield: Greenleaf Publishing.

Dunphy, D.C., Griffiths, A.B. and Benn, S.H. (2007) *Organizational Change for Corporate Sustainability*, 2nd Edition. London: Routledge.

Ellis, C.S. and Bochner, A. (2000) 'Autoethnography, personal narrative, reflexivity: Researcher as subject', in N.K. Denzin and Y.S. Lincoln (eds), *The Handbook of Qualitative Research*, 2nd Edition. Thousand Oaks, CA: Sage Publications. pp. 733–68.

Erfan, A. and Torbert, B. (2015) 'Collaborative developmental action inquiry', in H. Bradbury (ed.), *Sage Handbook of Action Research*, 3rd Edition. Los Angeles: Sage Publications. pp. 64–75.

Etherington, K. (2004) *Becoming a Reflexive Researcher: Using Ourselves in Research*. London: Jessica Kingsley Publishers.

European-American Collaborative Challenging Whiteness (2005) 'When first-person inquiry is not enough: Challenging whiteness through first- and second-person inquiry', *Action Research*, 3(3): 245–61.

Fals Borda, O. (2001) 'Participatory (Action) research in social theory: origins and challenges', in P. Reason and H. Bradbury (eds), *Handbook of Action Research*. London: Sage Publications. pp. 27–37.

Fisher, D., Rooke, D. and Torbert, B. (2003) *Personal and Organisational Transformations through Action Inquiry*, 4th Edition. Boston, MA: Edge/Work Press.

Flood, R.L. (1999) *Rethinking the Fifth Discipline: Learning within the Unknowable*. London: Routledge.

Foster, J. (2015) *After Sustainability: Denial, Hope, Retrieval*. London: Earthscan.

Frame, J. (1999) *The Complete Autobiography*. London: The Women's Press Ltd.

Galliz, K. (1999) 'Kazuo Ishiguro: The Sorbonne Lecture', in B.W. Shaffer and C.F. Wong (eds), *Conversations with Kazuo Ishiguro*. Jackson: University Press of Mississippi. pp. 135–55.

Garud, R., Hardy, C. and Maguire, S. (2007) 'Institutional entrepreneurship as embedded agency: An introduction to the special issue', *Organization Studies*, 28(7): 957–69.

Gaventa, J. and Cornwall, A. (2008) 'Power and knowledge', in P. Reason and H. Bradbury (eds), *The Sage Handbook of Action Research*, 2nd Edition. London: Sage Publications. pp. 172–89.

Gaventa, J. and Cornwall, A. (2015) 'Power and knowledge', in H. Bradbury (ed.), *The Sage Handbook of Action Research*, 3rd Edition. London: Sage Publications. pp. 465–71.

Goldberg, N. (1986) *Writing Down the Bones: Freeing the Writer Within*. Boston, MA: Shambala.

Goldberg, N. (1991) *Wild Mind: Living the Writer's Life*. London: Rider.

Gordon, G. (2007) *Towards Bicultural Competence: Beyond Black and White*. Stoke-on-Trent, UK: Trentham Books.

Guba, E.G. and Lincoln, Y.S. (2005) 'Paradigmatic controversies, contradictions, and emerging confluences', in N.K. Denzin and Y.S. Lincoln (eds), *The Sage Handbook of Qualitative Research*, 3rd Edition. Thousand Oaks, CA: Sage Publications. pp. 191–215.

Gustavsen, B. (2001) 'Theory and practice: the mediating discourse', in P. Reason and H. Bradbury (eds), *Handbook of Action Research*. London: Sage Publications. pp. 17–26.

Hall, E.T. (1977) *Beyond Culture*. Garden City, NY: Anchor Books.

Hardin, G. (1968) 'The tragedy of the commons', *Science*, 162: 1243–8.

Hardy, C. (1994) *Power and Politics in Organizations*. Thousand Oaks, CA: Sage Publications.

Hardy, C. and Clegg, S.W. (2006) 'Some dare call it power', in S.R. Clegg, C. Hardy, T.B. Lawrence and W.R. Nord (eds), *The Sage Handbook of Organization Studies*, 2nd Edition. London: Sage. pp. 754–75.

Hardy, C. and Maguire, S. (2008) 'Institutional entrepreneurship', in R. Greenwood, C. Oliver, K. Sahlin and R. Suddaby (eds), *The Sage Handbook of Organizational Institutionalism*. Thousand Oaks, CA: Sage Publications. pp. 198–217.

Harris, G. (2007) *Seeking Sustainability in an Age of Complexity*. Cambridge: Cambridge University Press.

Henriques, A. and Richardson, J. (eds) (2004) *The Triple Bottom Line: Does It All Add Up? Assessing the Sustainability of Business and CSR*. London: Earthscan.

Heron, J. (1979) *Co-counselling*. Guildford: University of Surrey.

Heron, J. (1996) *Co-operative Inquiry: Research into the Human Condition*. London: Sage.

Heron, J. (1999) *The Complete Facilitator's Handbook*. London: Kogan Page.

Heron, J. and Reason, P. (1997) 'A participatory inquiry paradigm', *Qualitative Inquiry*, 3(3): 274–94.

Heron, J. and Reason, P. (2001) 'The practice of co-operative inquiry: Research "with" rather than "on" people', in P. Reason and H. Bradbury (eds), *The Sage Handbook of Action Research: Participative Inquiry and Practice*. London: Sage Publications. pp. 179–88.

Heron, J. and Reason, P. (2008) 'Extending epistemology within a co-operative inquiry', in P. Reason and H. Bradbury (eds) *The Sage Handbook of Action Research: Participative Inquiry and Practice*, 2nd Edition. London: Sage Publications. pp. 366–80.

Hewitt, L.D. (1990) *Autobiographical Tightropes*. Lincoln, NE: University of Nebraska Press.

Holman Jones, S., Adams, T. and Ellis, C. (eds) (2013) *Handbook of Autoethnography*. Walnut Creek, CA: Left Coast Press.

hooks, b. (1990) *Yearning: Race, Gender and Cultural Politics*. Boston, MA: South End Press.

Hooper, D.U., Adair, E.C., Cardinale, B.J., Byrnes, J.E.K., Hungate, B.A., Matulich, K.L. ... O'Connor, M.I. (2012) 'A global synthesis reveals biodiversity loss as a major driver of ecosystem change', *Nature*, 486(7401): 105–8.

Hunt, C. and Sampson, F. (2006) *Writing: Self & Reflexivity*. Basingstoke: Palgrave Macmillan.

Hy, L.X. and Loevinger, J. (1996) *Measuring Ego Development*, 2nd Edition. Mahwah, NJ: Erlbaum.

Intergovernmental Panel on Climate Change (2014) *Climate Change 2014: Synthesis Report. Fifth Assessment*. Geneva, Switzerland: IPCC. Retrieved from www.ipcc.ch/report/ar5/syr

Ishiguro, K. (1982) *A Pale View of Hills*. London: Faber & Faber.

Ishiguro, K. (1986) *An Artist of the Floating World*. London: Faber & Faber.

Ishiguro, K. (1989) *The Remains of the Day*. London: Faber & Faber.

Ishiguro, K. (1995) *The Unconsoled*. London: Faber & Faber.

Ishiguro, K. (2015) *The Buried Giant*. London: Faber & Faber.

Jaggi, M. (1995) 'Kazuo Ishiguro with Maya Jaggi', in B.W. Shaffer and C.F. Wong (eds), *Conversations with Kazuo Ishiguro*. Jackson: University Press of Mississippi. pp. 110–19.

James, D. (2009) 'Artifice and absorption: The modesty of Kazuo Ishiguro's *The Remains of the Day*', in S. Matthews and S. Groes (eds), *Kazuo Ishiguro*. London: Continuum International Publishing Group. pp. 54–66.

Karr, J-B.A. (1849) 'Epigram: Plus ça change, plus c'est la même chose', *Les Guêpes* [*The Wasps*], January. https://en.wiktionary.org/wiki/plus_%C3%A7a_change,_plus_c'est_la_m%C3%AAme_chose

Kim, D.H. (1995) *Systems Thinking Tools: A User's Reference Guide*. Cambridge, MA: Pegasus Communications, Inc.

Kite, L. (2015) 'Every book feels like a big risk to me', *Financial Times*, 7 March. www.ft.com/cms/s/2/24786502-c29e-11e4-ad89-00144feab7de.html

Klein, N. (2015) *This Changes Everything*. London: Penguin Books.

Knight, P.T. (2002) *Small-Scale Research: Pragmatic Inquiry in Social Science and the Caring Professions*. London: Sage Publications.

Larkin, P. (2012) *The Complete Poems of Philip Larkin*. Edited by Archie Burnett. London: Faber & Faber Ltd; and New York: Farrar, Straus and Giroux, LLC.

Lather, P. (1993) 'Fertile obsession: Validity after post-structuralism', *Sociological Quarterly*, 34: 673–93.

Learmonth, M. and Humphreys, M. (2012) 'Autoethnography and academic identity: glimpsing business school doppelgängers', *Organization*, 19(1): 99–117.

Lewin, K. (1951) *Field Theory in Social Science: Selected Theoretical Papers*. New York: Harper & Row.

Lewis, B. (2000) *Kazuo Ishiguro*. Manchester: Manchester University Press.

Lincoln, Y.S. and Guba, E.G. (1985) *Naturalistic Inquiry*. Beverley Hills, CA: Sage Publications.

Ludema, J.D. and Fry, R.E. (2008) 'The practice of appreciative inquiry', in P. Reason and H. Bradbury (eds), *The Sage Handbook of Action Research: Participative Inquiry and Practice*, 2nd Edition. London: Sage Publications. pp. 280–96.

Ludema, J.D., Cooperrider, D.L. and Barrett, F.B. (2001) 'Appreciative inquiry: The power of the unconditional positive question', in P. Reason and H. Bradbury (eds), *The Sage Handbook of Action Research: Participative Inquiry and Practice*. London: Sage Publications. pp. 189–99.

Lukes, S. (1974) *Power: A Radical View*. London: Macmillan.

Lukes, S. (2005) *Power: A Radical View*, 2nd Edition. Basingstoke: Palgrave Macmillan.

McArdle, K.L. (2002) 'Establishing a co-operative inquiry group: The perspective of a "first-time" inquirer', *Systemic Practice and Action Research*, 15(3): 177–89.

McNiff, J. and Whitehead, J. (2009) *Doing and Writing Action Research*. London: Sage Publications.

Marshall, J. (1984) *Women Managers: Travellers in a Male World*. Chichester: Wiley.

Marshall, J. (1992) 'Researching women in management as a way of life', *Journal of Management Education and Development*, 23(3): 279–87.

Marshall, J. (1995) *Women Managers Moving on: Exploring Career and Life Choices*. London: International Thomson Publishing Europe.

Marshall, J. (1999) 'Living life as inquiry', *Systemic Practice and Action Research*, 12(2): 155–71.

Marshall, J. (2001) 'Self-reflective inquiry practices', in P. Reason and H. Bradbury (eds), *Handbook of Action Research*. London: Sage Publications. pp. 433–9.

Marshall, J. (2004) 'Living Systemic Thinking: Exploring quality in first person research', *Action Research*, 2(3): 309–29.

Marshall, J. (2007) 'The gendering of leadership in corporate social responsibility', *Journal of Organizational Change Management*, 20(2): 165–81.

Marshall, J. (2008) 'Finding form in writing for action research', in P. Reason and H. Bradbury (eds), *Handbook of Action Research*, 2nd Edition. London: Sage Publications. pp. 682–94.

Marshall, J. (2011) 'Images of changing practice through reflective action research', *Journal of Organizational Change Management*, 24(2): 244–56.

Marshall, J. (2014) 'Centre for Action Research in Professional Practice', in D. Coghlan and M. Brydon-Miller (eds), *The Sage Encyclopedia of Action Research*. Thousand Oaks, CA: Sage Publications. pp. 90–2.

Marshall, J. (2016) 'First-person action research and critical reflection', in J. Fook, V. Collingon, F. Ross, G. Ruch and L. West (eds), *Researching Critical Reflection: Multidisciplinary Perspectives*. London: Routledge. pp. 133–42.

Marshall, J., Coleman, G. and Reason, P. (2011) *Leadership for Sustainability: An Action Research Approach*. Sheffield: Greenleaf Publishing.

Marshall, J. and Mead, G. (2005) 'Editorial: Self-reflective practice and first-person action research', *Action Research*, 3(3): 235–44.

Marshall, J. and Reason, P. (1993) 'Adult learning in collaborative action research', *Studies in Continuing Education*, 15(2): 117–32.

Marshall, J. and Reason, P. (2007) 'Quality in research as "taking an attitude of inquiry"', *Management Research News*, 30(5): 368–80.

Marten, G.G. (2001) *Human Ecology: Basic Concepts for Sustainable Development*. London: Earthscan.

Martin, J. (1990) 'Deconstructing organizational taboos: The suppression of gender conflict in organizations', *Organization Science*, 1: 339–59.

Martin, J. (2000) 'Hidden gendered assumptions in mainstream organizational theory and research', *Journal of Management Inquiry*, 9(2): 207–16.

Mason, G. (1989) 'Inspiring images: The influence of Japanese cinema on the writings of Kazuo Ishiguro', *East–West Film Journal*, 3(2): 39–52.

Meadows, D.H. (1991) 'Change is not Doom', *ReVision*, 14(2): 56–60.

Meadows, D.H. (2002) 'Dancing with systems', *The Systems Thinker*, 13(2) (March).

Meadows, D.H. (2009) *Thinking in Systems: A Primer*. London: Earthscan.

Meadows, D.H., Meadows, D.L., Randers, J. and Behrens, W.W. (1972) *The Limits to Growth*. New York: Universe Books.

Meadows, D.H., Randers, J. and Meadows, D.L. (1992) *Beyond the Limits: Confronting Global Collapse, Envisioning a Sustainable Future*. Vermont: Chelsea Green Publishing.

Meadows, D.H., Randers, J. and Meadows, D.L. (2004) *Limits to Growth: The 30-Year Update*. Vermont: Chelsea Green Publishing.

Meyer, A. (1990) *Contraction and Convergence: The Global Solution to Climate Change* (Schumacher Briefings). Totnes: Green Books.

Meyerson, D.E. and Scully, M.A. (1995) 'Tempered radicalism and the politics of ambivalence and change', *Organization Science*, 6(5): 585–600.

Minogue, V. (1981) *Nathalie Sarraute and the War of the Words*. Edinburgh: Edinburgh University Press.

Norgaard, K.M. (2011) *Living in Denial: Climate Change, Emotions, and Everyday Life*. Cambridge, MA: The MIT Press.

Orr, D.W. (1994) *Earth in Mind: On Education, Environment and the Human Prospect*. Washington, DC: Island Press.

Pelias, R. (2000) 'The critical life', *Communication Education*, 49(3): 220–2.

Pimbert, M. and Wakeford, T. (2003) 'Prajateerpu, power and knowledge: The politics of action research in development. Part 1. Context, process and safeguards', *Action Research*, 1(2): 184–207.

Plumwood, V. (2002) *Environmental Culture: The Ecological Crisis of Reason*. London: Routledge.

Raelin, J.A. (2009) 'Action learning and related modalities', in S.J. Armstrong and C.V. Fukami (eds), *The Sage Handbook of Management Learning, Education and Development*. Thousand Oaks, CA: Sage Publications. pp. 419–38.

Reason, P. and Bradbury, H. (eds) (2001) *The Sage Handbook of Action Research*. Thousand Oaks, CA: Sage Publications.

Reason, P. and Bradbury, H. (eds) (2008a) *The Sage Handbook of Action Research*, 2nd Edition. London: Sage Publications.

Reason, P. and Bradbury, H. (2008b) 'Introduction', in P. Reason and H. Bradbury (eds), *The Sage Handbook of Action Research*, 2nd Edition. London: Sage Publications. pp. 1–10.

Reason, P. and Torbert, W.R. (2001) 'The action turn: Toward a transformational social science', *Concepts and Transformations*, 6(1): 1–37.

Revans, R.W. (1982) *The Origin and Growth of Action Learning*. Bromley, Kent: Chartwell-Bratt.

Richardson, J. (2004) 'Accounting for sustainability: Measuring quantities or enhancing qualities?', in A. Henriques and J. Richardson (eds), *The Triple Bottom Line: Does It All Add Up? Assessing the Sustainability of Business and CSR*. London: Earthscan. pp. 34–44.

Richardson, L. (2000) 'Writing: A method of inquiry', in N.K. Denzin and Y.S. Lincoln (eds), *Handbook of Qualitative Research*, 2nd Edition. Thousand Oaks, CA: Sage Publications. pp 923–48.

Rigg, C. and Trehan, K. (2004) 'Reflections on working with critical action learning', *Action Learning: Research and Practice*, 2: 149–65.

Rockström, J., Steffen, W., Noone, K., Persson, Å., Chapin, S., Lambin, E.F., … Foley, J.A. (2009) 'A safe operating space for humanity', *Nature*, 461: 472–5.

Rooke, D. and Torbert, W.R. (2005) 'Seven transformations of leadership', *Harvard Business Review*, April, 66–76.

Rosenwald, G.C. and Ochberg, R.L. (1992) 'Introduction: Life stories, cultural politics, and self-understanding': in G.C. Rosenwald and R.L. Ochberg (eds), *Storied Lives: The Cultural Politics of Self-understanding*. New Haven: Yale University Press. pp. 1–18.

RSPB and Birdlife international (2011) www.bbc.co.uk/nature/13681684 and www.rspb.org.uk/joinandhelp/donations/campaigns/albatross/problem/threats.aspx

Sarraute, N. (1963) *Tropisms and the Age of Suspicion*. Translated by Maria Jolas. London: John Calder.

Sarraute, N. (1964) *The Golden Fruits*. Translated by Maria Jolas. New York: Braziller.

Sarraute, N. (1983) *The Use of Speech*. Translated by Barbara Wright. London: John Calder.

Schön, D.A. (1983) *The Reflective Practitioner: How Professionals Think in Action*. New York: Basic Books.

Sebald, W.G. (2002a) *Austerlitz*. Translated by Anthea Bell. London: Penguin.

Sebald, W.G. (2002b) *The Rings of Saturn*. Translated by Michael Hulse. London: Vintage Books.

Senge, P.M. (2006) *The Fifth Discipline: The Art and Practice of the Learning Organization*. London: Random House.

Senge, P.M., Kleiner, A., Roberts, C., Ross, R. and Smith, B. (1994) *The Fifth Discipline Fieldbook*. London: Nicholas Brealey Publishing.

Shaffer, B.W. and Wong, C.F. (eds) (2008) *Conversations with Kazuo Ishiguro*. Jackson, IL: University Press of Mississippi.

Shepard, H.A. (1975) 'Rules of thumb for change agents', *OD Practitioner*, 7(3): 1–5.

Shove, E. (2010) 'Beyond the ABC: Climate change policy and theories of social change', *Environment and Planning*, 42: 1273–85.

Shove, E. and Walker, G. (2010) 'Governing transitions in the sustainability of everyday life', *Research Policy*, 39: 471–6.

Sinclair, A. (2007) 'Teaching leadership critically to MBAs: Experiences from heaven and hell', *Management Learning*, 38(4): 461–75.

Sinclair, A. (2009) 'Seducing leadership: Stories of leadership development', *Gender, Work and Organization*, 16(2): 266–84.

Sparkes, A.C. (1996) 'The fatal flaw: A narrative of the fragile bodyself', *Qualitative Inquiry*, 2: 463–95.

Sparkes, A.C. (2002) 'Autoethnography: Self-indulgence or something more?', in A. Bochner and C. Ellis (eds), *Autoethnographically Speaking*. New York: AltaMira Press. pp. 209–32.

Sparkes, A.C. (2012) 'Fathers and sons: In bits and pieces', *Qualitative Inquiry*, 18(2): 174–85.

Spender, D. (1980) *Man Made Language*. London: Routledge and Kegan Paul.

Stanley, L. and Wise, S. (1993) *Breaking Out Again*. London: Routledge.

Steffen, W., Richardson, K., Rockström, J., Cornell, S.E., Fetzer, I., Bennett, E.M. … Sörlin, S. (2015) 'Planetary boundaries: Guiding human development on a changing planet' *Science*, 347(6223), doi: 10.1126/science.1259855.

Stern, N. (2007) *The Economics of Climate Change: The Stern Review*. Cambridge: Cambridge University Press.

Swaim, D. (1999) 'Don Swaim interviews Kazuo Ishiguro', in B.W. Shaffer and C.F. Wong (eds), *Conversations with Kazuo Ishiguro*. Jackson, IL: University Press of Mississippi. pp. 89–109.

Tams, S. and Marshall, J. (2011) 'Responsible careers: Systemic reflexivity in shifting landscapes', *Human Relations*, 64(1): 109–31.

Taylor, S.S., Rudolph, J.W. and Foldy, E.G. (2008) 'Teaching reflective practice in the action science/action inquiry tradition: Key stages, concepts and practices', in P. Reason and H. Bradbury (eds), *Handbook of Action Research*, 2nd Edition. London: Sage Publications. pp. 656–68.

The Yes Men (undated) http://theyesmen.org

Torbert, W.R. (1973) *Learning from Experience: Toward Consciousness*. New York: Columbia University Press.

Torbert, W.R. (1976) *Creating a Community of Inquiry: Conflict, Collaboration, Transformation*. London: Wiley Interscience.

Torbert, W.R. (1987) *Managing the Corporate Dream: Restructuring for Long-Term Success*. Homewood, IL: Dow Jones-Irwin.

Torbert, W.R. (1991) *The Power of Balance: Transforming Self, Society and Scientific Inquiry*. Thousand Oaks, CA: Sage.

Torbert, W.R. (2001) 'The practice of action inquiry', in P. Reason and H. Bradbury (eds), *Handbook of Action Research*. London: Sage Publications. pp. 250–60.

Torbert, W.R. (2013) 'Listening into the dark: An essay testing the validity and efficacy of collaborative developmental action inquiry for describing and encouraging the transformation of self, society, and scientific inquiry', *Integral Review*, 9(2): 264–99.

Torbert, B. and Associates (2004) *Action Inquiry: The Secret of Timely and Transforming Leadership*. San Francisco: Berrett-Koehler Publishers.

Torbert, W.R. and Taylor, S.S. (2008) 'Action inquiry: Interweaving multiple qualities of attention for timely action', in P. Reason and H. Bradbury (eds), *Handbook of Action Research*, 2nd Edition. London: Sage Publications. pp. 239–51.

Trehan, K. and Pedler, M. (2009) 'Animating critical action learning: process-based leadership and management development', *Action Learning: Research and Practice*, 6(1): 35–49.

Turner-Vesselago, B. (2013) *Writing without a Parachute: The Art of Freefall*. Bristol: Vala Publishing.

Ulrich, W. (2000) 'Reflective practice in the civil society: The contribution of critically systemic thinking', *Reflective Practice*, 1(2): 247–68.

Van Maanen J. (1988) *Tales of the Field: On Writing Ethnography*. Chicago: The University of Chicago Press.

Vorda, A. and Herzinger, K. (1990) 'An interview with Kazuo Ishiguro', in B.W. Shaffer and C.F. Wong (eds), *Conversations with Kazuo Ishiguro*. Jackson, IL: University Press of Mississippi. pp. 66–88.

Wagstaff, P. (2007) Recorded conversation on the work of Nathalie Sarraute. 6 December. University of Bath.

Wakeford, T. and Pimbert, M. (2004) 'Prajateerpu, power and knowledge: The politics of participatory action research in development. Part 2. Analysis, reflections and implications', *Action Research*, 2(1): 24–46.

Wallas, G. (1926) *The Art of Thought*. New York: Harcourt Brace.

Waring, M. (1988) *If Women Counted*. San Francisco: Harper and Row.

Watzlawick, P., Bavelas, J.B. and Jackson, D.D. (1967) *Pragmatics of Human Communication*. New York: W.W. Norton & Company.

Watzlawick, P., Weakland, J. and Fisch, R. (1974) *Change: Principles of Problem Formation and Problem Resolution*. New York: W.W. Norton & Company.

Weick, K.E. (1979) *The Social Psychology of Organizing*, 2nd Edition. Reading, MA: Addison-Wesley.

Weick, K.E. (1995) *Sense-making in Organizations*. Thousand Oaks, CA: Sage Publications.

Whitehead, J. (1989) 'Creating a living educational theory from questions of the kind, "How do I improve my practice?"', *Cambridge Journal of Education*, 19(1): 137–53.

Whiteman, G., Walker, B. and Perego, P. (2013) 'Planetary boundaries: Ecological foundations for corporate sustainability', *Journal of Management Studies*, 50: 307–36.

Wong, C.F. (2000) *Kazuo Ishiguro*. Tavistock, Devon: Northcote House Publishers Ltd.

Wong, C.F. and Crummett, G. (2006) 'A conversation about life and art with Kazuo Ishiguro', in B.W. Shaffer and C.F. Wong (eds), *Conversations with Kazuo Ishiguro*. Jackson, IL: University Press of Mississippi. pp. 204–20.

Woolf, V. (1992) *The Waves*. London: Penguin Books. (Original publication 1931. London: The Hogarth Press.)

INDEX

Ellis, C.S., 8
emails, 57–58
equality, 9
ethics and ethical issues, xxi–xxii, 141
European-American Collaborative
    Challenging Whiteness, 62

facing into wind, 71
feedback, 12, 61–63, 107, 124–125, 131, 138
feminist reflective research, xvi
fictionalized accounts, 200–203
first person action research
    being as 'action' in, 44–45
    characteristics of, xv–xviii, 7–8
    cycles of, 45–46
    examples of, 140–167, 170–184
    form and voice in, xxii, 47, 98, 113
    framework for, 193–195
    identification of issues for, 42–43
    images of, 70–71, *70*
    as (im)possible, 68–69
    learning colleague-ship and, xx–xxi
    meaning of, 191–192
    multiple ways of knowing in, 46–47
    as political process, xix
    principles and practices of, 182–183
    propitious circumstances for, 43–44
    as relational and systemic, xviii–xix
    scope of, 43
    self-indulgence and responsibility in,
        xix–xx
    spaces for, 63–64
    style of, 41–42
    See also disciplines of inquiry; writing as
        inquiry; writing as representation
Fisher, D., 36
Flood, R.L., 10–11, 13
Frame, J., 100
Freefall Writing
    as applied to first person inquiry, 101–106
    examples of, 116–120, 123–139
    'going fearward' in, 59–60, 102, 104
    'sensuous detail' in, 102–103, 104–105,
        112–113, 116, 131–132, 187
Les Fruits d'Or (*The Golden Fruits*) (Sarraute),
    81–82, 84–85

Galliz, K., 93
Garud, R., 78
generative process, 23
'going fearward,' 59–60, 102, 104
'Going, Going' (Larkin), xxv–xxvii
Goldberg, N., 101–102, 103
grounded theory, 6
Guba, E.G., 4

Hall, E.T, 35
Harris, G., 10–11
heron, 70–71, *70*
Heron, J., 9
Herzinger, K., 92
hooks, b., 78

indeterminacy, 112
institutional theory, 77–78
Ishiguro, K., xvi, 87, 88–93

Johnson, P., 4

Karr, J-B.A., 15
Kim, D.H., 17–18
Klein, N., xxiii

Larkin, P., xxiii, xxv–xxvii
Lather, P., 198
Leadership Development Framework, 35–37
learning buddies, 61–62
learning groups
    example of, 123–139
    feedback in, 124–125, 131, 138
    overview, 62, 64
    qualities and importance of, 137–139
Lewis, B., 90
life narratives, 87–88
life patterns, 64–66
The Limits to Growth (Meadows et al.), 12
Lincoln, Y.S., xv, 4, 196
'living life as inquiry.' *See* first person action
    research
Loevinger, J., 35
Lukes, S., 27, 28

Marshall, J., xvii, xx, 42, 111, 124
Martin, J., 26
McArdle, K.L., 9
Meadows, D.H., 10–11, 12, 17, 24–25
mentoring, 61–62
Meyerson, D.E., 78–79
mindfulness, 66–67, 81

naive humanist realism, 114–115, 198
Naturalistic Inquiry (Lincoln and Guba), 4
note-taking, 57–58

Ochberg, R.L., 87–88
Orr, D.W., 140
outcomes, 66–67

A Pale View of Hills (Ishiguro), 88–90, 91–94
parts of speech, 33–34
peer supervision, 62